T0334978

INVESTING IN COLLEGE

INVESTING IN COLLEGE

A Guide

for the

Perplexed

Malcolm

Getz

HARVARD UNIVERSITY PRESS
Cambridge, Massachusetts
London, England
2007

Cataloging-in-Publication Data available from the Library of Congress
Library of Congress catalog card number: 2006050886
ISBN-13: 978-0-674-02464-9 (alk. paper)
ISBN-10: 0-674-02464-8 (alk. paper)

Contents

Preface

The stakes are high. Some families will invest more than $250,000 in higher education for each child. In thinking about college, a family faces a variety of choices: public or private, in-state or out-of-state, two-year or four, stop with an associates degree or proceed with a baccalaureate, or plan for more? How much financial aid might a family expect? How does the admission process work at selective colleges? This guide addresses these issues and more, with evidence from social scientists and some original exploration.

Parents who want to understand how higher education works will find more depth here than in college guides intended primarily for high school students. Nevertheless, curious prospective college students are welcome. And high school counselors, college admissions staff, college academic advisers, and others who want to help their students take advantage of opportunities in higher education will find insights they may not have considered before.

For these reasons, this book complements the standard sources from Peterson's, Princeton Review, The College Board, Barron's, and others. This guide does not provide lists or rankings of colleges, but it does provide specific examples of colleges that are similar in easily observed ways yet show important if subtle differences on close examination.

In a recent study, a colleague and I considered where the children of college and university faculty go for their higher education, a survey described more fully in Chapter 6. We found that although the children of faculty frequently choose, for the most part, to enter selective colleges—indeed, often the most selective—children of faculty from distinguished colleges are found in every sector of higher education, including the local public four-year campus, two-year colleges, and religious or ethnic schools. Every institution of higher education may be a good choice for some students.

For the most part, higher education in the United States is well organized, staffed by highly motivated, effective people, and housed in appropriate facilities. Nevertheless, while colleges serve their students well, there is room for improvement. Better-informed consumers who ask sharper questions and make more incisive choices will strengthen higher education. Colleges are responsive to students, and they evolve as circumstances and a demanding clientele change.

Data from the Bureau of the Census, the Bureau of Labor Statistics, and the National Center for Education Statistics have provided the essential underpinning for many parts of this book, and I want to thank the people who complete these surveys. I also want to thank Ashley Coleman, Michael Gleason, Peter McHenry, Stephanie Schacht, Tim Shuman, and Sheldon Steele for their help in preparing this work. Elizabeth Knoll and Susan Wallace Boehmer provided wonderful support in editing the manuscript. Several experienced counselors commented on drafts, including Bruce Breimer, Ruth Hagerty, Leonard King, Peter Latson, and Art Mandel. I thank as well Ronald Ehrenberg, David Mohning, Howard Sandler, William Shain, John Siegfried, and Jonathan Thornhill for helpful comments. Remaining flaws are mine, and any resemblance to specific people among the composite students and families described in the text is purely coincidental.

INVESTING IN COLLEGE

CHAPTER ONE

Introduction: The High Cost of Higher Education

Mary and Greg Smithson came to my office from Dallas with their son, Bill, to talk about his search for a college. Bill was a good student who played on his high school tennis team and aspired to a career in management. As a resident of Texas, he could attend the University of Texas in 2005 with 38,000 other undergraduates and pay in-state tuition of $5,735 per year. Undergraduate admission was "highly competitive," according to Barron's, and *US News & World Report* ranked Texas 46th among national universities. Of the 2,500+ four-year-degree-granting colleges in the United States, Texas—with its well-regarded, creative faculty who make significant contributions to knowledge every year—placed in the top 2 percent. In short, for Bill Smithson and his family, the University of Texas offered a tempting package.[1]

The Smithsons had also visited the University of Virginia, whose out-of-state tuition in 2005 was $22,700 per year. With its lower undergraduate enrollment of 14,000 students, a tradition of excellence going back to Thomas Jefferson, and a talented faculty, UVA was also an attractive choice. It had earned Barron's "most competitive" designation, and *US News* ranked it 22nd among national universities.[2]

But in addition to these public institutions, the Smithsons wanted to check out Vanderbilt, a private university where I teach economics. Vanderbilt has 6,000 undergraduates, a faculty who publish more than a thousand journal articles and many books every year, and a financial endowment of $2.6 billion. In 2005 Barron's listed Vanderbilt, with its $29,990 annual tuition, as "most selective," and *US News* ranked the school 18th among universities nationally.

During our lively conversation, Mr. Smithson asked if there is a difference in outcome that makes Vanderbilt worth the extra $24,000 per year in tuition over Texas or the extra $7,000 over UVA? Taking into account room and board of $6,184 at Texas compared with $9,826 at Vanderbilt and adding the extra cost of travel from Dallas to Nashville, the Smithsons estimated that Vanderbilt would add another $4,000 per year to the difference, beyond tuition. The Smithsons expected to pay full price—roughly $16,000 per year total expenditure (adding books and other necessaries) at Texas, $33,000 at UVA, or $44,000 at Vanderbilt. Over the course of four years, they were looking at an investment in Bill's college education ranging from $64,000 to $176,000 or more. Even for well-to-do families like the Smithsons, a differential of $100,000+ represents an investment decision not to be made lightly.

Hundreds of thousands of families raise the Smithsons' question every year, as the price tag for college continues to rise faster than the cost of living. Is spending *more* on higher education worthwhile?

The Smithsons' decisions about where Bill should apply, the colleges' decisions about whether to accept him, and ultimately Bill's decision about where to enroll are all part of a complex national process that matches high school graduates to colleges. Both students and colleges influence the outcome, and each responds to whatever information they have about the other. To help their sons and daughters devise a strategy for making a good match, parents need to understand the nature of this annual ritual.

One view of matching calls to mind the sledgehammer game at a county fair. The contestant hammers a steel bar with a sixteen-pound sledge to see how far up a pole he can drive a weight. Drive the weight all the way to the top, ring the bell, and win a prize. Like the contestant, most college applicants see colleges and universities arrayed along a pole by rank. They believe that getting their application higher up the pole will yield greater earnings over a lifetime, along with other good things. The college contestant swings the hammer of high school grades and national test scores, drives his application up as far as he can, and enrolls at the highest-ranked college where his application is accepted. A few contestants will ring the bell at the top and win admission to the number-one-ranked school.

In this image, the top college picks from among the applicants who push the weight highest, with each successive college choosing the hardest hitters from among the remaining candidates. Students are matched to colleges on the basis of academic merit; and their access to the nation's best colleges will yield, later on, the highest incomes in the land. Because colleges with the best-prepared students are the most desired and therefore can be the most selective, they can charge the highest tuitions.

The goal of this book is to expose what's wrong with this picture. It is a caricature of the matching process that leaves little room for strategy and causes many families to pay too much for higher education. In reality, the game on the ground offers more opportunities than simple brute strength. Students have many dimensions that matter to colleges, not just test scores and grades, and colleges have many dimensions that matter to students other than popularity and prestige. For many students, developing social skills, finding new interests, and gaining a more sophisticated sense of the larger society have significant value beyond the monetary gains. In terms of quality education, colleges and universities fall into broad groupings rather than a refined rank, and prices vary widely even among similarly ranked colleges, as the Smithsons learned when they compared tuitions at UVA and Vanderbilt. There are differences in quality worth paying for, but a high school student will not learn what those differences are if he focuses only on college rank.

Viewed as an investment, higher education often yields better returns than stocks and bonds. On average, investing in education is a sound financial move. However, families have many ways to spend money when shopping for an education, and some expenditures pay off better than others. Two-year degrees in programs such as nursing offer very high returns for the time and money invested, while some master's degrees perform poorly, from a financial perspective. Professional degrees in law and medicine generally yield strong returns but doctorates less so. To assume that more education is always worthwhile can lead to overinvesting and diminished returns. Chapter 2 provides some background to help parents weigh these costs and benefits and think about where to draw the line.[3]

The returns to education arise in part because a student gains skills through schooling that an employer values. On average, students with more skill earn more because they are more productive at work. However, the higher return may also arise because employers respond not just to individuals but to brand names. Employers have limited information about the productivity of individual job applicants, and so they look for some signal of a person's likely future success. If, in the employer's experience, graduates of particular colleges with stronger reputations perform better on average than other graduates, employers will be more likely to choose candidates from these schools, all other things being equal. Education is a sign of potential productivity, whose value may not depend exclusively on the achievement of a specific student but on the reputation of the school where the education was acquired.[4]

In determining whether higher-quality education pays off, economists have a difficult time distinguishing between these two sources of rewards. About the best we can do is interpret the observed returns on investment in a college education as a combined response to the student's personal skills and to the school's general reputation. But with an important caveat: College prestige often has its greatest value in helping a student land her first job. Over the course of a career, on-the-job performance becomes the determining factor, not one's alma mater. In helping their daughter or son choose a college, parents want to maximize the total reward over the long term, whether it originates in skill or signals or both.

In addition to productivity and brand name, employers may value other attributes that a college experience refines—the ability to relate to others different from oneself, the willingness to both lead and follow, the skill to listen carefully and respond appropriately, the curiosity to pursue new knowledge. Students themselves put high value on college experiences that pay off outside the narrow confines of a career path—in music, the arts, athletics, politics, religion, languages, travel, and volunteer work—along with a network of social contacts that may last a lifetime.

Some people get a high return from college not because they earn top money in their chosen careers but because their earnings would have been so much lower than average *without* college. This is often true for women and under-represented minorities. Without college, women and minority members of both sexes tend to earn much less at their jobs than white men; but with college, the differentials narrow. Because the gains are greater, the *rate* of financial return for women and minorities is higher, even though their peak earnings are not as high as that of white males, on average. The savvy investor will calculate the increase in earnings (and other advantages associated with financial security) likely to flow from the specific educational program to be completed, net of its costs, in deciding whether it is worthwhile, and not just the average earnings of people with college degrees. We might say that for some students, the weight starts out at a lower point on the pole, and the returns to education are measured by the distance the weight travels, not the top height it reaches.

The value of an investment in education depends very much on the choice of career. Chapter 3 describes eight benchmark careers and the average return from different levels of education in each. But few students have a substantial basis for choosing a career at age eighteen, and those who think they know where they're headed often change their minds as they mature. Some college programs are more successful than others in providing a range of experiences that help students explore their options, question their own assumptions, and choose careers where success and satisfaction are more likely. A curriculum with breadth as well as depth also facilitates flexibility over a lifetime, allowing easier movement among occupations as the economic landscape shifts. A general undergraduate education is well rewarded over the long term.

So how can prospective students evaluate the quality of a college curriculum? Too often, they and their parents leave this important job in the hands of college ranking services. But the notion that a student should enroll at the most highly ranked institution to which she is offered admission is a formula for spending too much and getting too little. With so much pressure from friends and relations, a family needs courage to understand that national rankings are a flimsy set of statistics at best. As Chapter 4 explains in detail, ranking is based on easily observed aggregates rather than the detailed specifics of different educational programs. Some magazines deliberately change their formulas frequently so that the ranks will jiggle, justifying fresh headlines to sell each new issue. Fighting back, colleges and universities manipulate their own numbers and behavior to influence their place on the pole. Scores that differ only in the third digit look much larger when converted to ranks, and these numerical scores, because they have the patina of precision, quickly take on a life of their own.

To gain enough control to deploy the strategies suggested in this book, a family must first understand the rankings, and then they must establish some psychological distance from them. When colleagues and neighbors are obsessing about getting their children into the top ten schools, a family needs to be able to say with conviction that it got a better deal by choosing a specific, strong program based on net price (that is, price net of grants-in-aid).

Quality in education matters, but it is very easy to pay too much for it. Differences in observed outcomes among graduates of dozens of colleges of similar overall rank and reputation do not vary in meaningful ways.[5] Indeed, the differences in outcomes among graduates of any one college among dozens of similar colleges dwarf the differences in average result across those colleges. The 74 colleges in Barron's "most competitive" category and the 109 in its "highly competitive" group charge substantially different tuitions, and their grants-in-aid vary as well from school to school. Paying significant extra tuition just to gain an extra ten to twenty places in rank does not yield a positive financial return. Instead of a pole with a notch for each college and a bell at the top, think of a pole with three-foot-wide bands of color and no bell (Barron's calls these bands most competitive, highly competitive, very competitive, competitive, less competitive, and not competitive). Driving the weight into a higher color usually delivers an extra financial reward. But you don't get an extra prize for moving up within a color band. This fact opens the opportunity to weigh carefully the price and services of programs within each group of schools.

Unfortunately, systematic information about class size, the qualifications of instructors, the academic culture among students, and a specific program's commitment to student success is difficult to find. Colleges and universities build brand names in many ways—by hiring public relations firms, televising athletic contests, providing lavish recreational facilities, landscaping their grounds, and hiring internationally renowned architects to design undergraduate dormitories. But a student's college experience occurs primarily within a specific educational program, and these programs can vary widely within a college or university. The medical school may be highly respected and flush with money, while the liberal arts college is lean and the school of music is underfunded and weak.

In the automobile industry, such differences are reflected in price: Toyota sells expensive Lexus and Camry models, but it also offers Corollas and Scions at a considerable discount. Universities provide little discount for their low-cost models. As a consequence, prospective students have to go beyond the viewbooks and tours and ask sharper questions about the details of specific programs that interest them. In the disciplines that matter to a student, whether it's English or anthropology, how large are the classes, who is teaching them, and how successful are the students? For women thinking about careers in science, the number of men and women who become physics and chemistry majors and the number of female faculty in each discipline may be of particular interest. What students may discover is that many programs aren't prepared to answer even the most basic questions. But if enough prospective students ask, the schools will learn to give more informed answers.

A crucial fact about higher education is that a university is a collection of highly variable colleges, and a college is a collection of highly variable departments. The most popular ranking services look at a university as a whole and include graduate schools of law, medicine, architecture, engineering, business, public health, dentistry, nursing, and theology in the overall scoring, alongside undergraduate programs. Having many famous faculty members, with productive labs, multiple publications, doctoral candidates, postdocs, and other research staff, will boost a university's reputation and improve its score. But those professors may play no role whatsoever in undergraduate instruction. Rankings are also influenced by the size of a university's financial endowment, yet most of the income from the endowment may be earmarked to support research efforts that rarely involve undergraduates.

Some well-regarded universities with able faculty and significant financial resources run some parts of their undergraduate program (and some graduate programs) as cash cows. A cash cow generates more revenue than the university spends to operate it; the university uses the surplus to underwrite its other goals. Of course, no university website touts its cash cows, but a prospective student will do well to avoid them. Shoppers need to ask pointed questions about the specific program they're considering if they want to get value for their money.

Cues about questions to ask are offered in Chapter 5—about the features of individual programs, the attributes of faculty who teach courses, the number of classes of various sizes, the curriculum offered and required, and teaching methods. A strong program with effective instruction on a campus with a lower overall reputation (that is, one that falls into a different color band on the academic pole) will often be superior to a cash cow on a more highly ranked campus. While it's undeniable that elite social networks and a school's reputation may offer a leg up in landing a job, in the long run a college education pays off primarily because *learning* pays off, and more learning takes place when the quality of instruction is higher, regardless of the rank, prestige, or popularity of the university as a whole.

Like the admission process, the college experience itself is sometimes seen as a brutal competition among students for high achievement and recognition. But in fact, a better college education involves teamwork—among students and their instructors, academic advisers, extracurricular coaches, and peers. Because students spend more time with other students than with faculty, the work ethic of students on a campus has important consequences for the amount that students learn. Students learn more when they engage one another both in the classroom and in outside study groups and other projects, ranging from community service to concerts. They also learn more when they are happy and confident. Anxiety saps energy and distracts students from academic pursuits.

If families are willing to consider colleges of similar reputation as close substitutes for one another, students can shop among them for more attractive levels of tuition (a subject explored in Chapter 6). Although private institutions dominate among the "most competitive" colleges and universities, an increasing number of public universities now fall into this color band. Among the next set of schools—the "highly competitive" institutions—public universities with their lower tuition have a very strong presence. Many students fortunate enough to live in these states can get an excellent education at a very reasonable cost.

While the sticker price of higher education has a powerful effect on the rate of return, how much of this price a family actually has to pay, and how a family chooses to pay its share, has a much greater effect. Choosing more expensive methods of finance can lower the value of an educational investment. Families who find the burden of debt too great will choose colleges that offer lower net price tags. For these reasons, a family should think carefully about the four main ways of financing a college education—saving, borrowing, working, and grants-in-aid (gift aid)—and how to maximize each one to the student's benefit. Chapter 7 offers details and gives examples.

Of course, families with lots of assets can use their personal wealth to pay for college. Because investment in college pays a higher return over the long run than stocks and bonds, a family that sold its stocks and bonds to pay for college would be making a sound financial decision. For families with high incomes but less accumulated wealth, increasing the rate of saving is the wisest course. Federal and state income tax laws allow investments dedicated to future college expenses to earn income without being subject to income tax. State-operated 529 programs offer the lowest-cost way to pay for college when a family is in the middle and upper tax brackets and is able to set aside money in secure investment accounts.

Like saving, borrowing can take many forms, each with its own price tag. Several federal programs make loans available to students to help with college expenses, and these loans are often part of a college's financial aid package. The federal government guarantees the lender against the student's failure to repay the loans, allowing the lender to offer the loans at low rates as though the borrowers had presented collateral.[6] PLUS loans, underwritten by the federal government, are available to parents. For many families, the federal loan programs are the most attractive method of borrowing for college. When mortgage rates are low, home equity or other collateralized loans can also be useful in paying for college expenses. The least attractive borrowing method is use of credit cards and other personal loans. The high interest rates on this uncollateralized debt may offset the potential financial gains from college.

Most college financial aid packages include an opportunity for students to earn money. Even a full-time student can commit some time to employment, though government-subsidized work-study programs set limits on both the hourly wage a student can be paid and the number of hours per week a student can work. About 40 percent of all college students attend college part-time to sustain themselves with employment as they gain an education.[7] Studying part-time means taking longer to receive degrees, and intellectually intense colleges tend to discourage it.

The fourth (and best!) method of financing college is through gifts or grants-in-aid that are offered by federal and state governments, private philanthropy, and the colleges themselves. Some grant aid may be offered on the basis of need—that is, a detailed consideration of the family's financial circumstances. Other grants are awarded on the basis of academic or other merit, such as musical ability or athletic prowess. Federal Pell grants are limited to students from families with incomes below about $42,000 per year, and their amounts are fairly predictable. However, some other sources of gift aid cannot be easily forecast.

Only about a few dozen colleges commit to meeting the full

financial need of all the students they enroll, and each one of these schools offers a unique mix of grants, loans, and student employment. Because a dollar of grant is much more valuable than a dollar of loan, understanding the mix a student is likely to get is essential to forecasting net cost. At colleges that do not meet fully demonstrated need, even the total amount of aid may be hard to forecast. And these schools will also vary the mix of loans, student employment, and grants they offer. For many colleges, the only way to determine a net price—that is, the college's charges less gift aid—is to apply for admission and financial aid and look at the offer. Many important decisions, including where to apply and whether to apply for early decision (a subject discussed in Chapter 8), must be made before knowing the net price a student will actually have to pay.

Grants based on academic or other kinds of merit are similarly difficult to forecast. Although colleges tout their merit awards, they will usually require a student to apply and be offered admission before a merit grant, if any, is offered. However, many states have very large merit scholarship programs that provide grants to all students who reside in the state, attend a college in the state, and meet a specified grade-point average. Overall, merit grants have become a very significant component in financing higher education in recent years.

The notion that a student should take a big swing at the academic anvil and attend the highest college he can reach, regardless of cost, is wrong if for no other reason than that less than 5 percent of the population can afford to pay full freight at the most expensive colleges. And even those people who could pay their way often get a higher return on their investment by choosing a less expensive education. For the vast majority of students, the specific terms of financial aid awards will have a material influence on the choice of college. Some students will find that their net cost is lower at a college with a much higher tuition, because of a generous financial aid award. But others will find that choosing a college with a lower stated price, even though it offers little financial aid, may be a better deal than enrolling at a much more expensive college with a financial aid award that leaves the student with heavy debt. For this reason among others, many colleges with lesser overall reputation nevertheless attract their share of outstanding students.

While many families obsess about their student's SAT scores and class rank, very few colleges reduce an applicant's dossier to a single score and offer admission by working down from the top of the heap. Of course, among the thousands of applicants to a college, some outstanding candidates will be readily admitted, and some applicants with doubtful qualifications will be rejected outright. But the bulk of the candidates will be of generally similar academic standing, and this large middle group is where the fine-grained decisions must be made. It's a bit like walking into a room fifteen minutes late, with just ten minutes left to line up fifty fidgety three-year-olds by height. A few tall ones and a few short ones can be easily identified, but in the middle group where the heights are similar, getting a correct ordering by height is impossible. And who will ever figure out whether you got it right to the first decimal, let alone to the second or third?

Admission officers know that test scores and grades are inherently fuzzy numbers—imprecise summaries of academic performance which vary considerably with repeated attempts at measurement and which predict college performance only modestly. So they group their thousands of applicants into broad categories by scores and then look for other information to weigh in making decisions. Qualitative information about the secondary school, the degree of academic challenge, the specific courses taken, and the success of the high school's recent alumni—all of these factors temper judgments about grades. Personal indicators of motivation, creativity, leadership, and curiosity appear in letters and essays. In addition to a concern for academic performance, colleges want to build and sustain lively campus communities, where artistic, athletic, political, social, ethnic, and religious activities are well represented. Among many applicants who are similar in their academic credentials, a college looks for students who add other things to campus life.

The result is that different colleges make different decisions. One may need an oboist, another a short-stop, a third a debater, and a fourth a student from Montana, each chosen from among the college's pool of well-qualified applicants. Academics are very important, to be sure, but other dimensions will appeal to different admission officers in different ways. From a distance, the process of matching students to colleges appears to have a good deal of randomness, as indeed it does. But applicants can turn this uncertainty to their advantage by shopping among similar colleges, by looking beyond published ranks and simple statistical measures, and by comparing details of tuition and financial aid, the educational program, and the social setting.

This book explores these ideas in more detail to help families understand the payoffs from college, the links between college and career, the downside of overvaluing college rank, some better ways to assess educational quality and campus social life, the wide variation in college tuitions, the many methods of financing higher education, and the nail-biting admission process. My bedrock advice is to shop carefully among colleges of generally similar reputation. A savvy investor needs to do more than stare at the sticker price and slam the doors: he needs to look under the hood and go for a test drive.

Ultimately, the decision of where to go to college should rest, as far as possible, with the student. Recognizing that the student is a critical decision maker can be a challenge for some families, as three contrasting stories make clear.[8] Lesley Drummond contacted me by email from St. Louis to ask about Vanderbilt's economics program. She came to see me on her visit to the campus and brought along her mother. Lesley asked thoughtful questions about the size of classes, what reading she might do in advance, the possibility of study abroad, and where alumni graduating with economics majors have pursued careers. Her mother listened but said little.

Steve Moselle phoned from Toledo to make an appointment to talk with me about economics at Vanderbilt. He arrived with his son, Trey, in tow. Mr. Moselle said that Trey aspired to a career in business and wanted to know why Vanderbilt doesn't offer an undergraduate business major. After a friendly chat, the Moselles left, Trey having said almost nothing at all.

Another student, Larry Simmons from Tampa, contacted me because he wanted to transfer from the University of Florida to Vanderbilt and was curious about the economics program. In his first two years in college, all his courses had been taught in a very large electronic format, with the result that he hadn't met a single faculty member. Before he entered college, if his parents had insisted that he visit several campuses and ask about the nature of the instructional programs, he would probably have made a different choice. Nevertheless, Larry successfully transferred to Vanderbilt as a junior and quickly got to know a number of his instructors, whose recommendations helped him land a consulting job in New York after graduation.

In matching a student with a college, parents have big levers, but a student who is pushed in an uncomfortable direction is likely to be frustrated and demoralized. Students who actively pursue their own interests, with parental advice and support, will usually make better choices and become more effective college students. Campuses have personalities, and prospective students perceive the differences quickly by sitting in the dining hall, listening to a student tour guide, scanning a campus newspaper, noticing how students dress, or walking across the quad. Students react to the personal chemistry of a campus in deciding where to apply, and they take into account different personal goals. How important is the social "fit" to me? What kind of classes and teachers do I like? How much effort will I need to make to succeed academically? Will I have time to pursue interests other than classwork?

And with a little parental coaching, students should also ask: Could I get a better deal? The Smithsons, whose search for a college opened this chapter, began with the national rank of universities as a shorthand indication of quality. But after making campus visits and having conversations with current and former students, they began to ask penetrating questions about teaching and to focus on specific programs of interest to Bill, rather than on whole universities. When Bill finally made his choice, he went to the University of Texas, where he is thriving as an accounting major.

CHAPTER TWO

Financial Returns: Does College Pay Off?

Joe Trello, a student in my public finance class, mentioned that his father intended to pay for his undergraduate and postgraduate education—and that of his three brothers—through whatever graduate program the sons chose, at the highest quality that each son could achieve. That commitment might well involve outlays of family wealth in excess of $1.2 million for postsecondary education. Although Joe's father surely had a variety of motives for his decision, let's view it solely as a financial investment and try to decide if it is a sound one. Will the Trello family's long-term wealth be greater with this investment in education than it would be if the funds were invested in a typical portfolio of financial assets?

The short answer is that, on average, higher education will give the family a higher rate of return. But there are important differences across the spectrum of degrees and careers, and (as usual) averages don't tell the whole story.

In the case of a typical financial investment, one saves money to purchase an asset, for example, shares in a mutual fund. In time, the asset may pay interest or dividends, and it may increase in value (a combination called *total return*). Historically, well-diversified financial portfolios of stocks and bonds have yielded 3 to 7 percent per year in total return over many decades after inflation, depending on the degree of risk an investor accepts.

Like a mutual fund, higher education has an investment value in the sense that the purchase of schooling in the present leads to higher earnings later in life. Let's call the purchase of schooling an investment in "human capital" and then try to estimate its total return. Of course, an investment in human capital (unlike a mutual fund) generates a stream of earnings only so long as the worker continues to live and go to work. Therefore, in our calculations we must adjust earnings at each age for the probability of survival and employment.[1]

Taking these factors into account, we can say that when the total return on investment in human capital exceeds the total return generally available on financial assets, the investment in human capital—in this case, education—has increased the investor's total wealth.[2] The sections that follow will explain this general relationship between education and earnings in more detail, as a prelude to describing the financial returns a student can expect at different levels of education and with different academic degrees. But first an important caveat, and it cannot be repeated too often.

For the vast majority of young people who head off to college and graduate school, financial returns are only part of the value of higher education. Most people choose to attend college because they expect to *enjoy* it, and for them tuition buys one of life's most complex and memorable experiences—"educational" and "valuable" in every sense. For many students, the college years are a time to engage with the larger issues of culture, social change, politics, and public policy, and to develop a commitment to broader goals. Personal challenges inside and outside the classroom contribute to a sense of independence, identity, intellectual curiosity, and responsibility. And when it comes time to choose a career, college graduates take these values and experiences with them. They look for returns from their work life that cannot be measured strictly by a paycheck. Some may seek opportunities for artistic creativity, travel and independent study, or community service. Others may choose to forgo high earnings in exchange for job security, self-employment, flexible schedules, family time, prestige, social connection, geographic location, or even benefits such as health insurance, parental leave, a retirement plan, or tuition assistance. So for many people—perhaps most—financial return is just one of many advantages they derive from the opportunities a college education opens up.

However, the discussion in this chapter sets aside these very important considerations in order to focus solely on the financial dimension: the monetary return to an individual from his investment in higher education. It also sets aside the financial returns that accrue to our economy as a whole, which extend far beyond the personal gains of individual earners. The level of income and well-being our society achieves collectively depends on the ease with which we communicate and the technological expertise we draw on to accomplish complex tasks. As citizens, we count on our shared understanding of how governments, laws, markets, and contracts work; we benefit from the global and historical perspective that individuals bring to their professional decisions; and we expect our leaders to be knowledgeable and ethical. These immeasurable returns from higher education work to everyone's advantage—including those who may never attend college.

But for the purposes of this chapter, we'll concentrate solely on the financial returns that come to individuals because of the educational choices they make. And what we will discover is this: more years of education and higher degrees are positively correlated with increased earnings, up to a point, and in certain fields more than others. And higher-*quality* education (which may also mean paying higher tuition) is also associated with increased earnings, but again only up to a point.

Furthermore, as Chapter 3 will demonstrate in more detail, different occupations show different patterns of income over a lifetime. Some, like nursing and engineering, pay off faster in the short term but provide less long-term growth. Others, like college teaching and medicine, show a smaller jump in earnings at the beginning but provide more sustained growth. So the question of how much higher education to buy is strongly influenced by the choice of career. Indeed, sometimes, choosing an education and choosing a career are essentially the same decision.

But the *first* decision a high school graduate must make is whether to enter college at all, rather then immediately joining the work force. Today, about 80 percent of high school graduates seek some kind of postsecondary education, either immediately or after a delay. (That only about 71 percent of young people finish high school reflects deeper social issues.) A high school graduate might choose to defer postsecondary education for many reasons—perhaps to mature, to gain confidence in a career direction, to accumulate funds to finance her education, or to join the military (though, in terms of an investment, a military career is no substitute for higher education, despite the promises that recruiters often make). Once she enters college, a student gives up much of the income she would have earned by working—a real cost that must be added to the other costs of schooling. Still, the vast majority of high school graduates choose some level of higher education, believing that later financial returns will more than compensate for tuition and lost wages while in college. Let's check the numbers and see just how right those graduates are.

Trends in Earnings and Education

Prudent investors look at the historical performance of an asset before deciding to buy, and Mr. Trello would be wise to approach his decision the same way. While "past performance is no guarantee of future returns," it can provide a useful perspective. Here's some of what we know about the past performance of investment in higher education.

From 1976 to 1983 the median earnings of both college graduates and high school graduates dropped, after adjusting for inflation. Still, in 1983 the median earnings of those with a BA or more were about 53 percent above the median earnings of high school graduates. From 1983 to 1994 this differential rose to more than 80 percent and has remained near that level. During the same time, the differential in earnings for high school graduates relative to those with less than a high school education widened even more markedly. The median earnings of people who did not complete high school peaked in the early 1970s and have been falling ever since, while the financial return to education has grown at every level, particularly the financial return to a college education.

Why is there now such a high premium on higher education? The short answer is international trade and advances in technology. During the last decades of the twentieth century, as trade barriers fell because of lower transportation and communication costs, the United States began to export more goods produced by American workers with high-level skills and to import more goods produced by foreign workers with low-level skills. U.S. employers in electronics, software development, biotechnology, and financial instruments demanded a highly skilled workforce and were willing to pay more to attract and keep those workers. At the same time, less-skilled American workers—those producing textiles and furniture, assembling consumer goods such as televisions, picking fruits and vegetables, or working as laborers on construction sites—had to compete with unregulated labor abroad or illegal workers at home, and as a consequence they faced fewer job opportunities and lower earnings. These fundamental changes in the structure of the economy are likely to persist and even deepen in the twenty-first century. Despite the exporting of many high-tech jobs to India and elsewhere in recent years, the American economy has become dependent on the higher education of its citizens for its long-term success.[3]

A generation or so ago, a low-skilled worker with a high school education might gain on-the-job experience in a corporation that would allow him to be promoted into a position of more responsibility. Today, as the proportion of high school graduates who enter college approaches saturation, few firms offer training to their low-skilled workers, and apprenticeships are uncommon. Over time, workers have responded to this shifting economic reality by purchasing more education. Adult workers with less than a high school education were more than 20 percent of the work force in 1976, but in 2002 they represented less than 10 percent. Those with at least some college have increased from less than 40 percent of the labor force in 1976 to nearly 60 percent today. The proportion of the work force made up of people with only a high school diploma peaked in 1980 and has declined gradually since. Nearly 60 percent of Americans born in the 1980s entered college, and today the population of the United States is better educated than at any time in its history.

One way to see how higher education pays off is to look at earnings in six large occupational groups that encompass all of civilian employment: managerial and professional; technical, sales, and administrative; service including food preparation; precision production, craft, and repair; operators, fabricators, and laborers; and farming, fishing, and forestry. For men, managerial and professional employment grew much faster than average between 1985 and 2002, and service and technical employment grew slightly faster than average. But the precision production occupations, as well as operatives, fabricators, and laborers (along with farmers, foresters, and fishermen), grew much more slowly than overall employment. While these jobs still employ many men, their fraction of the work force is shrinking.

For women, managerial and professional occupations (a large group) grew very rapidly during this period, as did farming, forestry, and fishing (a small group). Service jobs also expanded somewhat faster than average for women. Technical, sales, and administrative support, which employ many more women than men, grew a little less than average. Operators, fabricators, and laborers saw the slowest job growth for women.

Among men, earnings outpaced the cost of living only in the managerial and professional group. For other occupational groups, the median weekly earnings of men declined slightly in terms of purchasing power between 1976 and 2002. Among women, real earnings (earnings adjusted for increases in the cost of living) grew fastest in the managerial and professional group and slightly in the technical, sales, administrative support, and service occupations. Earnings declined slightly for operators, fabricators, and laborers and in farming, forestry, and fishing. Overall, the earnings of women grew faster than the earnings of men in every sector except farming, forestry, and fishing.

So for both men and women, growing job opportunities and rising earnings were found in the occupational group with the highest educational requirements—the managerial and professional category. This trend seems likely to continue. College-educated consumers have high expectations for the performance of the institutions they encounter, and this requires better management and professional services. Meanwhile, the demand for American factory workers seems likely to continue its decline. As production facilities in the United States become even more capital intensive, they will require fewer workers, and the employees hired will be more highly skilled. Consumers of electronic goods in particular are willing to pay more for better engineering and design—that is, for products with more managerial and professional inputs at the conceptual and planning stages. Component assembly, by contrast, will become increasingly an off-shore industry.

Do Undergraduate Degrees Pay Off?

How do the lifetime earnings of men and women with a bachelor's degree compare with those who have only a high school diploma? The age-earnings profiles shown in Figure 2.1—a picture of the earnings an individual might expect at each age of life—are a useful starting point for understanding the payoff from higher education. But for a variety of reasons this information is incomplete. First, the age-earnings profile is just a snapshot of earnings, which can change dramatically over time. Second, people who earn BAs may simply be more industrious, on average, than those who stop with a high school diploma—and if that were true, this characteristic, more so than the education itself, would be reflected in lifetime earnings. Third, these estimated returns may be influenced by reporting

Female Earnings Profile: BA

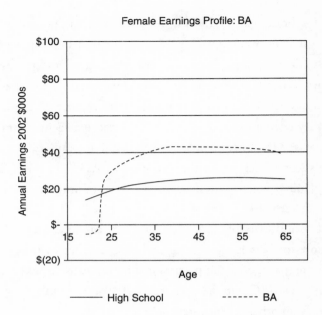

Male Earnings Profile: BA

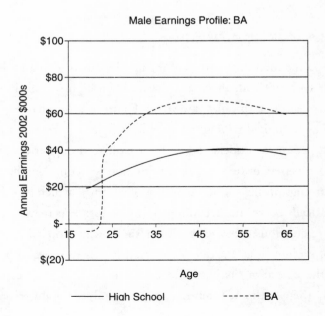

errors, or by differences in hours worked, overtime, and responsibilities rather than differences in education. Finally, these statistics include those with a BA who were working at one point in time; it does not include others who earned a BA but were not in the paid work force.[4]

To understand the relation between a college education and earnings in more detail, let's follow the story of a high school graduate, Clarissa Chin, who chose to earn her BA degree at a four-year state school and paid the annual tuition of $7,500 for each of her four years. She also took a part-time job, which paid about one-quarter of what she would have earned as an average high school graduate had she not gone straight to college. When Clarissa graduated, she went to work and was paid the average income of an employee her age with a BA degree; we can reasonably assume that had she not gone to college, she would have earned the average income of a high school graduate with no college education.[5]

What kind of financial return can Clarissa expect for the years she spent getting her BA degree? To make this calculation, we must take account of the likelihood that Clarissa will stay alive (for that, we'll use the Census Bureau's average survival rates) and the likelihood that she'll land a job and remain in the work force until age 65 (for that, we'll use average labor force participation and unemployment rates from the Bureau of Labor Statistics).[6] Given those assumptions, the payoff to her education can be calculated in two different ways.

One method uses the *present value* of different levels of education, and it starts by asking two hypothetical questions: (1) How much would Clarissa have had to put into a mutual fund right after high school graduation, in order to create a cash flow that would equal her lifetime earnings with a BA degree? (2) If Clarissa had decided not to enter college but rather had gone straight to work, how much would she have had to put into a mutual fund right after high school graduation, in order to create a cash flow that would equal her lifetime earnings with just a diploma? We'll assume an annual interest rate of 10 percent for these imaginary mutual funds, after inflation (the top of the plausible range). The sum of money that must go into each fund is called the *present value* of Clarissa's education.

We know from the Bureau of the Census statistics that the present value of her high school education is $142,000 (see Table 1). This is what she would have had to invest in her mutual fund right after graduation in order to duplicate her lifetime wages with just a diploma. By contrast, the present value of her college degree is $160,000. This number includes a present value of $142,000 for her earnings with a high school diploma, plus a present value of $70,000 for extra earnings because of her BA, minus $30,000 in tuition, and minus another $22,000 in lost earnings while in college. For Clarissa, the differential (expressed in present value) between earnings with just a high school diploma and earnings with a BA degree is $18,000. That might not seem like much, but remember this: whenever the dollar amount of this differential in present value is a positive number, the investment in higher education is returning *more* than 10 percent per year, net of inflation. Any serious investor will tell us that this is an excellent financial return.

The numbers look somewhat different for Clarissa's brother Steve, who did not go on to college. The present value of his expected lifetime earnings with just a high school diploma is $254,000—considerably higher than the present value of Clarissa's earnings, even with a college degree. For several reasons, men typically make more money than women over the course of a lifetime, at every level of education. Men choose somewhat different occupations, they have different rates of labor force participation, and they suffer less discrimination in hiring and promotion. Also, the choices women make may well be constrained by cultural and familial influences—a topic that goes beyond the scope of this book. If Steve had gone on to college, the present value of his gain in earnings from a BA would have been $58,000 ($254,000 plus an extra $129,000 from the BA, minus $30,000 in tuition and $41,000 in forgone earnings). This is considerably higher than Clarissa's $18,000.

A second way to evaluate Clarissa's investment is by calculating the *internal rate of return*. This method asks the question: What kind of annual return can Clarissa expect on her initial investment in tuition and lost wages during college, expressed as a percentage after inflation? Typical well-diversified mutual funds are unlikely to return more than 10 percent per year after inflation, calculated over many decades.[7] Investments with modest risk that yield 10 percent or more per year net of inflation are considered very good buys over the long term. By this standard, Clarissa's education should pay off very nicely. Among women, the internal rate of return for a BA is 13 percent per year. Among men, the return is even stronger, at 16 percent per year—well above the 10 percent annual benchmark of other investments. The difference between a 13 percent and a 16 percent return may not seem like much in one year; but over the course of several decades, the power of compounding becomes a huge factor in the larger lifetime earnings of men. Mr. Trello's commitment to an undergraduate education for each of his sons is quite likely to increase his family's wealth considerably.

The same methods of analysis can yield an estimated rate of return for each level of higher education. Students who enter college but stop short of a BA make smaller investments in higher education and yet earn good returns. Some of them earn two-year associate (AA) degrees in a technical area; some earn an AA degree in an academic area; and some earn college credits but no degree. Those with some college credits but no degree get the least return from their investment—a difference in present value of $4,000 for men and $2,000 for women. This is not huge, but it is positive nevertheless, which means that it surpasses the 10 percent benchmark for an excellent investment. The technical AA degree yields a bit more: $14,000 in present value for both men and women. And the academic AA degree yields even more: $19,000 for men and $17,000 for women. These returns translate into a strong internal rate of return of 16 percent for men and 15 percent for women for all AA degrees. So given the modest tuition and relatively short period of lost earnings, a two-year degree program can make a dramatic difference in lifetime income compared with a high school diploma.[8]

Do Postgraduate Degrees Pay Off?

The highest annual earnings accrue, on average, to holders of postgraduate degrees, particularly professional degrees in law, medicine, and business. Post-baccalaureate programs involve a larger investment of years in school without full earnings and with higher tuition. To see how well this investment pays off, let's assume that a master's degree requires two years of full-time effort after the BA and costs $8,000 per year in tuition. For the general class of all professional degrees, we'll assume an average of three years of full-time schooling at a tuition of $16,500 per year (though a JD and MD require more years and even higher annual tuition). For the PhD, we'll assume six years of study after the BA but with a stipend of $13,500 rather than tuition, since students in PhD programs often pay no tuition and receive a living allowance that varies depending on the field of study.

The earnings profile for master's degree holders shows a shape similar to that of the BA (Figure 2.1) but somewhat above it. For men who go from a BA to an MA, the difference in the present value of return is −$11,000, and the internal rate of 8 percent is less than the 10 percent benchmark. For women, the difference in the present value between a BA and an MA is $1,000, but because women with a BA earn less than men overall, that modest increase represents a 10 percent internal rate of return. In some fields, the MA pays off very well for both men and women, as we will see in the next chapter, and many people improve their rate of return by holding down a job while attending classes. Even a negative return doesn't necessarily mean that students made a poor choice. There are many reasons other than earnings to want a master's degree, and many master's degrees are in fields where nonmonetary rewards may be particularly important, as in social work, librarianship, and education. The calculations here merely provide benchmarks against which to compare alternatives in a general way.

The present value of the gain in earnings from the BA to a professional degree is $75,000 for men and $56,000 for women, with internal rates of return of 14 percent for men and 15 percent for women. This is a substantial gain, especially given the high cost of the years of extra schooling. Again, Mr. Trello is quite likely to see a satisfactory increase in his family's wealth if he invests in his sons' postgraduate programs. But given the rate of return for women, it's a pity (from a purely financial point of view) that he has no daughters to send to professional school.

The present value of return in lifetime earnings from adding a PhD to a BA is −$24,000 for men and $82,000 for women. The internal rate of return for men is just 7 percent, well under the 10 percent benchmark, but 100 percent for women. So a PhD has been a *very* good buy for women but not such a good buy for men. Again, there may be other advantages to holding a PhD degree that make it worthwhile for a given man, despite its lower financial return. And of course the financial returns on a PhD are not negative for the individual whose degree helps him land a choice job.[9]

A third way of looking at gains from education (in addition to present value and internal rate of return) is to consider the effect of education on the likelihood of earning a very high income. The Census's Current Population Survey reports the proportion of individuals at each level of education who earned more than $150,000 per year from 1996 to 2003. Among those who stopped their education with a high school diploma, 0.6 percent of males (6 in 1,000) and 0.1 percent of females (1 in 1,000) had earnings over $150,000, and this select group included a number of famous athletes and entertainers. Catherine Zeta-Jones, for example, began her stage career at age fifteen; LeBron James, with his tens of millions in promotional contracts, became a professional basketball player just after high school; the late Peter Jennings of ABC news didn't even complete high school. By comparison, among those with professional degrees, 25 percent of males (250 in 1,000) and 8 percent of females (78 in 1,000, to be exact) earned over $150,000 per year. The likelihood of very high earnings increases dramatically at higher levels of education.

Yet there is a considerable spread of earnings among people with the same level of education, and a large variation in earnings even among those of the same sex, age, and level of education. The top one-sixth of males with high school diplomas earn as much as the bottom one-sixth of males with PhDs. In addition to raw talent and intelligence, this wide dispersion reflects differences in the quality of education, the choice of more leisure versus work time, and the risks taken in pursuing careers. And of course we should not forget the role of mistakes and just dumb luck.

As the statistics cited above make clear, the earnings of women at every level of education are much lower over their lifetimes, on average, than the earnings of men. And yet female enrollment in college grew from 32 percent in 1950 to 50 percent in 1978 to 57 percent in 2004, and enrollment in postgraduate education increased as well. One possible explanation for this trend, as we saw in Chapter 1, is the higher rate of return for women on their investment in college, particularly as occupational opportunities have expanded over the last half century: Women's earnings increase at a higher rate than men's do as they become better educated. But there's an alternative explanation for the high enrollments of women in college.

Some have argued persuasively that, on average, women place a greater value on the nonmonetary rewards from education than men do—the opportunity to choose careers for their intrinsic satisfaction, a greater sense of serving broader civic goals and cultural advancement, the pleasure of learning for its own sake. In this view, education pays higher dividends for women than for men even if it doesn't necessarily lead to financial parity. Regardless of which explanation one favors, the high level of investment in college and postgraduate education by women is a fact of life today. With larger enrollments and significant academic success as stepping stones, many women will achieve financial parity with men in the coming decades, and in some cases exceed it. And in addition, women will likely take on more leadership roles in politics, religion, academia, the nonprofit sector, and the corporate world, with higher education playing a significant enabling role. Coca Cola's CEO isn't a woman, but Pepsi's is.

Does the Quality of the Institution Pay Off?

Mr. Trello's plan for his sons includes supporting high-quality education rather than seeking low prices. Is the extra outlay for extra quality worth the candle?

Two facts are clear from the studies we will examine. First, graduates of highly regarded nationally renowned colleges earn significantly more over a lifetime than graduates of lesser known local colleges. Indeed, the rate of return on the extra expenditure, estimated from simple salary differentials, is quite high. Second, students of greater talent, preparation, and ambition are more likely to apply to highly regarded colleges; those colleges are much more likely to offer admission to students with better prospects; and students with offers from a more prestigious school and a less prestigious one are more likely to accept the former. In other words, the process of application and admission sorts students among colleges, so that students who are more likely to enjoy lifetime success are also more likely to enroll in more selective—and more expensive—colleges.

Now, the question of whether extra quality is worth the price involves isolating the effect of the college from the effect of the student's background. How would the student who enrolled at a less expensive, less prestigious college have fared had she enrolled at a more expensive, more prestigious one? This is a difficult question to answer. A statistical approach to answering it would require following a group of people from college through their working years, taking account of their attributes as students and the attributes of the colleges they attended. Because an experiment that assigns students randomly to colleges is impossible to conduct, the investigator must find a way to control statistically for the personal attributes of students—not an easy task.

The study would also need to isolate the attributes of colleges that actually make a difference in a student's lifetime earnings, and to date no study has done this. Still, the major attributes are easy to list: the quality of the faculty and instruction, the talent and influence of the peer group, and the probability that a prestigious degree acts as a positive signal to prospective graduate schools and employers, independent of the accomplishments of the individual student. A family contemplating an investment in higher education could make sharper decisions about whether to spend more for a college with particular attributes if it were clear which attributes matter, but the available evidence is tantalizingly incomplete.

Social scientists have attempted to control for the attributes of students in three different ways. One group used data from Minnesota about identical twin girls who were raised together, to control for genetic, home, and educational backgrounds before college. In most cases where the two twins chose two different kinds of schools, the one who chose a private research university, with its well-compensated faculty and smaller student body, was earning more at midlife than her identical twin who graduated from a huge public university with limited selectivity. The estimated rate of return for attending a regional public institution like Minnesota State University Mankato was 20 percent; a nationally respected public research university like the University of Minnesota yielded 32 percent. A highly selective small liberal arts college like Wellesley College yielded 40 percent; a private, smaller research university like the University of Pennsylvania yielded a whopping 51 percent. The study of twins found large differentials across categories of colleges.[10]

Another investigation used national surveys that followed a group of students over many years. Drawing on information about how tuition and financial aid affected their college choices, the investigators were able to isolate the independent effect of the college experience itself from family background and other attributes of the student. They found that people who attended elite private colleges earned 40 percent more than those who attended regional public colleges. They also discovered a bigger effect in the 1980s than in the 1970s, suggesting that the advantages of quality have risen in recent decades. However, the statistical methods used may not have fully controlled for how students sort among colleges.[11]

The third study controlled not only for observed differences among students (grades and test scores, for example) but also for the possibility that other differences might have affected where students applied to college and which colleges admitted them.[12] The study matched students who were accepted and denied admission by the same colleges but who chose, in the end, to attend different ones. Each matched pair of students included only those who were looking for the same kind of colleges and who were viewed as comparable by college admission officers. The study controlled for other attributes of students, including parental income, race, and recruitment by athletic coaches, and measured the quality of colleges in several ways, including average SAT scores and tuition net of financial aid. It also considered whether returns on the educational investment differed by family income level.

In comparing the earnings a decade or so after college for students in matched accepted/denied sets, the study found little difference in earnings as a function of the quality of the college attended, when measured by the mean SAT scores of students or the competitiveness of the college as classified by Barron's. However, it did find significant positive earnings differentials for students at colleges with higher tuition net of financial aid. Most of the colleges in the matched accepted/denied sets were very similar, however, and that made it more difficult to distinguish the effect of any large differences in college quality.

This third study also found another interesting result that bears on the question of quality. It turns out that a student's rank in his college class had a positive effect on his earnings, other things being equal. Of course this effect may not be enough to overcome the higher earnings that come with graduation from a much more challenging school. Being a bigger fish in a smaller, less competitive pond has some financial advantages, but the size of the pond still matters.

These three kinds of evidence taken together lead to the conclusion that the financial returns on an investment in quality are quite high across broad categories of colleges, but the returns do not vary much among generally similar colleges. Individual programs within colleges might show significant differences in returns, even among generally similar colleges, but this kind of study has not been done.

The financial returns on quality in higher education appear to be greater for students from lower income and under-represented minority households. For a student from a lower income household, attendance at a highly ranked college moves the student toward incomes comparable to other graduates from the same college, yielding a higher gain and therefore a higher rate of return. Many leading colleges enhance this payoff from higher education by offering talented students from lower income households an attractive financial aid package.[13]

The higher earnings for students in matched accepted/denied sets who enrolled at more expensive colleges indicate that net tuition is associated with attributes of the colleges that influence lifetime earnings. (Just *how* tuition relates to college quality is a question addressed in Chapter 5.) But since the studies, taken together, show little or no easily observed difference in lifetime prospects for graduates of *generally similar colleges,* a student can confidently search among these schools for an attractive net price, for strong educational services in the program of interest, and for a comfortable social setting. And they should always bear in mind that the differences in lifetime earnings among graduates of any given college are much larger than the average differences in earnings across many colleges in a single category. Similar colleges give similar average results, and yet every one of them shows significant variation in results among its graduates.

Another important fact to bear in mind is this: the basic statistics used in ranking colleges, such as average SAT scores, the percentage of applicants offered admission, and the percentage of applicants who accept these offers (a statistic called *yield*), are poor measures of quality. A difference of dozens of places in published rankings does not produce discernible differences in the life prospects of students. But other features of colleges may indeed be important in shaping life prospects. A savvy investor will want to study the details, an idea explored more fully in later chapters.

Mr. Trello's commitment to paying extra for quality may indeed be a wise move if his sons consider their college and postgraduate choices carefully. By looking at dozens of similar institutions, the Trellos may find that a talented faculty, an intense intellectual atmosphere for students, and capable peers are available at varying prices. And each son may confidently make a different choice for his own personal reasons, without affecting his overall life prospects.

The Payoff to Higher Education

So to summarize: this brief interpretation of economic studies and surveys demonstrates a significant payoff to higher education. Indeed, in many cases the rewards are extraordinary. On average, higher education offers excellent value for the dollar spent, from the two-year degree through professional school. But with BAs now so prevalent, the quality of the college attended and the pursuit of advanced degrees have become two important marks of distinction in the work force. Forty-three percent of those who earned BAs in 1992–1993 continued their studies in masters, professional, or PhD programs within ten years of graduation, and 63 percent of that group completed these courses of study. About 20 percent of those who earned BA degrees also earned MAs. About 4 percent of BAs earned professional degrees, and about 2 percent earned doctorates. MA and PhD degrees, on average, yielded lower rates of return than professional degrees.[14]

In contemplating a point of entry into higher education, a prospective student will want to forecast how much education they are likely to complete. If two years of higher education is a likely end point, then choosing a less expensive two-year college will yield a higher return than two years at a more expensive four-year college. But if a postgraduate degree is the likely conclusion, then enrollment at a four-year college with a track record of placing students in advanced programs will be worthwhile, despite the extra cost.

The calculations here that account for age, gender, and level of education have explained only a small part of the total variation in lifetime earnings. To learn more, in the next chapter we will look at individual occupations.

CHAPTER THREE

Career Opportunities: The Choices that Matter

Susan Evans, one of the best students in my urban economics class, came to college with the intention of going to medical school, and she had started to accumulate the pre-med credits to make it possible. But after volunteering in two hospitals, she began to reconsider. She was disheartened by the hectic pace of clinical work and by the scant time physicians spent with their patients. Also, she was discouraged by the huge debt she would owe when she finished her medical training, not to mention the long years of work required to get there. She was beginning to think that a career in nursing might be more personally rewarding, but she wanted to talk with me about whether it would be a wise move financially.

Questions like Susan's occur at every stage of a person's work life—when high school graduates contemplate college, when college students consider their majors and career choices, and when graduates shift careers in the workplace or consider going to graduate school. In choosing an occupation, most people are drawn primarily by an affinity for the kinds of problems, materials, and colleagues they will encounter during their career. But as Susan's case makes clear, the economic return is also important, particularly when the cost of the necessary higher education is substantial.

Exploring how higher education pays off financially is a little like peeling an onion. The outer layer, described in Chapter 2, reveals how earnings vary with level of education, age, and gender. This chapter goes to the next layer, to look at how higher education pays off for men and women in different occupations. Eight benchmark occupations drawn from the 2002 Census Bureau Survey, with five others mentioned briefly, will be used to illustrate how education performs financially in a variety of career settings.

The occupations are (1) clergy, (2) elementary and secondary school teachers, (3) reporters and editors, (4) registered nurses, (5) policemen and detectives, (6) accountants and auditors, (7) insurance salespersons, (8) college and university teachers, (9) financial managers, (10) engineers, (11) marketing and public relations managers, (12) lawyers and judges, and (13) physicians. These occupations are just a few of hundreds to be found in the Census Survey, and they account for less than 10 percent of all civilian jobs (see Table 2).

There are deeper layers of the onion, of course, which reveal more detail about the relationship between earnings and education. For example, each occupation consists of individual groups with somewhat different incomes. All types of engineers do well financially, but civil engineers generally make less money than software engineers. When market forces change, the demand for certain industries, and their human capital, also waxes and wanes. In the photographic film industry, to mention one instance, the demand for chemists took a nosedive as digital photography replaced film. In addition, many personal factors, including family background, account for vast differences in the payout from higher education. But for now we'll focus on these thirteen benchmark occupations and see what we can learn about the financial rewards associated with certain career choices.[1]

The Benchmark Occupations

Some important differences stand out with even the most cursory examination of the Census Bureau data in Table 2, which were collected from 1996 to 2002. For example, clergy, who in the nineteenth century were learned professionals on a par with lawyers and physicians, now typically receive little college education, and their earnings are lower than for elementary and secondary school teachers. Teachers, like nurses, are a large occupational group dominated by women, and while teachers earn considerably less than nurses, they also work fewer hours. Male nurses earn about the same salaries as female nurses, despite being comparatively rare in this profession. And female police officers and engineers earn about the same as their male counterparts, even though there are far fewer women in these fields.

The difference in earnings between men and women is much greater in accounting, insurance, finance, and marketing, where women earn less than men even though they hold at least a third of all jobs. For women who choose law and medicine, earnings are starting to catch up with those of men, but the payoff of professional degrees for women is much greater than for men because the earnings they can expect in other careers are so much lower.

The benchmark occupations differ in growth of employment as well as earnings. From 1996 to 2002, employment for men grew faster than average among registered nurses and police officers and in marketing and finance. Earnings for men grew fastest for clergy and lawyers. Among women, employment rose in every benchmark occupation, but especially in law, medicine, marketing, and finance;

earning also increased rapidly in all occupational groups except K–12 and college teaching. Among men, *both* earnings and employment rose among police officers, financial managers, marketing managers, and physicians.

What this dual growth indicates is a significant increase in demand in these fields. When growth in employment is accompanied by stagnant earnings, as we find at all levels of teaching, this indicates an increase in demand but also an ample supply of willing workers (assuming that the quality of those workers isn't changing). Where both earnings and employment fall or grow more slowly than the aggregate, relative demand for these workers has declined. Male editors and reporters show this pattern.

Comparing average or mean earnings can be misleading because averages don't take account of the age and education of the worker. A better comparison—as the following analysis will show—comes from computing the internal rate of return for different levels of education for persons in each occupation. For the BA level, the base of comparison is all workers with only high school diplomas. For advanced degrees, the comparison is to holders of the BA. The rates are net of inflation and are most directly comparable to the rate of interest on inflation-adjusted Treasury bonds.

A quick scan of Table 3 shows that the highest internal rate of return for a BA and below comes from a two-year program for registered nurses, with an astounding 39 percent payoff. Returns are also very high for women professors, engineers, financial managers, and lawyers. The rate of return on education is relatively low for women who become teachers. For Susan Evans, the rate of return on a much smaller financial investment in nursing school will be higher than the rate of return on the much larger investment in medical school, if nursing continues to interest her.[2]

For men, the overall rate of return on their investment in higher education is often lower than for women, but it is relatively high for engineers, lawyers, and insurance sales; it is lowest for clergy and college teachers. Of course, each occupation has idiosyncrasies that influence employment and earnings and affect how the occupation is likely to evolve. The following discussion of eight benchmark careers looks more closely at some of these details.

Teachers

Betsy Rogers, National Teacher of the Year in 2003, couldn't "recall a time when she didn't want to be a teacher."[3] Though she earned an MA and doctorate, she continued to teach first and second grades near Birmingham, Alabama. Teaching has many rewards that go far beyond earnings, not the least of which is that people remember their teachers for decades, often with deep appreciation. Parents frequently express the hope that their children and grandchildren will have teachers as dedicated as ones they remember.

For several reasons, the salaries of elementary and secondary schoolteachers ought to be rising. With so many mothers now in the work force and other changes in families—higher returns to education, particularly for women; fewer children, with larger investments in each child; and more single-parent households—one might expect that the demand for school services would increase. As significant opportunities for women have opened in the professions and management, one would think that traditionally female occupations like teaching should start to pay more in order to compete for talented women and men. And given the need for better education in an electronic age, along with the strong financial returns education offers, one might expect that the demand for better quality schools would lead to higher pay for teachers.[4]

Yet teacher salaries have stagnated. Why is this? A countervailing force is that salaries for 97 percent of teachers are defined strictly in terms of education and years of experience, not by their performance in the classroom or other attributes. Such civil service compensation schedules embody rigid salary scales, salary compression (top talent is underpaid and bottom talent is overpaid), and stifling work rules. Although many people advocate more flexible pay plans to attract and motivate talented teachers—for example, pay more to those with training in math and science, to those with demonstrated higher levels of academic performance, and to those whom principals and colleagues judge to be more effective—successful implementation of these is likely to be unusual.[5]

About 60 percent of teachers remain in the profession for their entire work life, rather than switching to other occupations—a much higher proportion than in other fields, where only about 25 percent of women stay in their first career. Some of the reasons are obvious. Teachers work a nine-month year and so earn more per work day than those who put in an eleven-month year at comparable annual pay. Teaching accommodates childrearing better than many professions—and not just because teachers have their late afternoons and summers off. A person who withdraws temporarily from a law firm or medical practice to take care of small children (or for any other reason) is likely to see a 10 percent decrease in salary for every year she stays out of work. Teachers, by contrast, are able to exit and return to the classroom without taking a pay cut.[6]

But a more portentous factor in the high retention rates among teachers might be that civil service rules make the firing of ineffective teachers much more difficult. And if the skills learned in teaching have limited value outside the classroom, as some analysts have speculated, these combined factors would help explain why a disproportionately high percentage of teachers stay in the classroom, despite stagnant earnings and rapidly improving job opportunities for women in many other fields.[7]

The lifetime earnings profile for female teachers with a bachelor's degree is close to that for all women with a BA, but male teachers with a bachelor's make much less than other male college graduates. Teachers with MA degrees earn about one-third more per year than teachers with only the BA. But since they are, on average, about five years older, some of the differential in mean earnings reflects this gap in age. The modest rise in earnings profile with age for all teachers indicates that experience is somewhat rewarded in this profession. The state of New York and nineteen other states require the MA within five years of beginning one's career. The nation awards more master's degrees in education than it awards BAs in education, presumably because many teachers who earn other baccalaureate degrees use the MA in education as an entrée to the field. The financial rewards are even greater when teaching is combined with part-time study, which mitigates the cost of lost earnings.[8]

Private school teachers earn less than public school teachers (about 25 percent less for women, 17 percent less for men). The upside is that private schools typically do not require state certification, they feature smaller classes with formal and informal selection of students, and they offer a less bureaucratic work environment than public school systems.[9]

While the median earnings of teachers with college degrees have grown little over recent decades when measured in dollars of constant purchasing power, the earnings of women have grown a little relative to men. And, surprisingly, employment among women teachers has risen, even as other higher paying professional opportunities for women have expanded.

Registered Nurses

Students may prepare for careers as registered nurses by pursuing a two-year AA degree or a four-year BA degree and then sitting for the national exam (NCLEX). Although a BA isn't required of registered nurses, it opens opportunities for a master's degree, and with that credential comes the possibility of being a nurse practitioner, manager, or nursing school teacher.

In the face of a national nursing shortage, some economists and nurses believe that hospitals hire fewer registered nurses than they need in order to keep salaries low. But unfilled vacancies as high as 14 percent of budgeted positions have persisted since 1945—a sign that the current nursing shortage is not new or temporary. The underlying reason is monopsony (meaning literally one buyer, but more generally referring to employers with some control of the wages they pay). In a given metropolitan area, about two-thirds of all nurses work for just a handful of hospitals or hospital chains. Registered nurses make up about one-fourth of all hospital-based health care workers and about 30 percent of a hospital's wage bill. Hospital managers could attract more nurses if they raised salaries, but they would have to pay the higher salaries to all of the nurses they employ. Thus, the cost of hiring another nurse by offering a higher salary is much greater than the amount paid to the next nurse hired.[10]

Hospitals pursue a variety of strategies to attract new nurses. They offer signing bonuses, hire temporary nurses, and vigorously recruit in distant places rather than raise base salary, all of which allows hospitals to pay nurses less than the value of their contribution. As a consequence, hospitals are permanently understaffed, and nurses are chronically overworked and underpaid. This leads to further shortages, as burned-out nurses walk off the wards. The limited number of accredited schools of nursing further restricts the flow of qualified workers into this profession.

Some people have proposed that the federal government allow more immigration of nurses and provide more subsidies to train nurses. But if the shortages arise because employers restrict salaries, increasing the number of nurses is likely to lower the pay scale in the long run, and the shortages will persist. It is unclear how to make the market for nurses more competitive, particularly given the complex setting of regulations, negotiated contracts for services, and other peculiarities of the hospital and medical industry. The conventional wisdom that "You can always find employment as a nurse" may well reflect the permanent character of this dilemma.[11]

Among women, the earnings profile for RNs with a BA degree is quite similar to that for RNs with an AA degree. This means that the rate of return on a four-year program is much lower than that of a two-year program. (The net present value of an AA in nursing is $73,000 for women, whereas the net present value of a BA in nursing is only $36,000; see Chapter 2 for an explanation of net present value.) If a career as an RN is the final goal of post-secondary schooling, an AA degree is a much better investment than a BA. But a BA is a step toward a master's degree in nursing (worth an additional $37,000 in net present value). The return on an investment of a BA plus MA is worth pursuing, from a strictly financial perspective, and the nonmonetary professional rewards associated with an MA increase the value of this degree.

Median earnings for nurses dropped in the 1970s and recovered in the early 1980s, with modest growth since then. Employment for women in nursing has grown rapidly, while employment for men has shown modest growth. As the American population ages in the decades ahead, the demand for nurses is likely to accelerate. And if serious shortages loom, nursing may see substantial pay hikes, an expanded number of schools of nursing, and increased enrollment in two-year programs. A number of colleges are already adding or enlarging nursing programs in anticipation of this demographic shift.[12]

Accountants and Auditors

Because the corporate sector of the economy is large and people fill many different kinds of jobs, the Census Bureau has no occupation called "business." To get some insight into this diverse sector, we'll look at two reasonably well defined groups: (1) accountants and auditors and (2) financial managers. (Bookkeepers and clerks are a separate occupation.)

Accountants and auditors implement and verify systems that track the flow of cash and other assets through an enterprise. These systems are designed to discourage theft, improve decision making, and document tax liabilities. My student Valerie Johnson completed a double major in math and economics as an undergraduate and then enrolled in the twelve-month master of accountancy (MAC) program at the University of Arkansas, with the goal of becoming a Certified Public Accountant. But a person doesn't have to become certified in order to work as an accountant. Accounting jobs comprise a wide range of skills, and CPAs make up only about 22 percent of accountants in the Census Bureau's list of occupations.[13]

For men, mean earnings for full-time accountants are higher with more education. For women, the increments in mean earnings are more modest but still growing. The differential in earnings for men and women is larger in this occupation than among police, nurses, or teachers. Some of the gap in pay may reflect the number of hours worked, but there is also some evidence that women are less likely to take and pass the Uniform CPA exam. The proportion of female accountants grew substantially between 1970 and 2002—to the point where women seem to be taking over the field. This demographic change has had little effect on the gender gap in earnings: male accountants, though a shrinking fraction of the work force, still take home substantially more pay than women.[14]

Female accountants with just a high school diploma earn little more than average among women with a high school diploma. Women with some college credits earn more than their counterparts with just a high school education (net present value of "some college" for women: $20,000). Female accountants with a BA earn slightly more than the average woman with a college degree (net present value: $32,000). The MA in accounting, by contrast, is not a good financial investment for women in general, though again there may be nonfinancial benefits that make this degree worthwhile in individual cases. Male accountants with some college but less than a BA earn about the same as the average of all men with high school diplomas. College credits don't seem to improve the earnings picture unless men get a BA. Those who do start with considerably higher earnings, and they peak at age 48 (net present value: $54,000).[15]

The internal rate of return on a BA for men and women in accounting is 16 and 15 percent, respectively. When CPAs are self-employed or work with a few partners, their earnings are likely to be linked directly to the number of hours worked and the rates clients are willing to pay for services. Many accountants are salaried employees of accounting firms or businesses, however, and the rewards for extra effort are muted relative to some other business occupations. Although some raises and advancement may be tied to performance, and age has a modest effect on earnings, the lifetime earnings profiles of accountants are relatively flat.

Several indicators suggest that the accounting profession is not faring well. The *Occupational Outlook Handbook* notes a declining demand for "traditional [accounting] services." As most business information systems have moved to computers of increasing sophistication, the demand for paper and pencil ledger-sheet accounting has declined dramatically. Other evidence of decline is a 25 percent decrease in the number of accountants hired by CPA firms from 1995 to 2001 and a drop in accounting degrees awarded from 1995 to 1998. These declines were occurring before the corporate accounting scandals of the early 2000s.[16]

An annual survey sponsored by the American Institute of Certified Public Accountants confirms these trends. The number of people sitting for the Uniform CPA exam peaked in 1990 at 144,000 and fell to 127,000 in 2000. Some of the drop-off may reflect the new requirement of an extra year of study beyond the BA in order to sit for the exam; but the decline had set in before the new requirement went into effect. Another factor: the pass rate on the Uniform CPA exam is often less than 20 percent, much lower than the pass rate on the bar exam. And paradoxically, the number of credit hours of study in accounting appears to be unrelated to the likelihood of passing the exam. The decision of the AICPA to stiffen certification requirements in the face of modest or declining demand for accountants may have slowed the growth of this profession, and as a consequence the incomes of existing CPAs and those few who gain certification may increase.[17]

Financial Managers

The second business occupation we will examine closely is financial manager, a role that involves managing budgets, investing financial assets, controlling risks and liabilities, and evaluating investment decisions. Among men, financial managers with a high school diploma or some college credits show earnings profiles similar to all holders of the BA, and their mean earnings are not significantly different. For women, some college credits and the AA degree yield higher earnings compared to high school, but the present value of the gain does not justify the cost. A bachelor's degree for women, on the other hand, yields sufficiently higher earnings to make this a good investment. An MA in finance yields consistently higher earnings for men but not for women, but it is important to note that this does not include the MBA. In the Census Bureau database, an MBA counts as a "professional degree," alongside the JD and MD, rather than a master's degree.

Financial managers earn considerably more than accountants, on average. Among men, mean earnings of financial managers with a BA degree are 18 percent above that of accountants and auditors with similar education, and the average earnings of holders of the MA in finance are also 18 percent above similarly educated accountants. The differential in means for women is 30 percent more than accountants among those with the BA and 37 percent more with the MA.

The age-earnings profiles for men show a peak at age 46 with a BA and at 44 with an MA, and a gradual decline thereafter. The profile for women is similar, with peaks at ages 43 and 40, respectively. Although the age-earnings profile for a BA is similar for men and women, the profiles differ by gender at other education levels. The BA pays off better for women than for men, perhaps because employers are reluctant to hire women as financial managers if they don't have this credential.

Twenty-six percent of men and 7 percent of women in financial management earn over $150,000 per year, making this occupation a potential brass-ring career. Financial managers tend to earn more in larger firms, where they receive bonuses—an indication that individual performance matters. Controllers who are CPAs with an MBA degree earned about 20 percent more than the average financial manager.[18]

The median earnings for male financial managers rose slightly over the last thirty years, while the median for women rose more, narrowing the gender gap. Even though median incomes overall increased only modestly, employment grew rapidly over the last two decades, with extraordinary growth among women. This pattern suggests that workers are easily attracted to jobs in financial management.

Engineers

Interpreting the earnings of engineers is a complicated task. This occupational group includes licensed professional engineers (PEs) and others who do not hold licenses. Added to that is the fact that engineers are typically trained in a specialty from the outset. Petroleum, mining, and nuclear engineering are among the highest paid fields; chemical and electrical engineers fall in the middle group; and mechanical and civil engineers are among the lower paid members of the profession. Because the training is specialized, an engineer trained in one field of engineering would have difficulty finding employment in another field. Earnings and opportunities might rise for several years in electrical engineering, but civil and chemical engineers would not be eligible for those jobs.[19]

And here's another difficulty: About half of the people who start out as engineers jump to a managerial track midway through their careers. The shift to sales, production, or other occupations is often associated with higher earnings and may be viewed as a promotion. The early years of technical work often occur in groups where the contribution of individuals to the final product may not be measured well enough to award systematic bonuses; however, the possibility of moving to management may motivate entering engineers to perform well. An earnings profile that looks only at a person of a given age employed as an engineer understates the typical lifetime earnings for those who train for and enter the work force as engineers.[20]

That said, the age-earnings profile for men shows substantial gains in income with an AA (net present value: $97,722). (There are too few women in the group to allow reliable estimates.) Engineers with a BA degree earn an even better return, and MAs earn higher incomes than BAs, although not sufficiently high to make the MA a good investment. Perhaps that's because the most successful and highest paid engineers with MAs move over to management or into other roles, and their incomes are missing from this calculation. Engineers have higher average earnings than financial managers, but a much smaller proportion of engineers earn over $150,000 per year. To make that kind of money, people who train as engineers usually have to land managerial positions. Engineering itself seldom leads to very high earnings.

The median earnings of male engineers declined through the 1970s and regained ground in the 1990s. Female engineers saw earnings rise steadily from the early 1970s to 2002. Very few women were employed as engineers in 1970, but the proportion grew to about 10 percent by 2002. Employment for both male and female engineers increased during this period.

Earnings of engineers are often tied to specific markets, such as defense spending. Growth in the computing industry has expanded opportunities for electrical engineers. Because engineers often create new capital goods, they fare less well in recessions. The number of new engineers responds flexibly to changes in earnings and demand. Mid-career shifts in and out of engineering also seem to vary with changing salaries and demand.[21]

Lawyers and Judges

Because lawyers and judges are usually licensed, the educational requirements for this occupational group are enforced by the states. Most lawyers earn a JD degree, and most holders of this degree become licensed. Given the significant cost, in time and money, of investment in a legal education, many people who become lawyers will remain in the occupation, even if they shift from private practice to a government agency or to in-house counsel for corporations. However, some lawyers move to other roles, including managerial positions in the for-profit sector. By some estimates, more than 10 percent of the chief executives of the S&P 500 largest companies are lawyers. The link between education and career earnings is clearer for lawyers and judges than for most other workers.[22]

The wealth-value of a legal education is much larger for women than for men. While women with only the BA earn much less than their male counterparts, the incomes of lawyers are approaching gender parity. The internal rate of return of a legal education, given the BA, is 18 percent for men (net present value: $156,000) and 26 percent for women (net present value: $197,000, even taking the high cost of tuition and lost earnings into account). For men, the expected earnings peak of $133,000 occurs at age 54, while for women a peak of $112,000 occurs at age 47. The substantial returns to women who enter the legal profession may explain the recent surge in female enrollment in law schools.[23]

A significant proportion of practicing lawyers earn over $150,000 per year: 23 percent of males and 8 percent of females. These brass-ring earnings may reflect, in part, the nature of the incentives law-yers face. In most law firms, they receive bonuses and promotions based on the number of billable hours they rack up, not just the quality of their work. Some law firms expect their associates to bill 2,000 or more hours per year. A lawyer will work another unbilled hour for every two billed; these hours are spent maintaining rela-tionships within the firm, keeping current with legal developments not tied to a specific client's needs, and so on. A 3,000-hour work year translates into an average of about 60 hours per week, with even longer workdays as deadlines approach.[24]

Young associates face a strict timetable for being promoted to partner, often a five-to-seven year trial period. Those who do not make partner are invited to leave; it is an up-or-out decision. The winner-take-all character of the legal profession, at least as it plays out in large firms, rewards high levels of effort and high-quality per-formance. This is not a profession for the faint-hearted, and the pat-tern of high earnings reflects these occupational pressures, as well as the selectivity of law schools.

The median earnings of lawyers and judges have shown dramatic and sustained increases over the last thirty years. Among men, the median income for lawyers rose from $64,000 in 1971 (expressed in 2002 dollars) to $100,000 in 2002. For women, the growth in me-dian earnings was even more dramatic, from $34,000 to $75,000. Women accounted for 4 percent of lawyers and judges in 1971 and 25 percent in 2002. Employment of both men and women has grown significantly in this period, though growth has slowed some-what in the last few years.

A rise in earnings with growth in employment suggests that demand is increasing, along with some constraint on supply. The growth in demand can be traced to a number of causes. In an impersonal urban world, where many transactions of increasing complexity take place among strangers, formal contracts become crucial. Trademarks, copyrights, patents, and trade secrets require legal protections that were largely unnecessary when trade was mostly in goods whose quality was readily apparent and whose ownership was established by possession. Legal services play a significant and expanding role in making the postindustrial global economy work.[25]

In many states, only graduates of law schools that have been approved by the America Bar Association may sit for the bar exam. As the result of a lawsuit and action by the Department of Justice, the ABA has recently made accreditation easier, and more law schools have opened. But some observers continue to view the ABA accreditation process as a significant barrier to the profession. Raising the number of law graduates would depress the earnings of lawyers in solo practice, in small firms, and in salaried positions, but it would probably do little to reduce the fees and incomes of lawyers in large firms. As the financial stakes in a legal dispute rise, those who can afford to do so are willing to pay a premium for highly ranked service providers. Under these circumstances, lawyers earning top incomes will not be adversely affected by the total number of people in the occupation. We can see an analogous situation in the acting profession: moviegoers pay to see the performance of a few stars who earn tens of millions of dollars, while thousands of other actors with significant talent earn little. The winner-take-all character of some markets may give rise to high average incomes even though many practitioners earn comparatively little.[26]

Those who "make partner" in a large law firm with a strong reputation for quality can command an astronomical income. At the

Boston firm Ropes & Gray, partners averaged $910,000 annual salary in 2003. At one San Francisco firm with over five hundred attorneys, each partner earned nearly $1.2 million in 2000, and the firm paid beginning associates (that is, new law school graduates) $125,000 per year. The ability to attract talented young associates who meet extraordinarily high expectations leverages the reputation and enhances the earnings of partners. The continuing growth of large law firms indicates a rising demand in this sector of the legal market, a demand unlikely to be affected by the number of law school graduates.[27]

Physicians

As his senior honors thesis in economics under my tutelage, Alex Kidder did a cost-benefit analysis of a new treatment for children's cancer. He used data he helped gather at a summer post at a research hospital in his home town. He also majored in biology and eventually enrolled at Yale Medical School. Alex had a genuine fascination with medical issues and had planned to become a physician for a long time. But what kind of financial return could he expect on his investment?

The age-earnings profile for male physicians is similar to that for lawyers, peaking at $195,000 around age 50, followed by a moderate decline to $144,000 at age 65. For female physicians, the peak of $117,000 occurs at age 45. The medical profession rewards both an accumulation of skill and reputation with age, along with high performance. The median income of male physicians has increased remarkably, from $72,000 in 1972 (expressed in 2002 dollars) to $133,000 in 2002. Similarly, median earnings for female physicians rose from $52,000 in 1972 (in 2002 dollars) to $102,000 in 2002.

Employment of physicians has also grown steadily for both men and women, if significantly faster for women. This surge in demand for medical services is rooted in the demographics of an aging population, the emergence of new medical technologies and pharmaceuticals, and a general rise in incomes and expectations of quality among service providers.

Between 1977 and 1985, enrollments in medical schools surged and median earnings of physicians fell. After 1985 as the ratio of MDs to population declined, earnings moved upward, particularly for women. Although medical schools adapted to the entry of women, some analysts have expressed the concern that the American Medical Association, the Association of American Medical Colleges, and the state and national regulatory boards that are dominated by physicians operate as a guild to restrict entry to the profession in the name of higher quality. The only new medical school to open in the last twenty years is Florida State in 2002.[28]

If the accreditation process has played some role in the rising incomes of doctors, the widespread use of medical insurance, Medicare and Medicaid, and other financial innovations has also expanded the economic opportunities for physicians. Some of the growth in demand surely reflects advances in the medical sciences and the consequent improvement in the effectiveness of services. But medical outcomes in other industrialized countries where physicians receive much lower compensation are similar to those in the United States.

As with lawyers, most people who complete medical school are likely to remain employed as physicians throughout their working lives. Here again we see a tight link between schooling and career. The rate of return over the BA is 16 percent for men and 12 percent for women (net present value: $163,000 for men and $76,000 for

women). But differentials in median earnings across the specialties are large, as are the costs of training. In 2000 the median income of pediatricians was $125,000 and that of psychiatrists was
$135,000, while internists and anesthesiologists earned a median
of $250,000 and radiologists earned $289,000. Although orthope-
dic surgeons were not among the top five specialties in median
earnings, the arithmetic mean of their income at $335,000 suggests
that some orthopedists make huge incomes. In 2005 many ads at
www.physicianrecruiting.com show starting guarantees of $350,000
for orthopedists in Ohio and Michigan.[29]

In the 1990s the earnings differential for board-certified specialists
relative to others narrowed as the number of physicians with board
certification grew. The earnings of physicians respond to supply and
demand, and forecasting how public policies toward entry into
medical careers and specialties may change in the decades ahead is
difficult. As the baby boom generation moves into the over-65 age
group in 2011 and beyond, regulations about the provision of health
care and its financing are likely to change. In 2001, 88.1 percent of all
physicians had at least one managed care contract, and these contracts accounted for 40.8 percent of practice revenue. With managed
care and public insurance, rates are increasingly negotiated. Physicians are often compensated on the basis of the number of patients
seen and procedures performed. From 1989 to 2001, the number of
hours worked stayed about constant, but the number of patients
seen per week declined from 121.6 to 107.2. The earnings of physicians are further complicated by the limited information consumers
have to judge the value of services and the elaborate regulatory
structure deployed by both government and insurance companies to
contain costs.[30]

Physicians face a succession of challenges on the road to brass-ring careers. They compete with other students in gaining access to medical school, with other MDs in gaining access to favored residencies in desired specialties and, as chief residents, in gaining access to advanced training and favored entry-level jobs. The incentives for strong performance and the rewards for talent are substantial. There may also be an element of winner-take-all among patients willing to pay premium rates for top-ranked service. But with payments increasingly set by insurance companies, managed care firms, or the government, opportunities for top rates may be limited. Restrictions on the building of new medical schools and advanced training venues seem to be the most significant factors in maintaining high salaries among physicians, and have been since the 1920s.

If Mr. Trello puts one of his four sons through medical school, he will likely see a substantial return on this investment in higher education. But the initial outlay for tuition will be substantial. Add to that the lost earnings while in school, and the investment becomes even larger. Nevertheless, if his son succeeds as a physician, the average financial return will be higher than the typical return Mr. Trello would have received had he put all this money into financial markets.

Susan Evans will see a positive return on her investment in postgraduate education, whether she decides to go on to medical school or switch to nursing. But she will have a much higher income as a physician than as a nurse, and she may want to take that fact into account.

The Savvy Investor

As this review of a few benchmark occupations shows, more education usually pays off, sometimes extraordinarily well. Like a rock climber, the savvy investor will choose each educational foothold for its strength, accessibility to the climber, and its possibilities for further ascent. Each new position will offer a new perspective and may open a path previously unrecognized. A surprising number of engineering graduates enter medical schools. And a student who begins his schooling in a two-year community college may eventually complete law school. Yet, sometimes, less education may be the better buy.

Some occupations have attractive beginning salaries but relatively flat lifetime earnings trajectories, while others have steeper trajectories over a lifetime. Professionals in some fields have difficulty moving to other occupations, while in other cases movement to a different field is common. Access to some professions is severely limited by licensure restrictions, and others are wide open. Often, compensation is closely tied to individual performance, but just as often it is determined by union contracts, formal certification, and years of service. A few brass-ring occupations offer winner-take-all scenarios where compensation is essentially disbursed by lottery (even if the winners tend to downplay the high degree of luck involved).

The payoff from more education obviously depends on the students themselves, on the character of the education program, and on the details of the career they ultimately pursue. A high school student who wants to be an elementary school teacher and who hopes to make the most of his educational investment might consider spending less on his undergraduate program so that he can afford to complete an MA. For a student who aspires to a high-performance career in business, medicine, or law, with compensation to match, a professional degree may be essential. She will have to spend more on her education, but she can expect a high return on her investment—and possibly a very high income. Although fewer than one in twenty people who hold only a BA earned over $150,000 per year in 2002, one in five lawyers and two in five physicians did.

Students who are uncertain about a career—and most high school graduates fall into this category—should consider using their experiences in college to inform their next round of decisions. Liberal arts programs attract about 37 percent of all undergraduate enrollments—a larger share than any other program—in large part because they offer unsettled students a broad prospect from which to view their career options. During the college years, liberal arts students are encouraged, and often required, to experiment with different fields and experience different ways of learning and knowing. Unexpected success in college biology and organic chemistry might become a steppingstone to medical school for one student, while a new-found aptitude in calculus or economics might lead another student toward finance. Writing-intensive courses in history, philosophy, and literature may influence a student's thinking about law school (perhaps he'll decide *not* to go there).

But more important even than experimentation, the liberal arts provide general skills that are useful in a wide variety of occupations. Because many people move through several jobs over the course of their working lives as opportunities arise, general skills in communication, quantification, and analysis will serve them well. Two economic studies illustrate this advantage. One study found that among many groups of workers, the benefits of specialization declined over the course of two decades (from 1970 to 1990). General analytic ability, the facility to use computers productively, and adaptability to a changing workplace turned out to be just as important in blue-collar occupations as they were in service and professional employment.[31]

In another study, the 1980 graduates of universities in Scotland, where students begin with general studies and choose specialties later in their college program, were compared with those in England, where students enter a specialty at the beginning of college. The Scottish graduates were less likely to switch direction right after graduation, and since switching means accepting lower earnings for several years, the study concluded that the Scottish system yielded a higher financial return. Investing in general education pays off in allowing students more experience before they must choose a career.[32]

I have encountered recruiters from all sorts of businesses, ranging from a cafeteria chain to a large software house, who wanted to hire liberal arts graduates because they learn quickly and can understand customer and employer problems more readily than people with narrower training. The recruiter for the software company said that his new employees don't need to know how to write computer programs—the company can easily train them to do that. But finding people who can understand the customer's goals and can translate that knowledge into software design—that was the more valuable skill, and it was more commonly found among liberal arts graduates.

J. Carter Brown, director of the National Gallery of Art from 1969 to 1992, described his educational path to a career in arts administration, a goal he set for himself in high school. Before college, he sought the counsel of the director of the Metropolitan Museum of Art, who advised him not to study art history in college but rather to "get a broad cultural background." Brown studied history and literature as an undergraduate at Harvard and received his MBA from Harvard Business School before going to Europe to finally study art. But rather than complete his doctorate, he accepted a position as assistant to the director at the National Gallery, and he became director himself a few years later. He formed a career goal early, and his education played an important role in achieving it. But the path was indirect, with a prominent role for a liberal arts education.[33]

An emphasis in college on careful reading, persuasive writing, evaluating evidence, and integrating different kinds of knowledge builds a capacity for learning that transcends individual occupations and can last a lifetime. The value of a liberal arts education is about much more than simply finding a first job.

CHAPTER FOUR

College Rank: The Pitfalls of Prestige

One of my advisees, Trudy Tucker, graduated at the head of her class from a private residential high school for girls. She had taken the SAT I four times. She applied to eight colleges and was offered admission to five of them. She then chose to enroll at the college with the highest rank in national surveys among those where she was offered admission. She had visited none of the colleges, had gained no appreciation of the subtleties of social life on the various campuses where she was accepted, and she took little interest in possible differences in their educational services.

Trudy was determined to enter law school. At the end of her first term when she had earned good grades, she prepared applications to transfer to more highly ranked colleges. "It'll give me a better chance of admission to law school," she asserted. Her applications for transfer weren't successful, but she planned to try again the following year.

Although few students have Trudy's single-minded focus on college rank, many students view it as an important part of their calculus for success in a career. Families see colleges in rank order defined by the average qualifications of the entering class of students or a recent published ranking—much like the fairground pole described in Chapter 1. For many students, the college admission process is nothing more than a quest to get into the highest ranked college one possibly can. The race for rank can have a large effect on price and can cause families to pay too much for higher education.

This chapter explores college rank in more detail, both the substance of the selective admission process and the fuzzy measures that underlie published rankings. A first concern is how colleges select students to admit. Standardized tests have come to play a larger role in American education, with the SAT I and its sole competitor, the ACT, taking center stage in college admission. Here, we'll consider these tests carefully and critically and then conclude with a look at methods by which colleges and their faculty are ranked in national polls.

The race for rank reminds me of greyhounds chasing a mechanical hare at the dog track. No matter how fast the dogs run, they never catch the hare. If they all ran at half the speed, they would still finish in the same order at the same place. If order is all that matters, a lot of energy is being wasted on college admission, and too many students are paying too much for what they ultimately get.

Who Is Selected?

Here are three ways of thinking about how admission officers at selective colleges choose an entering class. These ideas informed the debate before the Supreme Court as it considered a lawsuit against the University of Michigan Law School in 2003. The issue before the Court was this: To what extent might race and ethnicity legitimately play a role in admission? In making a ruling, the Court considered a variety of opinions about what a selective admission process should do. A review of the Court's decision and the surrounding discussion sheds considerable light on the goals of the college admission office. With this information in mind, families can better weigh their student's prospects.

One view of selection is that students can and should be ranked by academic merit—that is, by grades and test scores. Colleges then seek to admit students starting at the top of the list and continuing downward until they have filled their freshman class. Because only a fraction of admitted students choose to attend any given school, each college makes more offers of admission than it has seats. Even so, the basic idea is that a college takes the students with the highest academic performance first. Call this the meritocracy principle.

Critics of meritocracy argue that academic merit has many dimensions and that the way we usually measure it—with grades and test scores—is highly imprecise. The differing dimensions may include mathematical reasoning and language skills, creativity and visual skills, knowledge of history or science, and much more. A single-file rank can be computed only by assigning weights to the individual components. Although weights might be devised from a statistical procedure, judgment also plays a part. Different colleges will weight the components differently, and as a consequence there is no single national pecking order among college applicants—or indeed any single rank order even within the applicants to a given college.

The measurement problem in testing arises in part because inexpensive timed tests capture only a fraction of a student's achievement. A student with the mental agility to seize a quick answer is at a distinct advantage over a student who works methodically and weighs each choice carefully. Yet much of the most productive work in college comes from deliberate thought and extended reasoning. From this point of view, test results are an imprecise (and some would say unfair) reflection of intellectual achievement and are of limited use in forecasting college performance (as we will see below). Indeed, the combination of high school grades and national test scores forecasts less than 25 percent of the variation in college grades. And even if the forecast were highly accurate, a student's college grade-point average is only a partial measure of the value of college education, and it's a modest predictor of success in a future career.[1]

A second view of selection contends that colleges and universities should take account of students' backgrounds in assessing their academic qualifications. This notion is akin to the process of developing top prospects in baseball. Native talent arises in all populations. To achieve as much as we can as a society, we want to develop everyone who has talent. Although the individuals who succeed reap great benefits, we all gain from their achievements, whether in jurisprudence, biotechnology, international diplomacy, or some other field. Advocates for this view argue that national test scores correlate poorly with innate talent but extremely well with the monetary wealth of the community from which a student comes. Using SAT or ACT scores as a measure of academic merit gives first place to those who are already well off. It's like offering soccer training in high school only to those who started playing the game when they were seven years old.[2]

If the benefit of an outstanding college education is measured by gains in lifetime income—that is, by how much a student earns with a degree, compared with what he would have earned without one—the benefit is at least as large for black students as for white students, who on average start out with more advantages. If our society as a whole wanted to maximize the return on its investment in higher education, we would design a system that selects students who show the greatest gains as a result of more investment. Students of high potential, industry, and curiosity from rural and inner-city high schools, where academic programs tend to be less challenging and whose SAT scores therefore are often not as high, may still have adequate preparation for selective colleges. And on average they will show more gains from a better college education than those who graduated from the best-endowed suburban or private schools and who earned 700s on their SATs.[3]

Critics of this view argue that adjusting for background is unfair to those families who have invested in the best high schools, and to those students who have put significant personal effort into achieving their academic goals under demanding circumstances. In a 1996 referendum in California, voters made it illegal for state-sponsored colleges to take any note of race or ethnicity in their admission decisions. As a result of lawsuits and legislative action, state-sponsored schools in Texas and Florida adopted similar policies. Shortly thereafter, the flagship universities in these states saw sharp declines in minority enrollments. Advocates of the referenda and legislative action and plaintiffs in the lawsuits against the universities pointed to the Fourteenth Amendment's guarantee of equal protection of the laws for all citizens and claimed that all government policies should be race-neutral.[4]

Plaintiffs in the University of Michigan lawsuit adopted the view that taking *any* account of background creates a disincentive for students to make a good effort in secondary school. Justice Clarence Thomas sided with them, arguing that African Americans achieve at their best when they are held to the same standard as everyone else. But several retired military officers, including Norman Schwarzkopf and Anthony Zinni along with former commandants of the service

cademies, argued that the military services need capable leaders
rom many backgrounds. A military where all the rank-and-file
ome from low-income nonwhite backgrounds and all the officers
re upper-income whites is unworkable. Leaders of corporations, in-
luding General Motors, made a similar point. To strengthen the
abric of our society, we need colleges that provide pathways to so-
ial advancement for persons from many backgrounds.[5]

The majority of the Supreme Court accepted the argument that
acial background, along with many other attributes, might play
ome role in admission on a case-by-case basis without violating the
onstitutional guarantee of equal protection of the laws. In the
Court's view, the state has a compelling interest in promoting diver-
ity in its educational institutions. Since race and ethnicity remain
owerful parts of a person's identity, selective colleges may give some
od to race and ethnicity in admission. The Court expressed its ex-
ectation that a fully race-neutral policy will be possible twenty-five
ears after its 2003 ruling, as the number of middle-class minority
nembers rises and as their children start out life with the same aca-
lemic advantages as white students.[6]

A third view of selection sees academic merit itself as too limiting
criterion. Given significant numbers of applicants whose academic
chievements, though variable, are nevertheless sufficient for success
t a given college, admission officers may choose to build a commu-
ity of students who will fill a variety of roles on campus and in later
ife. Artistic, athletic, and literary accomplishments, for example,
long with leadership abilities and other social or political skills, cor-
elate with lifetime success as well as college grades do. According to
his view, college should be a place where students learn how to
uild relationships with other talented people whose skill sets are
lifferent from their own. This ability of people with different kinds

of talent and intelligence to work together and get along is the glue that holds our society together.[7]

Critics of this "campus community" view of selection argue that colleges would do a better job of building a diverse community by simply lowering the academic threshold for all students and then picking its freshman class randomly from this larger pool, without regard to race, ethnicity, religion, or gender. Such a process would be fairer than using different academic standards for different groups. The colleges would become somewhat less exclusive and elitist, but all freshmen in the class would start out on an equal academic footing. This would create a stronger sense of community, since there would be no easily identifiable second-class scholars.

Of course, most undergraduate colleges already have easily identifiable groups who arrive with different academic qualifications and motivations. At many public colleges, the University of Oregon among them, out-of-state students are limited by a quota and therefore face higher admission thresholds than in-state students. They arrive on campus better prepared academically, on average, than most of the student body. Typically (though certainly not always), recruited athletes on campus have less academic preparation and less commitment to academic success than their fellow students. And at many colleges and universities, children of alumni who meet the school's academic standards are chosen over similarly qualified students who are not legacies, and some of these "preferential admits" fall into the lower quartiles of students in the freshman class. No student body is academically homogeneous.[8]

For the most part, though, colleges today seek academically talented students whose preparation and industry will allow them to succeed in their studies. Among qualified applicants, colleges seek to build communities by admitting students whose intellectual curiosity, leadership ability, extracurricular activities, and other talents will make them interesting classmates and productive members of society after college. As a result of the Court ruling in the University of Michigan case, admission officers have an incentive to reduce their reliance on numerical formulas and to get to know prospective students by reading each applicant's complete dossier. They may include race and ethnicity among the many background characteristics they consider, except where prohibited by law.

To summarize all of this another way, the selective colleges *themselves* downplay the notion that they rank applicants by test scores and grades. Even among those very selective colleges that admit only a small fraction of applicants, admission officers sift through the dossiers of all qualified students who apply, looking for those who will add unexpected dimensions to the college experience of their classmates. So if the colleges themselves do not use a simple ranking of students' grades and test scores in making offers of admission, it makes little sense for the national ranking services to compare these small differences in each entering class and to rank colleges accordingly. Trudy Tucker's use of published ranks to make fine distinctions among similar colleges is simply not consistent with what the colleges themselves say they do.

Standardized Tests

Still, national tests like the SAT I continue to play a much larger role in college admission than many people think they should, and this error is compounded when ranking services give great weight to the test scores of each freshman class. Prospective students who try to use these test scores to judge the likelihood that they will succeed academically at various colleges should do so with caution. The tests have a number of problems that limit their usefulness as a predictor of college success: they are imprecise measurements of academic achievement, they reward students for being savvy about the test itself, they correlate much better with the academic quality of a student's high school than with the individual herself, and the questions are biased in favor of white middle-class test-takers.[9]

Precision   Although the SAT I may represent the best that modern psychometrics can offer, the scores are less precise than their numerical values imply. Think of the test as a dartboard. Dead center is the student's underlying level of skill and knowledge, the point the test is supposed to reveal. Let's assume it's 500. For first-time test-takers, the dart will stick within a circle of 30 points from dead center about two-thirds of the time; some students will score 530, while others will score 470. To find a range likely to include the student's test score 95 percent of the time, the circle would need to extend from 440 to 560. In other words, on a very bad day—let's say a student was getting a cold or didn't sleep well because of anxiety about the test—the score could be more than 100 points lower than it would be on the very best day.[10]

Randomness in the performance of tests is typical whenever human attributes are measured. Body weight for an adult will vary a pound or two over the course of a day with the normal ebb and flow of life. A movement of 10 points in a person's blood pressure from one reading to another does not signal any change in fundamental health. Even body temperature drops a degree or so in early morning and rises in late afternoon. Big changes are important; small ones are meaningless.

When two average students score within 100 points of each other on the verbal section of the SAT I, there is a better than one-in-twenty chance that those scores have the same dead-center value. Such differences simply reflect the fundamental randomness of results among identical test-takers. The standard deviation is even higher when the scores being compared are closer to 800. Missing a single difficult question may drop a score by 20 points. A student whose dead-center score is 750 could just as easily show a 700 as an 800 in any given taking of the test.[11]

In the 1960s, ETS used a 601-point scale, with one-point values from 200 to 800. The move to ten-point increments in 1970 was an improvement, but it didn't go far enough. A better test would report scores on a five-point scale, just as the Educational Testing Service (ETS) does for Advanced Placement tests, where scores range from 1 through 5. The current practice of computing scores by tens, yielding a 61-point scale, gives a false impression of the precision of the test. Prospective students and their families often overinterpret minor differences that should not, and mostly do not, matter to the college admission office.

Test Savvy   A second problem with the SAT and ACT is that savvy test-takers have an edge that has nothing to do with academic achievement in high school or future performance in college but much to do with simply learning the test. Students who take the SAT I a second time gain on average about 13 points on the verbal section and 16 points on the math. Although this advantage is not large for an individual test-taker, it is highly significant across hundreds of thousands of students. It means that many applicants have an advantage in admission to selective colleges for no other reason than that they took the test more than once, or took a test-prep course. And this has upped the ante for everyone else. Students now believe that they must become test-savvy in order to compete. The speed of the mechanical hare has been turned up a notch, and all the dogs are running harder.[12]

About 50 percent of test-takers take the SAT I a second time, and upwards of 90 percent of applicants to the most selective colleges do so. They believe they'll be rewarded for repeat testing because many colleges consider only the highest recorded scores. But if colleges really cared enough about test results to get as close as they could to a student's dead-center value, they would average multiple scores. The higher score has greater variability and therefore provides less reliable information about a student's dead center.

The ETS knows that practice matters, and it sells old tests for just this purpose. Kaplan, Princeton Review, and other test-prep companies sell review material, cram courses, and practice tests that allow students to learn tricks for taking the test. Test-prep companies exaggerate when they say that their course can add more than 100 points to a test score on a second taking. But we're dealing in averages here, and a few students will indeed improve their score by this much after learning how to take the test. The tiny possibility of huge gains is what motivates hundreds of thousands of students to buy these materials and try to game the test.[13]

High School Quality   The best way to choose students who will do well in college is to select those who have done well in high school. Grade-point averages and class rank are the best predictors of college grades, because they identify students who thrive on academic work. Of course the problem with high school grades and class rank is that they are difficult to compare from one school to the next. A top student in a weak high school might have been a middle student in a strong high school. High school grades need to be adjusted, somehow, for the quality of the high school. This is a central problem for college admission offices, which have to evaluate high school programs in the nation's 25,000 public and 13,000 private schools (or at least the subset of high schools from which a college receives applications).

One recent study looked at the average SAT I scores of students as a way to compare the quality of different high schools. It asked this question: Is the *average* SAT I score of a student's high school class as good a predictor of his college performance as his own individual test score? The answer was yes. A forecast of a given student's college grades based on the average SAT I score of his class, combined with his grade-point average, was just about as accurate as a forecast based on a student's *individual* SAT I score, combined with his grade-point average. In other words, an individual's SAT I score provides little information about the student beyond indicating the quality of the high school he attended. So the third problem with national testing is that it mostly measures the academic quality of high schools, not the academic quality of individual graduates.[14]

Of course, experienced college admission officers have other methods of judging the quality of a high school. When a college has many alumni of its own who went to a particular high school and who worked out well, the admission office will tend to look favorably on other students from there. Colleges also look closely at the proportion of a high school's graduates who take Advanced Placement (AP) tests and go to selective colleges. Many high schools include in their students' application package a profile of the school, containing this kind of information about academic rigor. For students from lesser-known secondary schools where these ready indicators of quality are not available, the SAT I score provides a hint about the educational opportunities that a student was afforded. But to find out what the student actually did with those opportunities, large or small, admission officers have to read the full dossier.

Bias   A fourth problem for national tests is the possibility that they are biased in favor of middle-class white students. This possibility arises because of the method ETS uses to select questions. Every candidate question first appears in an unlabelled trial section of the SAT I, so that ETS can learn how students answer the new questions. ETS defines the "correct" answer to these trial questions as the one given more frequently by previous test-takers who did well on the scored part of the test. The directions say to "choose the best answer," but what this really means is "choose the answer most frequently chosen by test-takers who did well on the rest of the test," most of whom are middle-class white high school students.[15]

A sophisticated person might well argue that a particular question has several answers that are arguably correct; or sometimes a question has no correct answer at all.[16] Such philosophical discussions are irrelevant to ETS because it is simply looking for correlations. A savvy test-taker will know to use conventional wisdom in selecting an answer rather than conducting an internal philosophical debate. If most test-takers say the sky is blue, then a savvy test-taker will say the sky is blue, even if she's looking straight out the window at purple and gray clouds.

National Testing in Perspective

The SAT once stood for Scholastic Aptitude Test, but in recent years it has moved away from "aptitude" and toward "achievement." In 2005 the ETS dropped the dreaded analogies from the basic SAT I test, added more mathematics, and tied its questions closer to the typical high school curriculum (in imitation of the ACT, its chief competitor). That year, the ETS also added a writing sample that is available electronically to colleges where a student sends his test scores. The three component SAT I scores—verbal, math, and writing—now add up to a maximum of 2400. As time goes by, colleges will develop more experience with the writing scores and be able to judge how to use them appropriately in admission and in course placement.[17]

The ACT, begun in 1957 as American Collegiate Testing, focuses on reading, English, math, and science—skills found in the typical high school curriculum. The ACT is more commonly recommended or required by public colleges in the Midwest and South. Nationally, it has captured about a third of the market for college admission testing, while the SAT I holds two-thirds. ACT also added an optional writing test in February 2005 (in imitation of the new SAT I).[18]

Some selective colleges ask students to submit scores from two or three subject area tests known as SAT IIs. These tests are aligned to specific high school courses—for example, biology or French—and provide colleges more specific information about what a student has learned in her classes. A high score demonstrates not only knowledge in the subject area but also success as a student. Advanced Placement tests and International Baccalaureate (IB) programs are even more tightly bound to the curriculum and to mastery of a defined subject. None of these various subject-area tests measure aptitude or intelligence, and admission officers know that. The tighter focus of these tests makes them easier to interpret, however, and provides an even more explicit indicator of the quality of an applicant's high school than the SAT I. For these reasons, the SAT II, AP, and IB are of growing importance in college admission.

Because of so many problems with standardized testing, a few very selective colleges stopped requiring the SAT I some time ago, and their students who did not submit scores have performed as well in college as those who did. FairTest, an organization founded by critics of the test, provides a website with a list of colleges that do not require SAT I or ACT for many of their admissions decisions (730 colleges in 2006). Still, the average SAT I scores of colleges form the basis of a variety of national rankings of colleges, and deans of admission are evaluated to some extent on the rise and fall of the mean SAT I scores of the classes they enroll. Faculty also tend to imbue the SAT I with more symbolic importance than it deserves. Even firms that rate the bonds that colleges sell to finance their construction projects watch the SAT I scores of incoming freshmen as an indicator of institutional strength. Consequently, the SAT I scores get a lot of attention, and weak test scores diminish a student's chance of admission to highly competitive colleges.[19]

Strong scores, on the other hand, do not guarantee admission. Harvard University attracts nearly as many applicants with 800 scores on the SAT I verbal or math tests as it has places in its entering class. It does not offer admission to many of those with perfect scores—even those "dialing toll-free" (800 on both verbal and math)—because the admission staff looks at the entire dossier and tries to consider the student as a whole. Many selective colleges behave similarly but with somewhat lower informal thresholds. Students with high scores but poor grades are readily set aside, because the basic tests provide too little information to stand on their own. Those with high scores and good grades but few outside activities are of less interest than similar students who offer other accomplishments.[20]

The criticism here of standardized tests isn't a call for their elimination. Students take standardized tests from the time they can read through post-baccalaureate education and on to professional licensure. They are inexpensive, provide consistency across time and around the globe, and ensure a fundamental fairness in that every student who gives the same answers will get the same score, regardless of background. They do distinguish strong students from weak ones. Among such tests, those focused on the skills needed in a given program do better. The LSAT, for example, is better at predicting law school performance than the SAT I is at predicting undergraduate performance. In so far as they report scores for specific skills likely to be learned in high school and relevant to the college curriculum, the tests seem to be improving. But parents of college-bound students should understand that even a well-crafted, focused test has significant limitations.

Given the narrowness of the Supreme Court ruling in the University of Michigan case and the inherent weaknesses of the tests, many colleges are likely to move toward requiring deeper dossiers of materials from students as the basis for admission decisions: personal essays, high school grades, challenging curriculum, letters of recommendation, and samples of a student's work. Of course these items have their own inherent drawbacks. Some teachers don't express themselves well in letters of recommendation; some student essays are overedited by others; even AP courses vary in difficulty from school to school. If we add to all this the trend toward hiring "packagers" to get students (and their families) through the admission process, it's a wonder that colleges and students sort themselves out as well as they do.[21]

A student who reads widely, writes insightfully, has curiosity, motivation, and industry is likely to do well in the admission game and ought not to be discouraged by an SAT I score that is somewhat lower than that of a peer. But turnabout is fair play: Prospective students should not judge colleges solely by the average test scores of incoming students. They should make an effort to look beyond the numbers, to the quality of the educational community and services the college offers.

Rankings of Faculty and Departments

To judge the intellectual character of a college, a better gauge than average test scores might be the merits of the faculty. The central problem in judging faculty quality is that common methods of ranking primarily address faculty research rather than undergraduate teaching and advising. Particularly in universities, the ranking of departments and the aggregation of such ranks into the university's general intellectual reputation is a driving force on many of the most selective campuses. Understanding these forces will help prospective students assess where undergraduate education fits into a school's priorities.

Nobel laureates are often mentioned in campus tours, but these prizes don't say much about the quality of teaching. They are not awarded in all disciplines, they come late in life, they are relatively rare, and their holders almost never teach undergraduates. A slightly better source of information might be the behavior of presidents and deans, whose job it is to evaluate their own faculty, with the assistance of outside counsel. These administrators decide whether to add professorships and build new facilities to energize a program with strong leadership, or to withhold replacement faculty and trim support for a rudderless program. New building construction and new faculty appointments in a department are external manifestations of institutional commitments to a field, but the information they offer about the quality of undergraduate teaching is limited.[22]

How do national ranking services evaluate faculty and departments? One central component is a department's record of publication in scholarly journals and books. National ranking services aggregate the publication records of all faculty in a department to
come up with a score that can be compared with scores of similar
departments in other universities. Particularly in the sciences, some
rankings include the grant money that flows to the department.
Other rankings are based on surveys of faculty around the world
who are asked to assign a score to each department in their discipline.[23]

The widely recognized National Research Council (NRC) ranking of PhD programs uses the faculty survey method. The 1993
NRC survey (the most recent one available) ranked 3,634 programs
in 41 fields. Departments with stronger scores had more faculty and
faculty publications and produced more PhDs. Each faculty member in departments with PhD programs averaged 1.1 publications
per year. Departments where most faculty members publish something tend to score better than those where a few stars do most of
the publishing. Another study found that more recent publications
have greater influence on the opinion scores and that scores were
also related to citations of the faculty's work. But for a prospective
freshman who probably doesn't even know what his major will be,
much less whether he wants to go to graduate school, the ranking of
PhD programs doesn't offer much insight into the quality of classroom teaching.[24]

All colleges and universities face an essential tradeoff between
teaching and research, even though some faculty are extraordinarily
good at both and active scholarship imbues good teaching with
the magic of the latest discoveries. When the goal is to strengthen
their national reputation for scholarship, institutions tend to lighten
teaching loads, select faculty primarily for their research accomplish-

ments, produce more new PhDs, publish more articles and books, increase class size, and reduce the number of courses to undergraduates. Faculty in universities devote a significant amount of their time to research and publication, and during their limited mentoring hours they tend to focus on graduate students and postdocs. An increasing number of faculty, even in the liberal arts, do not teach or advise undergraduates at all. At the University of Chicago, the average faculty member in the social sciences teaches three courses per year, only one of which is for undergraduates.[25]

One way to evaluate a department's commitment to undergraduate instruction is simply to compare the teaching effort on different campuses. Here, for example, is a comparison of the philosophy program at New York University with that at Amherst College. NYU was ranked 34th by *US News and World Report (US News)* in 2006 and charged $31,690 in tuition in 2005–2006. Amherst was ranked 2nd among liberal arts colleges in 2006, with tuition at $33,035. The Philosopher's Gourmet (a well-known ranking of PhD programs) ranked NYU's philosophy department as number one in the English-speaking world in 2004.[26] In 2005–2006 NYU's Philosophy Department listed twenty regular (tenured and tenure-track) faculty on its website, plus four "regular visitors," one visitor, and two fellows. NYU offered twenty-eight courses in philosophy for undergraduates, twenty of them taught by regular faculty, three by visitors and fellows listed on the department website, and five by persons not mentioned on the website. NYU's undergraduate enrollment was just under 20,000 students.

In comparison, Amherst listed eight faculty in philosophy on its website, seven of whom are regular faculty (one was on leave in 2005–2006); the eighth is a visitor. The department offered twenty philosophy courses to the school's 1,600 students in 2005–2006.

Clearly, NYU's commitment to scholarship in philosophy is significant, but its more numerous and expensive faculty produce an undergraduate program that is similar in offerings to that at Amherst. Taking the undergraduate enrollment and dividing by the count of undergraduate courses in philosophy shows one course per 714 students at NYU and one per 80 students at Amherst. On a per-student basis, Amherst's undergraduate program in philosophy dwarfs NYU's.

Anyone with access to the Internet can create this kind of comparison for any discipline that interests them. College websites list the specific undergraduate courses offered each term and give the name of instructors. Matching the names of instructors from the current course list to the names of faculty on departmental websites will often reveal how many courses are taught by tenured and tenure-track professors, how many by lecturers, and how many by adjuncts, graduate students, or persons not named on the departmental website. These comparisons provide a counterpoint to published rankings based on institutional averages or research records.

The NRC ranking appropriately gives considerable weight to research and publication because these are central to successful PhD programs. Apprentice scholars have a better chance of learning the research trade by associating with faculty members who have stronger records of published research. But in evaluating an undergraduate program, one might ask how many of these famous investigators also teach undergraduates. And even if they do, the question remains whether faculty who are active in the production of new ideas are also likely to be successful teachers of undergraduates. The best available evidence indicates that successful teaching and successful research are not highly correlated.[27]

To assess how colleges and universities establish priorities between research and teaching, a national survey asked faculty members if they agree with these two statements: "Teaching effectiveness should be the primary criterion for promotion of faculty/instructional staff at this institution"; and "At this institution, research is rewarded more than teaching." The responses made clear that at doctoral institutions, the rewards for research are substantially higher than the rewards for teaching. And in liberal arts colleges, teaching is a much higher priority than it is at research universities. We'll look at this question again in Chapter 5.[28]

Incidentally, philosophy can be a very valuable discipline. One of my students, Roger Berger, returned excitedly from taking the GMAT, the test required for application to many MBA programs. The test is electronic, and test-takers get their score as they leave the test site. Roger scored high, he said, because the symbolic part of the test came straight out of his logic course in philosophy, and the essay was "pure Aristotle." Roger was an economics major, but his coursework in my department did not play much of a role in his final score. Roger went to business school at Wharton.

Rankings of Undergraduate Programs

The most popular rankings of undergraduate programs are not nearly as well-grounded as the rankings of graduate programs. *US News* began publishing its influential lists in 1983. Each year, the number of undergraduate applications jumps at colleges whose rank goes up and plummets at colleges whose rank drops. Despite its enormous popularity among prospective students and their families, the *US News* rating has come in for heavy criticism from statisticians.[29]

At the heart of its system is a survey of senior administrators which asks their opinions about other colleges and universities. But it is not clear how much information the respondents actually have about the colleges they score (or whether their answers are entirely candid, given the competition). This survey becomes, to some extent, a measure of reputation, or even branding, as much as quality. *US News* also gathers data about faculty, finances, admission ratio, graduation rate, and alumni donations but assigns weight to each component in an arbitrary manner. From one year to the next, *US News* changes the weights in its formulas, dropping some elements and adding new ones frequently so that the rankings shift even when little has changed on campuses. *US News* wants to sell magazines, and changes in rankings boost sales.[30]

Many students apply simultaneously to research universities, liberal arts colleges, and master's colleges, but *US News* uses a somewhat different formula for these different groups, making comparisons across types difficult. It's impossible, for example, to know how Carnegie Mellon University, ranked 21 among national universities in 2007, compares with Macalester, ranked about the same among liberal arts colleges that year. The *US News* ranking of universities applies to whole campuses, even though the medical school, law school, and business school may be largely irrelevant to undergraduates.

A particularly pointed critique of this aspect of the *US News* rating system comes from its former director of data research, Amy Graham. A better rating system, she says, would focus specifically on the educational services undergraduates receive in the specific programs they consider. And finally, because *US News* doesn't report the standard errors in its scores (that is, a measure of the essential randomness in the measures it uses), trivial, statistically insignificant differences become magnified into enormous gaps in the minds of students and their parents.[31]

Is there a better way to rank colleges and universities? A group of economists addressed this question by looking at the choices made by students who were admitted to the same colleges. Their survey of 3,240 high-achieving high school students gave points to the college where a student chose to enroll and took points away from the colleges where he was admitted but did not enroll. Weighting these choices statistically allowed the economists to rank colleges and universities by student preference. So, for example, if among fifty students who are admitted to both Hamilton College and Wesleyan University, twelve chose Hamilton, ten chose Wesleyan, and twenty-eight chose somewhere else, Hamilton would receive more points than Wesleyan.

Student preference ranking has the advantage that admission offices have more difficulty gaming it by artificially inflating the number of applicants or by accepting a larger proportion of its freshman class in early decision (strategies which increase the school's "selectivity" and "yield," as we will see). But student preference ranking doesn't tell us whether a college's popularity makes a difference in students' lives. If twelve students choose Hamilton and ten choose Wesleyan, are any of them worse off than if they had made the other choice? Student preference ranking also doesn't take account of financial aid offers. If the twelve choosing Hamilton got more attractive financial aid offers at Hamilton, and the ten choosing Wesleyan got more attractive aid offers at Wesleyan, then their choices may say little about preference, other than a preference to pay less rather than more.[32]

Another problem is that the respondents are self-selecting. If only students from elite private or suburban public schools complete the survey, then the preference rankings will reflect their tastes, not that of all students. But the biggest problem with student preference ranking is that students themselves have limited information about the schools they finally choose and those they reject. Many applicants do not visit all the schools that accept them, and some visit none.

Ranking schools on the basis of student preference is a lot like ranking chocolate ice cream without opening the carton. It has a lot to do with successful branding (colorful cows, exotic origins, clever names) and very little to do with comparative quality. And it ignores the chance that thoughtful students may be looking for something different in a college—a special taste that doesn't exist in the competing brand.[33]

Racing Out of Control?

Suppose lots of students were like Trudy Tucker. If published rank was all that mattered, the highest ranked colleges could dramatically increase tuition. Students who can afford to ignore financial return would buy in even when the returns were negative. Students with little intellectual curiosity wouldn't worry about the quality of teaching and might wind up paying large sums for a steady diet of huge classes taught by video. If the SAT I scores of the entering class were taken as the single measure of a college's success, colleges would devote their dollars to attracting and sustaining enrollment of students with high average SAT I scores, while ignoring the quality of campus life. If philanthropists donated only to the top-ranked colleges, the quality of educational facilities and services for most undergraduate programs would plummet.

A race for rank can turn ugly. As George and Harry run from the grizzly, George yells: "Do you think we can outrun the bear?" and Harry responds, "I don't know, but *I* only need to outrun *you!*" When only rank matters, sabotage becomes a real threat. Students may refuse to participate in collaborative study, hide critical library materials before a test, or cheat. In Japan, where a test score places students by rank order in the prestigious schools and universities, teenage suicide has been linked to the pressure of the tests. Japanese students spend years in private after-hours cram schools to prepare for them, and some students take an extra year of study in order to sit for the exam a second time. Even in the United States, many private schools offer an extra year of study after high school (called a postgraduate or PG year) to help students get into a higher-ranked college than they otherwise might.[34]

When rank is all-important, colleges use sophisticated methods to game the system. In providing data, a college exercises discretion whenever it can. For example, until *US News* became more specific in its requests, colleges with a summer remedial program for entering students could report the mean SAT I score of only the students who entered in September. Because a low acceptance rate raises rank, a college can offer a low fee for online applications from students with little prospect of being accepted. When student-faculty ratio is a factor, colleges can exclude students who are studying abroad and include faculty who are on leave or doing full-time research or teaching only graduate students. When the rate of alumni-giving is a factor, schools will go to great expense to get a little something from a lot of alumni, even if the amount of each gift doesn't offset the cost of soliciting it. Gaming the ranking system has moved from a cottage industry in the admission office to a permanent item on the agenda of almost every college's senior leadership.

Fortunately, American higher education isn't completely absorbed in the race for rank. The decisions of admission officers are multidimensional, because these professionals know that test scores are fuzzy and incomplete measures of preparation. University deans recognize that ranking faculty by research output isn't well correlated with the quality of undergraduate teaching, and they take steps to remedy the situation. And students, with help from their parents and advisors, make an effort to avoid chasing the mechanical hare by considering costs and benefits carefully.

CHAPTER FIVE

The Learning Environment: What Your Money Really Buys

Wally Linden spent a year after high school as a hired hand on his Uncle Jim's ranch in Colorado. He became fascinated with western culture and used some of his spare time to read U.S. history and the Klondike and cowboy poems of Robert Service and Baxter Black. One night Wally had a long conversation with his uncle about the risks and rewards of raising livestock, and after that talk he started following the price of cattle and grain futures in the *Wall Street Journal.* Because the local water table was falling and Jim had to drill deeper and deeper wells, Wally grew interested in the geology of underground water, as well as the politics of pumping it out. Meanwhile, he improved his Spanish by talking with the neighbors, and one weekend he helped his cousin Sally autopsy a downed heifer at the state veterinary lab.

When Wally came to Nashville to talk about college, his approach was both deliberate and searching. Although he wanted to study biology and geology, economics and political science, Spanish and poetry, he was open to other subjects as well. He planned to use his college experience to learn as much as he could about many different things. Wally's central question was: How much will I learn here?

It's not an easy question to answer. Chapter 4 pointed out some of the problems that arise in trying to assess colleges and universities as a whole. In this chapter, we'll look at specific aspects of the campus learning environment, focusing on ways to judge the intellectual challenge and depth of learning in individual programs of potential interest to applicants. There are few published statistics to help us out. A prospective student will have to frame questions and interpret the responses he gets.

We'll begin by considering how people learn. Students have different learning styles, and schools have different approaches to the curriculum; we'll try to see how these two sets of variables mesh. Next, we'll ask whether course requirements, class size, grading systems, and extracurricular activities, including intercollegiate athletics on campus, have a significant impact on how much students learn. Our final concern will be the qualifications of the teaching faculty, because these are the men and women who design and deliver the educational program.

How People Learn

Understanding how people learn is helpful in thinking about what colleges are designed to do.[1] Here are six basic ideas about learning.

Additive Learning   When we learn something new, our minds connect it with what we already know. Effective teaching builds on the foundation of the student's prior experiences. This fact has important consequences for admission to college and placement in courses. In considering applicants, colleges seek to define the general level of preparation needed for academic success on campus and to screen out unqualified students. They also specify prerequisites for courses. An economics course that uses calculus will be frustrating to a student who hasn't mastered the math. Good college programs provide a sequence of courses and experiences which assure that seniors are challenged in different ways than entering freshmen.

Active Learning   Although memorizing lists, rules, and facts plays a role in education, learning more often occurs when a student uses new ideas for his own purposes. When students pose their own questions, solve new problems, and write original essays, they put ideas to work in ways that are likely to have lasting effects. Colleges that offer tutorials, seminars, and student research projects provide more opportunities for active learning than colleges that serve up a steady diet of huge lecture classes and multiple-choice tests.

Motivation   Of course, active learning means that students must work at it. Effortless learning doesn't exist. The most enduring education consists of the internal mastery of ideas, and that takes effort. When colleges read the dossier of an applicant, they look for signs that the student truly desires to achieve this mastery. Taking the most difficult courses in high school, spending summers in productive pursuits, and volunteering for community service are just a few ways that college-bound students encounter new ideas and demonstrate the effort they're willing to make to master them. Wally Linden's reading and exploration show a high degree of enthusiasm and motivation for learning.

The Learning Community   Education is social, and being in a community of scholars improves the chances that learning will take place. Of course there are famous instances of brilliant minds achieving great insights while working alone (Gregor Mendel's discovery of heritability is just one example). But most of us, most of the time, find that we learn best in a collaborative, supportive, nurturing environment where ideas are exchanged and debated. In a classroom where students are well prepared and well motivated, students learn from the questions, responses, and disagreements of their classmates. College is a combination of individuality and collaboration, much like a professional basketball team. Covering one's position, passing the ball to the open man, and playing defense as well as offense enhance the performance of the team as a whole and allow each player to perform better than he otherwise would. Good colleges promote teamwork in their classes, not just competition.

Multiple Ways of Learning   Understandably, students are drawn to disciplines whose ways of thinking come more easily or more naturally to them. As a consequence, students sort themselves across disciplines and across colleges in part according to their abilities. Some of the gains from higher education come from just this kind of sorting—people who discover they actually hate higher math are not likely to go to engineering school. But effective learning also comes from using several strategies to tackle a problem from multiple angles, using words, numbers, symbols, and images simultaneously. A good college encourages experimentation in multiple ways of thinking and learning—not just to help students sort themselves out but also to expose them to people with different approaches to problem-solving and gaining knowledge.

Two physicists chatted in Stockholm while waiting for their Nobel prizes. One said he had taken a first course in economics and found it so easy that he switched to physics. The other said that he had taken a first course in economics and found it so hard that he switched to physics. Happily, many able students find economics to be just right and enjoy pursuing the subject in some depth. The fact that each of us is better at some things than others isn't a character defect. Good colleges encourage intellectual exploration, and they impose little penalty on adventurous learners who don't excel in one area, as long as they are doing well in something else.

The Concrete and the Abstract   Most students learn first from examples, and only later discover the abstract ideas behind them. Yet abstract thinking may have the greater value. For example, a student can learn to solve the classic algebra word problem about how much time a boat takes to go upstream, given different rowing and current speeds. But it is more useful to see that the same tools can solve many time and distance problems, and that time and distance are themselves just instances of a set of relationships among variables. Memorizing abstract rules without connecting them to examples is a difficult way to learn and is of limited value. But understanding only concrete examples without discovering how to use the deeper ideas is equally limiting.

This interplay between concrete and abstract ideas has a number of implications for higher education. One is the unavoidable tension between general education and preparation for a specific career. A good general education helps students develop abstract ideas by drawing on a variety of examples taken from many fields of study. Education focused exclusively on a specific career may do less well at fostering abstract thinking. A second implication concerns the choice of instructors. Instructors committed to a life of scholarship are more likely to develop abstract ideas and to use nuanced language and complex symbols to communicate them.

Classes taught by these scholars are likely to offer more intellectual challenge and teach deeper thinking skills. An instructor whose life work is elsewhere—for example, a practicing architect who teaches an occasional class in construction administration or structures—may share valuable practical experience, but he is less likely to demonstrate or require abstract thinking.

Core Curriculum   Most four-year liberal arts colleges use these six fundamental ideas about learning, to varying degrees, in the pursuit of three general educational goals: core, breadth, and depth. Core skills include reading, writing, speaking, and mathematics. Breadth allows students to explore different ways of knowing. Depth helps students develop detailed knowledge in one or two areas gof concentration (a major or minor). For a student of average preparation in a typical liberal arts program, as much as a fourth of the undergraduate experience will be devoted to developing core skills, and a like amount to breadth. At least a quarter will be in a major, and the balance will be allocated to electives or to the addition of a minor or second major.[2]

Core Courses

The idea of requiring college students to master a core set of skills has been around for a long time. Students frequently complain about these "GenEd" ("General Education") requirements, and the whole edifice regularly comes up for reform. Critics claim that core courses are ineffective because, among other things, they ignore one or several of the basic ideas about learning discussed above. In this section we'll look at some new classroom approaches in three core areas—writing, mathematics, and second-language study.

Writing   My students say that improving their writing skills is among the most important outcomes of their college experience. When I was in school, the study of composition meant learning the rules of grammar, diagramming sentences, identifying and correcting grammatical errors, and practicing accurate word usage. The philosophy was that one should learn the rules at the sentence level before applying them to the writing of paragraphs and coherent essays. Certainly, not knowing the difference between "affect" and "effect" can be embarrassing, and recognizing a dangling modifier or lack of agreement between subject and verb has its value.

But in recent years many colleges have shifted to writing as a process, not as a one-shot end result. Students are urged to express their thoughts on topics of interest, to get feedback, and to edit and rewrite. Writing-intensive courses have appeared in many disciplines under the flag of "writing across the curriculum." The idea behind this phrase is that, while some biology majors may never be very good at writing about poems, by the time they graduate they should be proficient at writing about mutagenesis or bonobos or whatever they studied in their chosen field. The goal of the core writing program (called expository writing in some colleges) is to help students transform their interconnected, multidimensional thoughts into a single line of written exposition, from beginning to end of an essay, journal article, report, or thesis. The core writing program is typically separate from creative writing courses, where students compose novels, short stories, poetry, plays, or film scripts.

The process approach to expository writing draws on the ideas of additive learning, active learning, and motivation. Its first principle is that students should have something to say before they begin to write. History students write in history courses, and archaeology students write about archaeology. A student who has something to say is more likely to be motivated to express it well. Second, the process approach coaches writers to make incremental improvements in their work. It introduces rules about grammar and usage only as they are needed. Third, the process approach emphasizes editing, a key skill for a writer. First drafts are rarely masterpieces. Most good writers create drafts, revise them, seek comments, and revise yet again. The process approach anticipates imperfection at initial stages and builds a round or two of revision into the assignment—the way most writers actually work.

Finally, the process approach treats writing as a collaboration. The teacher, acting as a coach rather than a disciplinarian, gives the student tips for improvement and opportunities to restructure and revise; she doesn't just sit in judgment and issue a grade. Peer editors may also provide useful comments on the drafts of other students. Becoming a constructive critic is a vital part of becoming a better writer, and working with peers makes the writing process more engaging. For all of these reasons, writing-as-process is the dominant paradigm on college campuses today.[3]

Mathematics Attempts to reform instruction in mathematics along analogous lines has had limited success. The largest effort, which began in the 1980s with backing from the National Science Foundation, is called the calculus reform movement. The impetus for it grew in part from the observation that more than half of students who attempt to learn calculus fail to earn satisfactory grades. Among those who do reasonably well in the introductory course, few have sufficient mastery to use calculus in subsequent courses.[4]

Several fundamental ideas about learning drive this new approach to calculus. One (multiple ways of knowing) is the importance of combining words, numbers, graphs, and symbols as methods for understanding mathematical relationships. Students are encouraged to use computers and graphing calculators aggressively: to manipulate mathematical symbols more easily, to integrate words, animation, three-dimensional graphs, and symbols into their thinking and final reports, and to save and share their work.

A second idea about learning calculus (the concrete and abstract) is to have students confront real data and concrete problems and invite them to puzzle out a conclusion, for example, an analysis of the growth of a population of rabbits. By working through a sequence of elaborate and well-developed problems that are anchored by storylines, students discover the mathematical principles for themselves. In effect, calculus is taught as a laboratory course, with the instructor in the role of guide and critic rather than lecturer.

A third idea (the learning community) is to have students work on challenging puzzles in small groups and produce a written report of their methods and conclusions. Working in groups allows students more time to formulate questions, propose answers, and get feedback. Although the instructor may have to help a group learn to work together productively, most students become highly motivated to learn in this setting.[5]

Implementing a reform-based calculus course takes considerably more effort on the part of faculty than continuing the conventional lecture method. Learning a new way of thinking about teaching, changing goals to focus on deeper thinking skills, and dealing with students' anxiety when they begin to work in new ways takes courage and determination. The calculus reform movement has achieved a permanent place on many college campuses but is far from dominant.

Its critics argue that students who succeed in a reform calculus class have less experience in conventional symbol manipulation and can use fewer formulas than students who spend a term in a conventional class. Indeed, students themselves who have earned good grades in conventional math classes and scored well on standardized tests are often critical of the reform approach because it de-emphasizes drill on symbol manipulation (at which they can excel by memorizing) in favor of exploration, writing, and developing intuition. Proponents of reform decry the "mindless symbol-pushing mode" as the central failure of conventional instruction in mathematics.[6]

Given Wally Linden's interest in geology and economics, he should inquire about a college's approach to teaching calculus. Whatever method it uses, a college should be willing and able to report the proportion of all recent graduates who have attempted a calculus course and the proportion of those students who passed it. Not all calculus courses are the same, of course, and grading standards differ. Even so, failure rates in calculus courses have motivated much of the calculus reform movement and are a good starting point for learning about how a college teaches mathematics. Wally might go on to ask more probing questions: What proportion of calculus students take subsequent math courses, and what kind of success do they have when using calculus in other disciplines like biology, economics, and geology?

Second Language   Instruction in second languages has shown a reformation (and a renaissance) similar to that in writing. A generation ago, students learned new languages primarily by studying grammar and memorizing vocabulary so as to translate texts. In recent decades, language instruction at many colleges has moved to a whole language approach, with students learning the four language skills at every stage of their study: listening, speaking, reading, and writing. Instruction often involves no English at all but rather introduces the new language interactively, much as a child learns her first language. Computer software also plays an important role. Students learn to use the new language in a cultural context, so that their language skills are relevant to everyday life.

The goal of the whole language approach is to bring students to the point where they can function comfortably in their target language. In modern languages that use the Roman alphabet, 240 hours of classroom time (which translates into two years of intensive instruction, at five classes per week) should allow a student to converse with native speakers about common topics. In non-Roman phonetic languages like Russian, the goal takes a little longer to reach. Nonphonetic languages like Mandarin require still more time.[7]

Proficiency in a second language adds a global dimension to a college education, and it may widen a graduate's career prospects as well. A substantial number of study-abroad programs are conducted in languages other than English, and most foreign-language departments provide opportunities for total immersion when studying abroad.[8]

Colleges spend tens of millions of dollars to build new instructional facilities in language study and many other fields and to hire faculty with strong intellectual reputations. But a college's commitment of significant resources to transform the way instructors actually teach their subject is rare, and faculty members themselves often have little professional incentive to innovate. Savvy prospective students will want to ask how faculty are recognized and rewarded for teaching, and whether they incorporate the latest educational techniques.[9]

Breadth and Depth

In career-oriented undergraduate programs, such as those offered at a maritime academy or design school, the issue of breadth hardly arises. Courses are in the curriculum because they relate to students subsequent careers. In the liberal arts, the issue of breadth takes two forms, which we might call substance and style. Some schools require that all students study a common set of important ideas. Others require that all students study a common set of ways of knowing.

The "ideas" approach can be found in the great books programs. Robert Maynard Hutchins, president of the University of Chicago from 1929 to 1945, advocated a general education based on classic texts, which serve as the springboard for discussing and writing about the great ideas of civilization. Students read works ranging from Aristotle and Dante to Kant and Einstein. This program continues today at the University of Chicago, St. Johns College, and Thomas Aquinas College, among others. To some critics, it is ironic that a curriculum requiring every student to read the same great books is viewed as broad; but those who advocate a great books approach to breadth argue that these authors address questions for all ages. For a great books program to be successful, the college must attract distinguished faculty who are excited about teaching in this format.[10]

A more common approach to breadth is to define broad categories of knowledge and to require students to select from each, much like picking dishes off a menu at a Chinese restaurant. Liberal arts students must take some courses in at least four areas: the humanities, the sciences, the social sciences, and non-Western, gender, or ethnic studies. The notion here is that each area represents a different way of knowing, a different style of learning, or a different angle of perspective on the world. Students get a rich sense of the variety of questions that scholars in different disciplines ask, and the kinds of evidence they seek in order to answer them.[11]

Some colleges, including Marquette University, require a specific two-semester course in Western Civilization and a course in religion. At the other extreme, Brown University requires basic skill in writing and completion of a major but has no other specific skill or breadth requirements. At most institutions, courses taken for breadth may extend over all four years of college, and there is some value to spreading them around. A senior with a few economics courses under his belt might view an introductory American history course quite differently than he would have as a freshman.[12]

The breadth requirement typically entails a significant amount of reading and close analysis of individual texts. A student who completes a strong college program should expect to learn to read materials critically on many levels. The great books programs involve both extensive and intensive reading, but many other approaches to the breadth requirement build reading skills, particularly in history and literature courses.

Listening and speaking well are usually not explicit goals of the college curriculum, but participation in class discussions inevitably improves these essential intellectual and social skills. Some few colleges require students to take a course in public speaking, where the emphasis is on the development of logical arguments as much as oral presentation. Although rhetoric—the skill of making an effective oral argument—entered the school curriculum with Plato, very few colleges require a course in rhetoric.[13]

Majors Students in the liberal arts usually take about one-fourth of their undergraduate courses in a single field. A student who completes a major stands at the entry level of specialization. He's sort of a junior-grade historian, mathematician, or biologist.

As it turns out, though, a student's choice of major is not a particularly good predictor of his later career. Philosophy majors enter law school, engineering students make their living as managers, economics and Spanish majors go to medical school, and music majors become architects. A major helps a student deepen his intellectual insights, and it allows a greater accumulation of knowledge than randomly chosen courses. Perhaps most important, it gives students a glimpse of the frontier between what's known and what's not.

A major typically begins with an introductory course or two in the first or second year of college, moves through a sequence of intermediate level courses, and sometimes culminates in a seminar or thesis wherein a student does original work. Colleges able to offer many small classes are more likely to expect a thesis or a topping-out seminar in the student's major. In some fields like the sciences and economics, majors typically have longer cascades of prerequisites and courses that must be taken in sequence.

Most liberal arts colleges offer twenty-five majors or more. Many colleges allow students to create a "contract major," carved out from existing courses in several departments that cohere in some defensible way. For example, a contract major in environmental studies might include courses in botany, plate tectonics, and meteorology along with macroeconomics and the history of modern Africa.[14]

Completion of a major provides a significant credential. Employers, graduate schools, and even the general public understand how a film major differs from a physics major. Doing well in a major may be the most important academic achievement in college, after mastery of basic skills, both from the point of view of personal satisfaction as well as life prospects.

On some campuses, undergraduates have opportunities to undertake academic work in their field outside the standard curriculum. Students who assist in faculty research projects often find the experience more valuable than a course. Paradoxically, this may be more likely on liberal arts campuses than at research universities because, with no graduate students at hand, faculty at liberal arts colleges may employ undergraduates to perform some of the roles played by graduate students at universities. On the other hand, pre-med students on campuses with medical centers may land simple jobs in labs that grow into more substantial roles as their knowledge deepens. Some undergraduates who participate in faculty research publish the results of original investigations under their own names while they are undergraduates.

For a number of years I have selected and trained undergraduates to lead small weekly sections in a large statistics course that would otherwise offer only large lectures. The section leaders present some new ideas, help students review, and promote active class participation. Several have enjoyed their roles so much that they pursued PhD degrees with the view of becoming college teachers. But are undergraduates good teachers? In written evaluations of my statistics course, several students have exclaimed, "I learned everything on Fridays!" My lectures were on Monday and Wednesday.[15]

How College Students Spend Their Time

For an intellectually voracious student, the course catalogue is a candy store. A student at a liberal arts college will complete between thirty-two and forty regular courses over eight semesters to earn the baccalaureate degree. Since a college may offer eight hundred or more individual courses, a graduate will have sampled only 5 percent or less of the offerings. Programs that focus on specific careers have a more prescribed curriculum and less choice. A future chemical engineer will face a pre-set sequence of courses for each of her eight semesters, with only a few slots for electives along the way. She will have relatively little opportunity to study electrical, civil, or structural engineering, much less a second language or music theory.[16]

How Many Courses?   The accreditation process imposes a lower limit on what constitutes a course and how many courses are required for a degree. Once per decade, a group of elders from other institutions visits the campus, reviews its operations, and decides whether to renew or withdraw accreditation. A college that recasts its instructional program in a way likely to reduce student learning below a minimum threshold risks having its accreditation withdrawn. Without that credential, the school loses access to government-supported financial aid programs and has difficulty attracting students. Although accreditation is a voluntary, nongovernmental process, it has teeth. Self-regulation maintains the reputation of quality colleges and separates them from diploma mills that sell bogus degrees on the cheap.

Nevertheless, the number of courses required for graduation varies widely among accredited institutions. Washington University in St. Louis requires forty courses or the equivalent, Yale requires thirty-six, Lafayette College thirty-two, and Williams College thirty-two semester courses plus four winter study projects. Some colleges measure academic activity by the credit hour. One fifty-minute class that meets each week for fourteen weeks counts as a one-credit-hour semester course on many campuses. A normal course with three fifty-minute class meetings per week is a three-credit-hour course. In my experience, students learn more from three fifty-minute classes per week than from two seventy-five-minute classes or one lecture of 150 minutes.[17]

Colleges package their instructional time in a wide variety of ways. Some schools have a two- or three-semester system, others have a three- or four-quarter system. Between semesters, some institutions require minicourses. At Colorado College, students take one course at a time, each for $3\frac{1}{2}$ weeks, eight times per year. At St. Johns College, a fixed curriculum based on the great books is delivered in small seminars and tutorials. All 450 students at the college take the same four courses: a philosophy-humanities-social science seminar, a laboratory tutorial, a language tutorial (Greek for the first two years, French for the last two), and a mathematics tutorial. Each Friday evening the entire college attends the same lecture—the only lecture offered on campus. At any moment the entire student body is engaged in a common discussion of history, literature, philosophy, language, and more.[18]

Class Size   In their promotional materials, many liberal arts colleges put a lot of emphasis on class size, but what are the real implications for learning? The available evidence suggests that an instructional program with only large classes yields the least learning, but a mix of small and large classes produces more learning than a regimen of all middle-sized classes. This relationship was discovered in studies of elementary and secondary schooling, but it probably holds for higher education as well. What the investigators found was that the effect of class size is not linear. The increase in learning is quite pronounced as class size drops from twenty to below ten. By contrast, the increase in learning is modest as class size falls from one hundred to twenty. A college that wanted to maximize its investment in learning would put students in a few large lecture classes, in order to free up instructors for several very small seminars. This combination of a large class with three small classes for each student yields nearly 5 percent more total learning than four middle-sized classes of twenty students each.[19]

In this study, learning was measured by standardized tests. But improvement in writing skills, in the ability to make effective oral presentations, in participation in discussions, and in original application of ideas are not measured well by this method. Small classes allow more varied outcomes and increase engagement; and engaged students are more likely to choose more challenging courses later and go on to graduate study. These significant but usually unmeasured outcomes should be taken into account when comparing class size from one campus to another and when choosing courses for the upcoming term. I usually advise my students to take some smaller classes every semester.[20]

Tutorials—defined as one-on-one or very small group classes where students lead and faculty question—are relatively rare. At Williams College, about three hundred students participate in tutorials annually, and Williams is expanding its faculty in order to support more tutorials. Seminars of ten to fifteen students are frequent in some programs and rare in others. Many colleges now offer or require a seminar for first-year students, and others include a seminar in the requirements of a major. Some colleges post a maximum class size; for example, Colorado College puts a limit at twenty-five.[21]

Many colleges and universities report the size of undergraduate classes in a "common data set" they make available on their website. Although these counts are not specific to individual programs, they do allow some comparison. What may be more helpful to know are the sizes of classes at specific points in the curriculum. How large are the groups in courses where writing is expected? What is the group size for introductory calculus and French? One way to find out the upper end of the distribution of class size is to ask about the number of seats in the largest classrooms, identify the classes that meet there, and inquire about their value.[22]

Suppose 500 students are each to take four classes—a total of 2,000 seats—to be taught by 50 instructors, each teaching two sections. They might all be served by 100 sections of 20 students. Alternatively, they might attend four large classes of 250 students each and 96 sections that average 11 or fewer students each. Each student, then, would have one class of 250 and three classes with 11 or fewer students. The average class size, from the institution's point of view, is 20, that is, 100 classes with a total of 2,000 seats. Yet from a given student's point of view, one class of 250 and three classes of 11 gives an average class size of 71.

But focusing on averages misses the point. Having several small classes combined with a quite large one yields more learning than having all middle-sized classes, even though the middle-sized classes boast a lower faculty-student ratio. A prospective student should ask specifically about the number of quite small classes he is likely to encounter each year in a given program. Colleges that offer many sections with fifteen or fewer students should be pleased to report the fraction of student seats that are in such sections. Some large classes may have to be part of the program to keep it affordable, but they have their own value for certain kinds of material.[23]

The pattern of class sizes is often embedded in the culture of a given institution, where the preferences of the faculty and the expectations of students fix on particular methods of instruction. The important point is that the style of instruction should match the size of the class. If the lecture mode is the only teaching method a given instructor can bring to bear, the class might as well be quite huge.[24]

And sometimes large lecture courses are spectacular. One of the most popular courses at my college is an introduction to ethics taught by an award-winning professor, John Lachs. It has three hundred students. Alumni parents advise their children to take this course, saying it changed their view of the world. If class sizes at Vanderbilt were all small, relatively few students would have contact with this outstanding professor.

I once asked a group of middle-aged college staff members from around the country to recall the most valuable class of their undergraduate years and to note the size of that class. Many of the respondents recalled that their most valuable classes were quite large. Law schools famously use classes of a hundred students in which professors lead an active dialog, calling on students by name and expecting them to respond thoughtfully in light of their reading. The classrooms are well-designed amphitheaters so that students can hear one another. One hundred students is about the maximum number that allows eye contact as well as ample space for notebooks, computers, and reading material.

The skill to interact with a substantial class in the manner of *The Paper Chase* is a rare gift, but it also takes practice. Some award-winning lecturers prepare each day's talk with great care and rehearse its delivery. They succeed in making compelling presentations to a live audience of up to seven hundred students at a time. The large class gives many students access to great thinkers, and students often prize such experiences in later life. A prospective student should ask about the number and quality of large classes, rather than just assume they have little value. A class that meets for a large lecture twice a week will usually break into small weekly sections for discussion, review, and testing. Graduate or undergraduate students may lead the sections. A lecture with sections yields more learning than a lecture alone.[25]

Grades   Grades are the most immediate, tangible outcome of college. Many college students track their grade-point averages to the third decimal and choose courses and allocate study time to achieve their GPA goals. At the same time, many students at selective colleges are shocked to earn Bs and Cs in college after having been straight-A students in high school. When selective colleges admit only students with strong high school records, nearly all of their students will have lower grades in college than in high school. Because the pattern of grades differs significantly across colleges, prospective students ought to know the outcomes at colleges under consideration, and they might even tilt toward colleges where grades carry more meaning.

Many people assume that a grade reflects demonstrated mastery of an established body of knowledge—a sort of dipstick to measure the amount of learning. An A indicates that the student learned all the important ideas; a B signals knowing most of the ideas. The dipstick notion has significant shortcomings because education works best when a teacher works from his or her own experience but adapts it to meet the interests and skills of the students at hand. Education is the process of taking students from where they are and moving them forward. In this view, grades are a more useful measurement of effort than of learning. The major goal of the grading regime is to encourage behaviors that are likely to increase learning and discourage those that are unlikely to do so. It is not intended to measure learning per se. An instructor may award points for tasks that induce learning but will not be on the final test—formal presentations in class are one example.

Grades can also indicate a student's effort in relationship to the other students. A grading system that always assigns some As, Bs, and Cs (grading on the curve) gives students an incentive to make an effort, and it identifies top performers. Simple mastery of key ideas may not win an A when all students in the class can readily master the key ideas. The A may be reserved for students who show an extra measure of creativity, insight, and polish. The down side of basing grades exclusively on the relative positions of students in a local group is that it creates rivalry, it discourages collaborative work, and it can even lead to sabotage. Recognizing these potential problems, a wise teacher will create tests and assignments that include many elements everyone has mastered and a few elements that almost no one has mastered. This will tend to produce a range of grades without artificial weighting of the scores. Some colleges take extraordinary steps to limit the destructive consequences of student rivalry for grades. During their first year at MIT, all students are graded on a pass/fail basis in every course, to lower the pressure on their very talented and competitive freshman class.

At the other extreme, some colleges have come to award much larger proportions of As. At the proprietary (for-profit) colleges, nearly one in four grades is an A, compared to only one in ten at public four-year colleges. But the most selective colleges have the same problem with grade inflation as the for-profit colleges. In June 2001, 91 percent of the graduating class at Harvard received Latin honors, that is, graduated *cum laude* (with honors), *magna cum laude* (with high honors), or *summa cum laude* (with highest honors). Under its new policy, no more than 60 percent of Harvard's graduates receive Latin honors. In 2004 Princeton also moved to limit A grades to the top 35 percent of students in each course. On some campuses, no more than 25 percent of graduates, those with the highest grade-point averages, receive Latin honors.[26]

A few colleges, such as Emory University, reserve honors for students who not only make excellent grades but also design a research project, write a thesis, and defend it before an interdepartmental faculty committee. An Emory student whose thesis is deemed worthy of presentation to professionals in the field receives high honors, while one whose thesis is considered publishable receives highest honors.[27]

When nearly all students earn top grades, an A loses much of its value to recruiters, postgraduate schools, and prospective employers. The most able students are better served by a grading system that differentiates students by level of performance.

Time Management   College students need to eat, sleep, exercise, play, and sometimes earn a little money. To fit so many activities into their schedule, students learn to optimize the payoff by devoting more time to more productive activities, so that, on the margin, the extra payoff from a little more time spent in each activity is about the same. We often assume that the more time a student commits to each learning activity, the more he will learn. But in fact, if time is used effectively, the contribution of extra time diminishes as more time is applied. Although some students may not use their time effectively at first, most quickly master the necessary skill.

Students are likely to spend more time on courses in their major, somewhat less time on purely elective courses, and much less on required courses in areas of questionable interest. Time spent attending class, formal review sessions, and labs have higher payoff on average, as measured by grades, than time spent in self-study, reading, writing, and reviewing, though it must be said that students tend to calculate the payoff from different uses of their time somewhat differently than their parents or instructors, and some students do well even though they attend class rarely.[28]

Social norms among the community of students have a huge effect on academic performance, as measured by grades. On a campus where a student finds the coursework easy and where the other students make modest time commitments to academics, a student is likely to commit fewer hours to learning. When attending class is voluntary (as it usually is), many students skip at least a few meetings. When grades are based on tests that reward drill and memorizing, some students will cram before exams and slack off at other times.[29]

By contrast, a student in an environment where the courses are challenging and where his peers commit many hours to study is likely to make more effort, with greater payoff. When a student writes essays or does other original work, the upper boundary on learning is open-ended. But there are important differences from college to college in the effort required to do well, and this can vary from one program to another on the same campus. A school's undergraduate architecture program may be extremely demanding, even for a talented designer, while the psychology major may be a cakewalk. In choosing a program, a student should consider how much time and effort she wants to commit (and, in some cases, how much cut-throat competition she can endure) and then choose a college accordingly.

Students who work for pay up to twenty hours per week show little or no decrease in grades compared with those who do not work, given otherwise similar backgrounds. Also, students who participate in intramural sports, theater productions, student government, musical performances, and other extracurricular activities show no reduction in grades, other things being equal. Indeed, many students with these outlets for their energy do better in class. Those who do volunteer work also show somewhat higher grades. Intercollegiate athletes post somewhat lower grades than average, for a variety of reasons that we'll explore in the next section.[30]

Athletics   Intercollegiate athletics stands apart from most other student activities because of its external visibility and its enormous expense. Clark Kerr, when chancellor of the University of California, quipped that the job of a university president was to provide "parking for the faculty, sex for the students, and athletics for the alumni."[31] Of course sports are important to students as well, and not just the players. Admission offices see a considerable jump in applications after the football or basketball team wins a big championship.

But intercollegiate sports cost a lot of money. Only football, men's basketball, and (in some regions) ice hockey generate significant revenues. A number of schools subsidize their extensive athletic programs from general funds at a rate of as much as $1,000 per enrolled undergraduate. James Duderstadt, former president of the University of Michigan, reported that the school's participation in intercollegiate athletics was not financially self-supporting across the board, even when Michigan's football team went to the Rose Bowl.[32]

The National Collegiate Athletic Association (NCAA) organizes play in twenty-two sports, seventeen of which are played by both sexes. NCAA Division I colleges offer athletic scholarships and must support at least seven sports each for men and women. Division II colleges offer athletic scholarships and must support four sports for each gender. Division III colleges do not offer athletic scholarships but provide need-based financial aid to athletes, as they do to other students. To the surprise of many people, Division I and II recruiting is intense in all sports, including bowling, softball, and lacrosse. Recruiting is less intense in Division III, but intercollegiate competition is often taken very seriously by alumni, and admission officers play their part in fielding teams. A surprising number of major research universities, including Caltech, Carnegie Mellon, Case, Chicago, MIT, NYU, Rochester, and Washington University, support a wide range of athletics at the Division III level rather than Division I or II.[33]

Some small schools, such as Seton Hill and Shenandoah, recently added football programs in order to draw male athletes to campuses where enrollment tips toward women. As JoAnn Boyle, president of Seton Hill (formerly a women's college) put it, "I started a football team, brought in hundreds of paying students, added a vibrant piece to our campus life and broadened our recognition factor. And in the long history of American higher education, one thing you can count on is football's longevity. Football is here to stay." At Swarthmore and a handful of other highly selective liberal arts college, however, events moved in the opposite direction. Swarthmore's football team, which had played 120 seasons, was discontinued in 2000, in part to reduce the percentage of students who participate in intercollegiate athletics. Reed College in Oregon—another successful liberal arts school—has no intercollegiate athletics whatsoever.[34]

Still, coaches at highly respected schools, from Colby to Southern Cal, actively recruit students for their athletic rather than academic potential. Students who are not specifically recruited rarely "walk on" to teams at any level of NCAA competition. A talking point for colleges is that athletes won't be admitted who are not expected to graduate, and coaches at selective colleges are limited to recruits who meet the school's minimum academic standard for admission. Nevertheless, recruited athletes typically come to campus with lower (sometimes much lower) academic credentials than average for the school, and graduation rates of athletes trail those of other students, even when campuses mount extensive tutoring services primarily for the athletes' convenience.[35]

Across the board, recruited athletes are more likely to major in the social sciences, to take easy courses, and to earn grades below what their academic credentials would forecast. In strong liberal arts colleges where outstanding intellectual work and class participation are the norm, some faculty complain that recruited athletes sit silently in the back row and belittle academics. A strain of anti-intellectualism is most prevalent among men in the money sports, but it can be detected in the nonrevenue sports and in women's athletics as well. These attitudes and behaviors contrast with those of students in music, student government, and journalism, who tend to earn higher than expected grades despite large commitments of time to extracurricular pursuits.[36]

Athletes typically train and play more than twenty hours per week, often over more than one term of the year. On some campuses, they live and eat apart from the rest of the student body and are isolated from many aspects of campus life. But after they graduate, athletes outearn nonathletes, and sometimes by a considerable margin. (These conclusions are little affected by the very few graduates who become professional athletes.) They succeed particularly well in the financial services sector, where their psychological profile has its advantages.[37]

As James Shulman and William Bowen put it, "One of these characteristics can be thought of as drive—a strong desire to succeed and unswerving determination to reach a goal, whether it be winning the next game or closing a sale. Similarly, athletes tend to be more energetic than the average person, which translates into an ability to work hard over long periods of time—to meet, for example, the workload demands placed on young people by an investment bank in the throes of analyzing a transaction. In addition, athletes are more likely than others to be highly competitive, gregarious and confident of their ability to work well in groups (on teams)."[38]

A high school athlete whose career plans require strong academic preparation in college—an engineering or pre-med student, for example—will probably do better in school if she avoids making an obligation to a coach (who, in any case, may prefer a dedicated athlete of somewhat lesser skill to a more capable but distracted one). Club sports offer an outlet for physical competition that many former high school stars find amenable.

Prospective freshmen may want to ask current students what position sports play in the social and intellectual life of the campus and then figure out if the answer fits their own interests. They should also ask what percentage of students play intercollegiate sports—the answer may be surprising and, for some students, disconcerting. At Swarthmore in 1999, for example, the figure was 30 percent—much higher than at large Division I universities. Finally, a prospective freshman who just wants to work out and stay in shape should pay attention to the athletic facilities provided for the student body as a whole. In recent decades, these elaborate amenities—worthy of an elite health spa—have become major stops on campus tours, a part of the intense competition for rank and tuition dollars.[39]

Buying Faculty

In addition to asking about class size and the way students allocate their time, Wally Linden should ask college representatives about the tenure status and scholarly achievement of the faculty. Who teaches the key courses in biology, economics, history, Spanish, political science, and the other subjects he's interested in?

Faculty members—those who write the books, manage the curriculum, and teach the classes—define higher education. Colleges compete fiercely for stellar faculty, and this market creates differentials in pay which account for some of the variation in expenditure per student. In a sense, a prospective college student is buying the services of a faculty. And for this reason, understanding the goals and incentives of faculty and how they differ by type of college is important in assessing the learning environment.[40]

The PhD   Every recipient of a PhD has written an original work of approximately book length or the equivalent that has passed muster with the department's faculty committee. Many holders of the PhD present work from their dissertations in one or more of the 19,000 academic journals published worldwide. Sometimes the entire dissertation is revised for book publication by a scholarly press. A first benchmark for judging the faculty of a college is to observe the proportion of the faculty who hold a PhD. Faculty who have earned a doctorate have shown the capacity for creative intellectual work. For students who want to learn to think creatively themselves, having teachers who model this behavior has significant value.[41]

Between 60 and 70 percent of faculty at doctoral and masters universities and at liberal arts colleges earned the PhD, and small differences in the proportion of PhDs from one campus to another do not matter.[42] Fewer than 20 percent of the faculty at two-year colleges hold doctoral degrees. Many research and doctoral universities have professional schools with holders of first professional degrees as their primary faculty. The JD and MD are appropriate and usually sufficient degrees for faculty roles in law and medical schools. In creative areas like music, art, and writing, many colleges hire successful people whose creativity comes through their art rather than scholarly publication. In some fields, an MFA (Master of Fine Arts) is the highest terminal degree. Some colleges count librarians and coaches among their faculty, though they are not expected to publish. For these reasons, excellent colleges seldom have 100 percent of their faculty with a PhD. Harvard reports that 98 percent of its faculty hold PhDs, while Yale lists 96 percent (an insignificant difference).

Tenure   A prospective student may want to give weight to the proportion of the faculty who are tenured or on a tenure track. The tenured and tenure-track faculty differ from other instructors in ways that affect the educational program.

Colleges choose new PhDs as assistant professors with the expectation that the young scholars will continue to produce new ideas. An assistant professor holds an appointment for, say, six years, with an up-or-out decision made by the end of this probationary period. Those professors who demonstrate a significant flow of creative work, usually in scholarly publications, receive promotion to the rank of associate professor with tenure. Tenure is a lifetime employment contract that may be terminated only in extreme cases. After a further period of creative work and publication, an associate professor may be promoted to the rank of professor. Some few full professors are awarded named chairs—in effect, a rank above professor.

The tenure system plays several roles in an institution of higher learning. Tenure grants a faculty member academic freedom—the ability to pursue unpopular, unorthodox ideas without fear of losing his job. Creativity often comes from adopting a fresh point of view, challenging, in some fashion, received wisdom. Although much of this winnowing is private, often scholars test their radical ideas in public forums. If the penalty for error or simply disagreement is too great, the likelihood of a creative breakthrough goes down.

Often the most important ideas are unorthodox enough to be

misunderstood or dismissed as implausible even by one's colleagues. Protecting academic freedom allows people to pursue heretical approaches to problems, sometimes with big payoffs. Many important essays by people who would later garner Nobel prizes and other prestigious awards for their work were rejected, sometimes repeatedly, by the editors of scholarly journals (who are also professors) before finally being published in other venues. Academic journals typically publish at most one-third of the submitted essays, following review by other scholars. The selection reflects the editor's judgment about the quality and originality of the work and the interest readers are likely to have in the topic. Widely read journals may publish less than 10 percent of submissions.[43]

At research universities, half or more of a faculty member's time is devoted to research leading to publication. Universities hire and promote faculty primarily for their past performance and prospects for future success in research. The faculty's publication history is the dominant feature by which research universities are evaluated. Faculty at other colleges publish their work as well, but usually at lower rates. One way to judge the value of a professor's research is to count how frequently others cite it as they pursue their investigations. In biology, the discovery of the double helix as the structure of DNA is one of the most important ideas of the last century. The short article by James Watson and Francis Crick announcing this discovery in 1953 has been cited tens of thousands of times. John Nash's discoveries in game theory (recall the book and movie *A Beautiful Mind*) are of similar importance in economics and have also been cited repeatedly. Every discipline has its seminal thinkers. The rest of us make lesser contributions, measured in part by the rate at which other scholars subsequently cite our work.

After academic freedom, a second reason for the tenure system is that faculty members must make long-term commitments in narrow specialties in order to make original intellectual contributions. A specialist in nineteenth-century French literature may have no career path other than as a professor that would draw on her knowledge about this subject. Just as a railroad insists on a long-term contract for services before it agrees to construct a spur to a coalmine, the faculty member needs a long-term commitment from a college in order to justify his sustained investment in the discipline. The college offers tenure as a method of encouraging and supporting highly specialized research. In the late nineteenth century, American colleges shifted from a faculty of talented generalists producing few new ideas to a specialized faculty for whom production of new ideas is an important goal. In recent decades, specialization has become even more important. Tenured faculty devote their lifetimes to esoteric scholarship.[44]

A third reason for the up-or-out tenure system is that it forces the college to make a careful evaluation of faculty performance after a specified period of time. In considering a decision to offer tenure, more than a dozen people within the college may read the candidate's publications and render careful judgment about their importance. Experts from other schools will be asked to evaluate the published work as well. Although expectations differ from college to college, in part reflecting the salary levels the schools can afford, the tenure decision is usually well considered. Those few colleges that do not have a tenure system tend to put much less effort into evaluating faculty and to renew term contracts on a continuing basis.[45]

Tenure is a highly desirable attribute of a job. For this reason, a college can pay less to faculty with tenure than would be needed to attract comparable experts without tenure. Colleges find that tenure is an economical method of attracting and sustaining high-quality faculty. A prospective student will ask how many courses are taught by tenured and tenure-track faculty. At some liberal arts colleges, more than 95 percent of teaching is done by tenured and tenure-track faculty, compared with as little as a third at some research institutions. Although few colleges routinely report these statistics, those colleges where research-grounded faculty teach more of their undergraduates should want to show their numbers. It's worthwhile to inquire.

Full-time and Part-time   Just as tenure encourages commitment to scholarship, full-time faculty are also more likely to show a deeper commitment to their institution, to stay abreast of their field, and to be effective teachers. However, the percentage of faculty who are part-time is increasing. Except for the research universities where part-time instructors do about 22 percent of teaching, all types of colleges showed an increased use of part-time faculty in the 1990s. In 1998 about two-fifths of instructors at MA and BA colleges, including liberal arts colleges, were part-time. At two-year colleges, about three-fifths of the faculty are part-time.[46]

A headcount of faculty doesn't fully describe a college's teaching resources. Research and doctoral universities use graduate students to teach, though they are not counted as faculty. Graduate student teaching assistants were responsible for 8 percent of undergraduate credit hours at doctoral and research universities in 1998, while at nondoctoral four-year and at two-year colleges less than 1 percent of credit hours were taught by graduate teaching assistants. Some colleges employ lecturers and adjunct faculty (usually people with other careers) in teaching roles without the expectation of sustained original scholarship.[47]

Although many faculty with active research programs also teach undergraduates, on some campuses they account for a minority of the instruction, and a significant number of research faculty teach no undergraduates. Persons who are specialized in teaching undergraduates may provide a significant amount of all instruction. They may be on term-limited appointments or otherwise not on a tenure track and are not expected to produce research. A survey in 2004 reported that 45 percent of full professors at private research universities taught at least one undergraduate class in fall 2003, compared with 88 percent of full professors at private BA colleges. But research universities often include law, medical, and other schools that have no undergraduates; the mean number of courses taught of all kinds (not just undergraduates) was 1.6 for full professors at private research universities, compared with 2.8 at private BA colleges.[48]

An increasing proportion of faculty at research universities are in specialized roles, some focused on teaching, others focused on research. Aggregate measures such as student-faculty ratios provide little insight into the educational services delivered in a given program. In fall 2002, Yale listed 836 tenured faculty, 826 term appointments (including those who may be considered for tenure), 847 non-tenure-track faculty, and 540 research faculty (those with no regular teaching responsibility), for a total of 3,049.[49]

Salaries and Tuition   A higher sticker price for tuition buys more expensive faculty in both the private and public sectors. Higher tuition correlates with higher faculty salaries, from the lower salaries at two-year colleges to top salaries at research universities. Across the categories of private colleges, extra dollars of tuition are strongly associated with higher salaries of full professors. Because the intellectual prowess of the faculty is a primary ingredient in the quality of a college, it is not surprising that students who pay for more quality are bidding for more highly compensated faculty.

Higher salaries don't necessarily mean that the faculty do more teaching, however. At two-year, general BA (other than liberal arts), and master's colleges, higher salaries are associated with more classes taught per term, on average, but at research universities the relationship is the opposite: the better paid a faculty member is, the less he will teach. The liberal arts colleges and the second-tier research campuses show no relationship between courses taught and salary, on average.[50]

Faculty are paid more where the emphasis on research is greater, and with more research comes less teaching. Think tanks like the Institute for Advanced Study, where Albert Einstein was a faculty member, are the most extreme cases. The institute has a distinguished, well-compensated faculty but no students. In paying more tuition at research universities, students are, in effect, buying the prestige that comes from association with distinguished faculty who produce original ideas, even if the students never meet those faculty members or take their class.

The much-touted aggregate student-faculty ratio is useless, then, in forecasting class sizes or the likelihood of interaction with a school's most distinguished intellectuals. It is entirely possible that average class sizes are smaller in two-year colleges with higher student-faculty ratios than in research universities with lower student-faculty ratios, because the faculty at two-year colleges teach so many more courses to undergraduates. Added to that is the fact that the student-faculty ratio can be computed in a variety of ways, making comparison across campuses difficult. To learn about the size of classes and the chances of working with an eminent faculty member, Wally will have to ask direct questions of admission officers and anyone else he encounters in the programs that interest him.

CHAPTER SIX

Sticker Shock: Will You Pay Too Much?

Meghan Barnes, a marketing manager from Benton Harbor, Michigan, visited my campus with her daughter, Rosemary, as a first step in getting acquainted with the college marketplace. Rosemary had taken an economics course in high school and wanted to learn more. She also enjoyed French and asked about our study abroad program in Aix-en-Provence. Her mother had graduated from a private college in the Midwest and was surprised at the cost of tuition, room, board, and other fees. She asked, "Are there any bargain colleges in higher education?" Even families that can afford to pay full fare often want to find less expensive alternatives that deliver comparable services. Why pay more when a similar product is available for less? In this chapter we'll look at the sticker price of a college education and ask why it varies so much and where families can look for bargains.

Some consumers see high price as a sign of high quality. But, just as often, what high price really buys is prestige. If the objective is to acquire a status symbol, overpaying is itself the goal. Hermes sells handbags with its block H logo often for more than $4,000. The exorbitant price buys the cachet of the expensive brand. For some families, colleges have a lot in common with handbags: the point is to impress acquaintances with the fact that you can afford the logo. These consumers are happy to pay full sticker price for a spot in a top-ranked college or university, and the higher the price and rank, the better. But for many families in the college market, it pays to shop around.

With some products and services, price is only weakly associated with the quality of materials or workmanship. In housing, for example, $400,000 buys a very different number of square feet in San Francisco than in Houston, primarily because of location and scarcity. A bottle of wine with the same label bears different prices in different cities because of variations in local taxes and regulations. Similarly, in higher education, the announced price—tuition—is only weakly associated with the quality of services in an undergraduate program. There are at least three reasons for this.

First, state governments provide direct support to the public educational institutions they own and operate. Therefore, tuition at a state school pays for only a fraction of what the college or university actually spends on the education of each student. Quality of services in a state school may be quite high even though tuition is comparatively low.

Second, philanthropy underwrites a significant share of the cost of many colleges and universities, particularly private ones. Bowdoin College in Maine has a financial endowment of $313,181 per student that supports about $15,000 of expenditures per year per student in real dollars. Current giving provides nearly $16,000 more per student. In addition, Bowdoin has 117 buildings and 423 acres of land that serve its 1,642 students. Thus, the college supplements Bowdoin's tuition and fees of roughly $33,000 with a similar amount in income from endowment, current gifts, and the services of the land, buildings, and equipment it owns. Despite its high sticker price, Bowdoin is actually a bargain, in that the services it provides cost almost double what the college charges its students. Many private colleges and universities with large endowments and significant philanthropy offer similar good deals, as measured by expenditure per student.[1]

A third reason that price is a poor signal of quality is that colleges differ in their success at turning revenues into effective educational programs for undergraduates. Quality comes from carefully choosing faculty and operating facilities to advance learning. While dramatic architecture and cutting-edge research programs address important goals of a university, including the recruitment of desired faculty, students, and donors, the presence on campus of signature buildings and outstanding researchers who don't teach does little to promote undergraduate education. Research universities, both public and private, attract large revenue streams from government and the private sector to underwrite the investigation of new ideas. The research enterprise is so huge that it often dwarfs the undergraduate program in terms of cash flow and may dominate the identity of the institution. The challenge to the prospective student is to look beyond the block letter to the stitching. Does the university also deliver high-quality instructional services to undergraduates?

This third problem, which asks how expenditure per student relates to quality, requires understanding the curriculum, class size, grading system, faculty, peers, and much more—topics addressed in Chapter 5. In this chapter, we'll start with the simplistic assumption that expenditure per student is indeed a preliminary marker for quality, and we'll compare that number to tuition and financial aid. If a lot more is expended on a student's education beyond what she pays for out of her own pocket, then the school is likely to be a bargain. After that, we'll look at selectivity and ask why some students might be willing—even wise—to pay a premium for a highly selective college or university with a very high sticker price.

Public Colleges and Universities

State governments are the primary driving force in higher education, with public colleges and universities accounting for more than three-fourths of the nearly 17 million students enrolled at all levels in degree-granting institutions in 2003–2004. Yet the states differ dramatically in how they finance and manage their schools, and this has implications for bargain hunters.[2]

For in-state residents, public colleges and universities in some home states offer much better deals than those in other home states. Tuition and fees for in-state students at the University of Arizona (ranked about 98th nationally in *US News*) was $4,494 for the academic year 2005–2006. The University of New Hampshire (ranked about the same) charged $9,778 to in-state students in the same year. If we look at tuition only and go simply by *US News* rankings (both big ifs), Arizona looks like a bargain for its residents.[3]

At a state-sponsored school, in-state rates are always a deal relative to the tuition that out-of-staters have to pay. But tuition is not the only factor to consider, and some people will get a better education, dollar for dollar, by going to a public college outside their home state—one where expenditures per student are higher. Public colleges in Iowa, for example, spend more than twice as much as public colleges in Florida on every student they enroll. These funds go directly from the state treasury to the budget of the college.

Expenditure per student is one way to judge a state-sponsored school system. But some states choose to spend their education dollars by offering a larger number of seats relative to their population. This allows a higher proportion of high school graduates to attend college in-state at low tuition. California's enrollment in its public colleges and universities is 54 percent of its population who are 18 to 24 years of age; Kansas, New Mexico, and Arizona are not far behind. At the other extreme, the District of Columbia offers the fewest seats relative to population (10.7 percent). Pennsylvania, Massachusetts, Rhode Island, and New Hampshire enroll between 27 and 31 percent. The average for the nation is 38.8 percent (see Table 4).

Some states set as their primary goal keeping tuition low for all students, regardless of need or ability, as in Nevada and Florida. Other states, such as Georgia, provide direct scholarships to the top tier of its high school graduates who choose an in-state school. California and Illinois, with their three-tiered system of higher education (two-year programs, four-year colleges, and full research universities scattered throughout the state), try to juggle all four goals: high expenditure per student, high enrollment, low tuition, and financial aid.

To discover bargains as we look at these huge variations across the states, we'll focus on schools in each tier—two-year colleges, four-year colleges, and universities—and consider differences in how much states spend on each student attending these public schools, how many students they enroll at every level, how they set their tuition, and how they dispense financial aid.

Expenditure per Student   This number is not readily available from the institutions themselves, but Gordon Winston and his colleagues have used the federal survey of expenditures in higher education to create estimates. Expenditure per student counts all students who are enrolled, not just in-state residents and not just undergraduates, because many colleges don't track expenditures separately by level of program.[4]

Ideally, a prospective student would prefer to know the expenditure per student in the specific program he's considering. Since a liberal arts college has essentially one program, its expenditure per student is a fair representation of the services delivered to each student. But a university with a medical school and other post-baccalaureate programs will have large expenditures that are irrelevant to undergraduates. Another layer of ambiguity arises when the same faculty members serve graduate students and undergraduates (as is frequently the case in schools of business, education, engineering, and arts and sciences) and when graduate students also teach. Published university accounts and federal surveys of college expenditures do not attempt to sort all this out—an impossible task.[5]

Public universities show the highest expenditure per student, 27 percent higher than four-year colleges. This group also has the broadest dispersion, suggesting considerable heterogeneity within the group. These results are not surprising. Graduate programs usually require more specialized and more highly compensated faculty. Their faculty put more effort toward research, not all of which is funded by grants and contracts from the National Institutes of Health, the National Science Foundation, and other sources that support specific investigations.[6]

Public four-year colleges are more homogeneous across the country in their expenditures per student, and on average they spend 26 percent more per student than two-year colleges. But there is also considerable overlap across the three tiers. Maine, New Jersey, and Virginia spend more per student on their two-year colleges than Kansas, Rhode Island, and Mississippi spend per student on their universities. This raises the possibility that two-year colleges in some states offer a substantially higher-quality education than universities do in some other states. Low-spending universities may not be great bargains, even with low tuition. If undergraduate instruction is almost exclusively in large groups and if graduate students, adjunct instructors, and others with limited credentials are doing most of the teaching, a student who desires a more intense intellectual experience may want to look elsewhere. Of course, graduate students and adjuncts may be effective in some roles, especially with native speakers in foreign language instruction. The problem arises with over-reliance on these instructors.

Enrollment as a Percentage of Population   In public education, quantity and quality always involve a tradeoff. With a given budget, some states tilt toward fewer seats with higher spending per seat, while other states tilt toward more seats with less expenditure per seat. A prospective student looking for access to less intense services will be better served if he lives in a quantity-oriented state, where he is more likely to be offered a seat at comparatively low tuition. These states include Arizona, California, Florida, Kansas, and Wyoming (though all of these have their pinnacles of excellence as well). On the other hand, a well-prepared ambitious student seeking a four-year in-state college is likely to be better served if she lives in a quality-oriented state like Delaware, Iowa, Louisiana, Pennsylvania, and Vermont, where the two-year tier is smaller and soaks up fewer funds.

In eighteen states, more than 50 percent of all undergraduates enrolled in public colleges attend two-year colleges, while thirteen states have less than 30 percent. In Wyoming 66 percent of undergraduate enrollment is in two-year colleges, and in California it is a whopping 74 percent. The District of Columbia has no public two-year college, but the University of the District of Columbia offers two-year degrees. For a prospective student looking for a low-cost way to enter higher education, the in-state two-year colleges are good bargains.

But if she is looking for a highly regarded national university at in-state tuition rates, she should ask which public universities in her home state place the most emphasis on their graduate and professional programs. These flagship schools are more likely to receive ample state funds, to draw students from out of state who pay higher tuition, and to place graduate students in jobs out of state. Only 21 percent of MBA students at the University of Virginia's Darden Graduate School of Business Administration are from Virginia, for example, where out-of-state tuition and fees are $37,300. Only 10 percent of Darden's 2004 graduates took jobs in the South.[7]

In nine state-sponsored systems of higher education, including Alabama, Colorado, and Maryland, one student in eight is studying at the graduate or professional school level. This represents a significant investment in post-baccalaureate education, and it is a mark of high quality in a public university. Six state-sponsored systems, including California, Utah, and the District of Columbia, have made a more modest commitment—one student in twelve is in graduate or professional school. States such as Alaska, where undergraduate enrollment relative to population is large, tend to have lower enrollments in graduate and professional programs. States such as Arizona, which put special emphasis on two-year colleges, are also less likely to have relatively large post-baccalaureate offerings.[8]

Tuition   Tuition at public colleges and universities varies widely. At the high end, Pennsylvania State University charged $11,024 per year for in-state students in 2005–2006 ($21,260 out-of-state). At the low end, the University of Idaho charged $3,968 in-state ($12,738 out-of-state) in the same year.

Four-year schools charged an average tuition of $5,491 in 2005–2006, which paid for nearly 30 percent of expenditures per student. Public two-year colleges averaged $2,079, which paid for only 19 percent of expenditures per student. In this tier, among the highest tuitions were the Community College of Vermont, with annual rates of $5,130 in-state ($10,560 out-of-state) for 30 credit hours. At the low end was California, at $780 for 30 credit hours for in-state students. The low tuition at two-year public colleges reflects both lean operations, with a 20 percent lower rate of expenditure per student, and heavier subsidy, with 81 percent of the expenditures coming from sources other than tuition, primarily from state and local governments. In most states, the two-year colleges are a tremendous bargain for the right kind of student.[9]

Higher tuition at public schools leads to higher expenditures per student on average, but the increase is not dollar for dollar. States with higher tuitions tend to trim tax support for their colleges, with the net effect that each extra dollar of tuition yields about $0.50 more expenditure per student, on average. However, as public support drops toward zero, the offset of tax support by tuition diminishes to the point that most of the extra tuition stays on campus.[10]

Financial Aid   States with low tuition in effect provide subsidies to all students regardless of income. States with high tuition often award more student-specific financial aid and so focus their subsidies on students with financial need. Consequently—and this point is important—low-income households tend to pay less in high-tuition states, while high-income households tend to pay less in low-tuition states. To put it another way, states with higher in-state tuition actually turn out to be better bargains for low-income students. But states with low in-state tuition are better bargains for high-income students, all other things being equal.

Most public colleges and universities offer some financial aid based on need. On average, about 60 percent of students at more expensive four-year public colleges receive aid, while at two-year colleges the rate is about 40 percent. Selective four-year colleges generally have more wealth and aggressively seek better prepared students. But at all three tiers in the public sector, students at colleges with higher stated tuition are more likely to receive need-based financial aid. That's partly because, for purposes of computing need, the more expensive the college, the greater the need (holding a family's circumstances constant).[11]

What other factors increase the likelihood of receiving financial aid at a public college or university? Although surveys rarely show it, less family wealth (that is, fewer assets, as opposed to lower income) tends to increase the likelihood of aid. Students with younger siblings or only one parent also have an advantage, as do students from rural areas, along with black, Hispanic, and Asian students. At two-year colleges, students who have taken an AP course are more likely to receive aid. At universities, students with higher SAT or ACT scores are more likely to receive aid. Those who are more highly ranked in their high school class and have higher grade-point averages are more likely to receive aid at every level.

So to sum up, in the public sector the sticker price of tuition is a weak signal of quality because of the varied policies of state governments and the diversity of programs and financial aid. Public colleges and universities in some states are significant bargains, and most families will start their college search by gauging the price and quality of the public schools in their home state. When the home state doesn't offer appropriate quality at an attractive net price (and this varies by income level), application to strong out-of-state public schools or to private colleges and universities may offer better prospects. But admission to public schools for out-of-state students is often highly competitive, with out-of-state enrollment limited by quota. Getting into the College of William and Mary, a highly selective state-supported school in Virginia, may be as difficult for an applicant from Massachusetts as getting into Stanford.

Private Colleges and Universities

Private colleges and universities are an important and successful part of higher education. Nearly one-fourth of enrollment at all levels of higher education is in the private sector, about 4.3 million students in 2004. Price is a stronger signal of quality among private institutions than among public schools, and for those paying full price at private colleges, bargains in tuition from one school to the next are rare.[12]

Religiously Affiliated and Ethnic Colleges   The private sector includes much more than leafy New England liberal arts colleges or stately universities with Gothic or Greek Revival architecture. The private sector also includes colleges that serve particular religious or ethnic affinity groups, as well as the proprietary (for-profit) schools.

About half of the enrollment in the private not-for-profit sector is in religiously affiliated institutions. These colleges and universities are a diverse lot, ranging from national research universities like Notre Dame to hundreds of small Bible colleges like Asbury in Wilmore, Kentucky. The role of religion differs significantly from school to school. At one end of the spectrum, some colleges have a commitment to training students for careers as pastors. The Freewill Baptist Bible College in Nashville, for example, lists as its first goal the preparation of students for full-time ministry. These colleges try to hire faculty and staff who adhere to their affiliated religion.

At the other end of the spectrum, religious affiliation is largely a matter of history. The campus supports active religious communities of students and faculty from many faiths, just as do most nonsectarian colleges. Boston College is a research university committed to its Jesuit heritage; 105 of its 645 faculty are Jesuits. Yet its admission website says: "You do not have to be Catholic to feel accepted on campus." Many nonsectarian colleges, public and private, seek out students from diverse backgrounds. Emory University is an affiliate of the United Methodist Church, but it has many Jewish students and faculty, a strong Jewish studies program, and a kosher food option in its dining hall.[13]

Schools with religious affiliations can be found at every level in national rankings, including the top twenty national universities. Choosing a religiously affiliated college doesn't imply a less intense intellectual experience. Nor does it guarantee a lower tuition. Because religion can be a motive for philanthropy, a family might hope to find bargains among schools affiliated with religious groups. But in fact, tuition at some religious affiliates is indistinguishable from similar nonsectarian colleges. For others, roughly speaking, the stronger the religious influence, the lower the tuition.

The 242 Roman Catholic colleges are the largest group, with a total enrollment of 684,000. Georgetown University is ranked 23rd nationally by *US News* and has tuition of $32,199 (2005–2006). The 98 colleges affiliated with the United Methodist Church enroll 180,000 students. Duke, Southern Methodist University, and West

Virginia Wesleyan are examples. The Baptists, with 70 colleges and 120,000 students including 14,000 at Baylor University, are third largest. Brigham Young University, ranked 70th nationally, is the flagship university of the Church of the Latter Day Saints, with an enrollment of 31,000. BYU's tuition is a minuscule $3,410 (2005–2006). Yeshiva, the oldest university operating in the United States under Jewish auspices, is ranked 44th nationally, with tuition of $26,100. Brandeis is a nonsectarian Jewish-sponsored university, ranked 31st nationally, with tuition of $32,500 (2005–2006).

Some colleges and universities serve specific ethnic groups, not necessarily based on religion. There are at least 120 historically black colleges and universities.[14] The Atlanta University Center Consortium is an example in the private sector. Its Morehouse College for men is ranked by *US News* as a third-tier liberal arts college with tuition of $16,684. Spelman College for women, also part of Atlanta University, is ranked among the top 75 liberal arts colleges in the nation, with tuition of $15,945 (2005–2006). In the public sector, several historically black colleges date from the time of segregation under the second phase of the land grant program begun in the 1890s. Prairie View A&M in Texas, Kentucky State, and South Carolina State are examples. The historically black colleges have enjoyed a resurgence in the last decade as philanthropists like Bill Cosby have given support and as African-American students have sought to emphasize their heritage during the college years.

Colleges for Women   From the 1830s to the middle of the twentieth century—a period when all-male colleges were dominant—colleges dedicated exclusively to the education of women developed in parallel with colleges that served both sexes. As women came to more prominent economic roles after 1945, coeducation gained ground for both men and women. By 1996 only two independent, non-affiliated male-only colleges remained, Wabash and Hampden-Sydney, and the number of exclusively female colleges continued to decline. Some traditional women's colleges such as Vassar in 1969 and Randolph-Macon Woman's College (Lynchburg, Virginia) in 2006 chose to admit men, while others, including most recently Marymount College, made the decision to close their doors.

Colleges vary widely in their ability to attract women, from only 20 percent female enrollment at Rose-Hulman Institute of Technology, to 75 percent at Parsons School of Design, to 100 percent at the several dozen remaining women's colleges. Nationally, 58 percent of undergraduates are women, and many schools have female enrollment well over 60 percent. Most women prefer to be on campuses with men, just as they were in secondary school and expect to be after college graduation. Knowing this, coed colleges actively seek a gender-balanced student body, and the under-represented sex is frequently given preference in admission. Shenandoah University, with a large female enrollment and a notable music conservatory, moved male enrollment from 35 percent in 2000 to 41 percent in 2005 when it launched an intercollegiate football program. Meanwhile, Stevens Institute, which first enrolled women in 1971, recently added women's swimming, soccer, and field hockey in an effort to increase female enrollment to 40 percent.[15]

Do women perform better in colleges where women fill all the leadership roles and give less weight to the consequences of classroom performance on their social lives? Some research supports this view. But even in coed colleges and universities, women usually outnumber and earn higher grades than men and often pursue educational goals with more dedication.[16]

The most selective women's colleges report particular success in

inspiring students to pursue PhDs in the sciences, and strong traditions in language instruction. They are also among the most expensive liberal arts colleges. Wellesley posted a 2005–2006 tuition o
$31,348, and Bryn Mawr's sticker price was $30,330. Wellesley ha
need-blind admission and meets the defined need of all its students
Bryn Mawr is need-blind for up to 95 percent of its students and fill
the remaining seats with students who can pay full price. Overall
about 60 percent of their students receive financial aid.

Women's colleges with religious affiliations have somewhat lowe
costs. For example, the tuition at Wesleyan College (Methodist) in
Macon, Georgia, was $14,500 in 2006–2007. At Trinity College
(Catholic) in Washington, D.C., the undergraduate college for wo
men had tuition of $17,716 in 2006–2007. Although philanthropy
makes these colleges less expensive and allows them to have sig
nificant financial aid programs, they generally are unable to mee
the full demonstrated need of all of their students.

Some women's colleges developed in a coordinate role with
neighboring college. Of these, Barnard, which shares courses with
Columbia University, is quite selective, drawing 4,431 application
to enroll 558 new students in 2005–2006. Spelman College share
classes with Morehouse and other members of the Atlanta Univer
sity Center Consortium but retains its own admission office, faculty
and curriculum. Yeshiva University operates separate campuses and
programs for men and women. In rural Collegeville, Minnesota
the College of St. Benedict enrolls 2,033 women with tuition a
$23,454 in 2005–2006, while St. John's enrolls 1,895 men with simi
lar tuition. St. Ben's and St. John's offer a common academic pro
gram with separate campuses, residence halls, and traditions. A
with the other attributes of a college, programs designed exclusively

or women differ in the all-important details, and they continue
to evolve.

Proprietary Schools   The proprietary sector, with 629 accredited colleges, is growing under aggressive management. The Career College
Association—a trade group of institutions, many of which do not
offer accredited degrees—lists 1,270 schools among its members.
Roughly half of the proprietaries are not accredited by the same organizations that accredit public and not-for-profit colleges, with the
result that course work there may not count toward an accredited
degree. ITT Technical Institute has a national chain of seventy-five
campuses. The University of Phoenix offers extensive course work
online.

Although many proprietary colleges serve their missions well, a
story that aired on CBS's *60 Minutes* in February 2005 highlighted
some concerns. Because they receive neither direct tax support nor
philanthropy and they spend a significant share of revenues in
marketing, many proprietaries deliver educational services that cost
less than the tuition charged. CBS also claimed that recruiters receive bonuses for students they attract, even if the students' prospects are poor. Some proprietaries raise capital by selling shares of
stock rather than calling on philanthropy or public support. Tuition
at proprietaries, unlike in the public and nonprofit sectors, often
covers both marketing and capital costs in addition to the cost of the
educational services.[17]

The proprietaries are always on the lookout for market opportunities. In anticipation of an increased demand for nurses as the population ages, several proprietary colleges are expanding to offer nursing education. They respond rapidly to changing conditions, look

for ways to hire inexpensive faculty, and make aggressive use of technology. Their programs and prices vary to meet demands.[18]

Tuition and fees for proprietaries depend on location and type of program. Strayer University in Washington, D.C., had annual tuition of $12,150 for ten courses in 2006. DeVry University (Philadelphia-Washington, D.C.) charged $13,700 for annual tuition and fees in 2005–2006. The University of Phoenix charged $18,360 in tuition for ten three-credit hour courses in its MBA program in Philadelphia in 2006–2007. The proprietary colleges appeal primarily to nontraditional students, and in this respect they fill a significant and growing niche in higher education. But they're no substitute for a high-quality full-time undergraduate program.[19]

Selective Liberal Arts Colleges and Universities   The race for rank is the defining feature of highly competitive private colleges and universities, though many public schools also participate in this competition. Private schools generate as much revenue as they can in the pursuit of donations, and then deploy their resources in ways that attract highly qualified students. Cutting the sticker price is almost never done, because it gives the appearance of reducing quality; but financial aid is prevalent in this group. Colleges gain in many ways by attracting more academically capable students. They can charge higher tuitions, attract more benefactors, and hire outstanding faculty while offering lower salaries, because working with better students is more engaging. The top colleges pay top salaries, of course, but they would have to pay even more if their students were boring.

Selective colleges define excellence, in part, by the talent in their student body, and they define success as attracting the most accomplished students relative to other colleges. More than a hundred colleges consider themselves contenders for the top twenty spots in national rankings, and the schools shape many of their academic goals accordingly. In the next section we'll look more closely at selectivity in both private and public institutions and then ask why some students and their families are willing to pay extra—sometimes a lot extra—for a spot in a highly selective college or university.

Measuring Selectivity

Any college or university—public or private—that attracts more qualified applicants than it has seats is defined as selective. Dartmouth College began the selective admission process in 1921. Active selection on the basis of academic merit spread to many colleges in the 1950s, and selectivity has become more extreme in recent decades, especially on campuses in the private sector.[20]

Selectivity is usually measured as the proportion of applicants who are accepted, a ratio that falls with rising applications. Barron's breaks down selectivity into categories of competitiveness; of these, the "most competitive" colleges accept less than one-third of applicants, and only 7 percent of students entering four-year colleges are enrolled in this group (Table 5). Another 14 percent enroll in the "highly competitive" colleges, which accept between a third and a half of their applicants. About 26 percent enroll in "very competitive" schools, which accept between half and three-fourths of their applicants. Schools that accept three-fourths of their applicants or more account for 52 percent of all students at four-year colleges or universities. (The remaining 1 percent is made up of students in the "Special" category—art schools, conservatories, and so on which vary in selectivity.) Selectivity is most important in the private sector, keenly important for out-of-state applicants at strong public campuses, and also important (sometimes very important) for in-state admission to flagship state schools, especially honors programs.[21]

The fact that each college in the most competitive group accepts only one-third or fewer of its applicants doesn't mean that two-thirds of applicants are frozen out of this group. The high rate of selectivity derives in part from the fact that students apply to several colleges. Suppose that 10,000 prospective students were interested in places in ten colleges, each of which will enroll 1,000 new students. If each student applies to five randomly selected colleges in the set, there will be 50,000 applications, and the ratio of new enrollments to applicants will be one to five at every college (20 percent), even though all 10,000 students will exactly fill the places in the ten colleges. If all the students apply to six of the ten colleges, the "enrollment rate" will drop to 17 percent. Applicants to less competitive colleges generally apply to fewer colleges because their chances of getting in seem quite high. This accounts in part for lower ratios of applications to new enrollees and lower "selectivity" at these schools.

The noncompetitive institutions listed in Barron's generally admit all in-state applicants with high school diplomas who have completed a college preparatory program in English, math, science, and social studies. Some of them winnow students more aggressively during the first year of study, resulting in higher than average attrition among enrolled students. The open-enrollment colleges also enroll more part-time students and students with weaker academic credentials who are less likely to complete their studies on any campus.

Of the "special" institutions listed in Barron's, art schools usually examine an applicant's portfolio, and music schools often require an audition. Schools in this category vary widely in selectivity, but the selective ones give weight to artistic and other kinds of merit in the admission decision.

Among the "most competitive" schools, 67 are private research universities and liberal arts colleges and 7 are public institutions. The Ivy League schools, a set of technical schools (CalTech, Cooper Union, MIT), and research universities from around the country (Case Western, Georgetown, George Washington, Rice, and the University of Rochester, for example) are in this category. Of the 7 public institutions in this group, 2 are service academies (at West Point and Annapolis), along with UCLA, UNC Chapel Hill, UVA, and others. The most competitive liberal arts colleges include Bates, Carleton, Connecticut College, Kenyon, Occidental, and Pomona, to name a few.

Privates also dominate the "highly competitive" set (74 of 109), which includes many liberal arts colleges (Grinnell, Skidmore, Wofford) and universities (Boston University, Lehigh, Syracuse). However, several flagship public universities are also in this highly competitive group (Florida State, Georgia Tech, Illinois, Michigan, Penn State, Rutgers, four SUNY campuses, UC Berkeley, and UC Irvine, among others), along with the three remaining service academies.

The selectivity of a college or university is strongly associated with its stated tuition for both private and out-of-state public institutions. The mean tuition among Barron's very competitive campuses is nearly 24 percent above the mean in the competitive group; tuition in the highly competitive group is more than 50 percent above the competitive group; and mean tuition among the most competitive colleges and universities is nearly 90 percent above the competitive group. Mean tuition in the less competitive group is 14 percent below that of the competitive group, and mean tuition in the noncompetitive group is 30 percent below.

Out-of-state tuition and fees averaged $9,616 at noncompetitive public four-year colleges in 2004 but $14,116 among very competitive public four-year colleges. Tuition and fees at private colleges averaged $11,219 per year at noncompetitive four-year colleges but $29,195 among the most competitive colleges. Public in-state tuition and fees averaged $5,000 in 2004 and did not vary systematically with the selectivity of the institution. Choosing a college in the higher quality group, as measured by selectivity at least, usually comes at a higher sticker price for private and out-of-state public schools.[22]

But stated tuition as a marker of quality has its limitations. Although the most competitive colleges have the highest tuition, their other revenue streams are also higher per student, compared with less competitive colleges. In the private sector, tuition is leveraged with philanthropic support and income from endowments. Ironically, high tuition on the most competitive campuses buys the most leverage. As a consequence, a dollar of stated tuition buys more than two dollars' worth of educational expenditures at the most competitive private colleges but less than $1.40 of educational expenditures at less competitive colleges. Educational quality is most heavily subsidized at the high end of selectivity and at the highest stated tuitions.

A college's endowment is a financial fund that is invested to yield income to support a college's operation in perpetuity. Endowment income supplements tuition and other revenues to allow a college to spend much more on educational services. At the most competitive research universities and liberal arts colleges, average endowment *per student* was over $200,000 in 1998. In the highly competitive category, however, while the endowment at liberal arts colleges averaged a hefty $135,000 per student, that of the research universities dropped to less than $50,000 per student. Schools typically spend about 5 percent of the value of their endowment on current operations each year. From their endowment income, the most competitive liberal arts colleges and universities contribute more than $10,000 per student per year to operations. At liberal arts colleges and universities listed as competitive (Barron's fourth category from the top), endowment provides only about $3,000 per student per year.

For students who qualify for financial aid, the stated tuition vastly overstates the net price a family will have to pay. Among research universities, those in the most competitive category tend to be the wealthiest and to provide more aid than those in the highly competitive and less competitive categories. Among the liberal arts colleges, by contrast, those in the highly competitive and less competitive categories offer more aid on average than the most competitive colleges. The latter have quite significant aid programs, but these schools are not as aggressive in using aid to attract students.

Paying a Premium for Selectivity

Many students enter college not simply to develop marketable skills but also to test themselves against other students for access to top-tier jobs and post-baccalaureate programs that depend on academic success. Being among the top performers on a campus of strong performers places a student among the best of his national peer group. Very selective colleges and universities effectively signal that their students are high achievers. The same student might have achieved an even higher rank among graduates at a less competitive college, but that position would have less clout on the national job market or in competition for a spot in graduate or professional school. When relative position is the name of the game, testing oneself against stronger competition counts, and a college's reputation comes into play.[23]

Recently the *Wall Street Journal* tallied a "feeder score" for schools which approximates the proportion of undergraduates from a given college who enter the top five medical, law, and MBA programs. The top twenty colleges and universities in terms of feeder score included seven of the eight Ivy League schools, whose undergraduate programs are primarily in the liberal arts. Six more of the top twenty are private research universities, including Stanford, Duke, and Chicago, where undergraduate programs are similar to the Ivy League set. The remaining seven of the top twenty feeder schools are leading liberal arts colleges, including Middlebury, Haverford, and Swarthmore. Of the top fifty feeder schools, twenty-one are private liberal arts colleges.[24]

The analysis has limitations, of course. That only four of the top fifty are in the public sector may reflect the greater diversity of programs in large state schools. Students who enter colleges of agriculture or nursing may have less interest in post-baccalaureate professional degrees in medicine, law, or business from the outset. At most public universities, the liberal arts college enrolls only a fraction of the university's undergraduates. The small, highly selective honors colleges at many public universities are quite successful in placing students in post-baccalaureate programs. The *Wall Street Journal* analysis would be more reliable and informative if it included more years and more graduate professional programs. And of course a college that places its graduates in leading professional schools may simply attract talented students who would perform well wherever they went to school.[25]

Competition for top jobs or professional schools is one reason some parents will choose to pay a premium for selectivity, but it is not the only one. Another reason may have to do with peer effects. Just as rivals in the Tour de France benefit by working together at times to reduce wind resistance, most students learn more when they collaborate with peers, even as they compete with them for grades. Writers learn from other capable writers, musicians play better around accomplished musicians, laboratory biologists are more productive when they work in teams. College, as its Latin root suggests, is about cooperation, even when there is stiff competition for rank. So in addition to the value of a school's reputation in the marketplace, another reason for choosing a more selective college is to gain access to more talented peers.[26]

A number of statistical studies have found that students with more academically accomplished roommates earn higher grade-point averages in college, when other student attributes are held constant. This roommate effect on academic performance is strongest among high-achieving students. So increasing the chances that their son or daughter will get a high-achieving roommate may cause some parents to favor a more selective college.

Many parents also know that students of high-earning families are more likely to attend more selective colleges, and that graduates of these schools are more likely to play leading roles in politics and the professions. Association with a set of well-placed, highly ambitious peers is another reason, in the minds of some, to pay top tuition.[27]

Educators know too little about how peers influence performance and outcomes in the long run. But they know enough to see that more selective colleges generally offer more positive peer effects.[28]

What Will Tuition Be Next Year?

Tuition per student at public colleges has grown remarkably since 1971 relative to the other things households buy. The average annual rate of growth of tuition in dollars of 2004 purchasing power over the twenty-one-year period was 3.4 percent for in-state students at public two-year colleges and 4.4 percent at public four-year colleges. The rate of increase from 1995 to 2000 was 3.6 percent per year, but from 2001 to 2005 it accelerated to 7.9 percent per year.[29] Private college tuitions grew similarly, albeit from a higher base. Private tuition showed little growth from 1970 to 1980 but increased steadily from 1985 to 1995 at 3.2 percent per year. The pace of increase accelerated to 6.0 percent per year from 1995 to 2000 and fell back slightly to 5.2 percent from 2001 to 2005.

Tuition has increased because the demand for college education has grown. Colleges and universities have responded by expanding enrollments, adding campuses, and improving quality, but there are limits to the supply response, and so prices rise. The demand for quality has accelerated along with tuition. That tuitions at four-year colleges have grown faster than those at two-year colleges reflects this increased demand. Although the return on investment for associate degrees is very good, the return on baccalaureate degrees is excellent, and the returns on certain post-baccalaureate degrees are astronomical. Add the nonmonetary dimension of status and social mobility, and we begin to see that the personal reward to higher-quality education is substantial. This is why consumers are willing to pay more for it. Knowing that the market for quality will bear higher prices, colleges put more resources into faculty, computers, and libraries along with gymnasiums, food services, residences, and other indicators of quality.

Tuition in the public sector has grown faster than in the private sector in recent years, and financial aid programs have shifted from grants to loans and tax credits. With the personal payoff to education rising (and the gap in incomes between more educated and less educated persons growing), perhaps voters think individuals should bear more financial responsibility for their own education. And perhaps legislators want families to bear more educational expense directly, so that states can shift tax support to health care, prisons, and other activities.

If tuition continues to increase at 4 percent per year beyond inflation, as it did over the last twenty years, tuition will more than double in a generation. The college that costs $25,000 per year today will cost $66,000 in today's dollars twenty-five years from now. It's hard to believe that demand will continue to grow at a rate to sustain such increases in prices without setting off a variety of countervailing forces. If trivial differences in services have little effect on life prospects, might consumers shop more carefully? When consumers are more sensitive to price, prices are likely to increase more slowly.

Although 40 percent (and in some cases up to 60 percent) of students at the most expensive colleges receive financial aid, the rest are paying full price. Consequently, the growth in tuition at the highest priced colleges and universities is driven by the income levels of the top 10 percent of the population. If the earnings of those who are best off begin to slacken, the rate of growth of top tuitions will slow somewhat. The upper end of plausible rates of increase in tuition for the generation ahead is 4.5 percent annual increase beyond inflation. The lower end of plausibility may be 1.5 percent. That puts a 3.0

percent annual increase beyond inflation as an optimistic best guess for the most competitive colleges and universities. Rates of increase will be less at lower-tier colleges and two-year programs.

Finding True Bargains in Education

People buying higher education don't necessarily choose the lowest bidder. Smart investors try to balance net price with quality. Expenditure per student, selectivity, and high stated tuition are just a few of the markers that are correlated with the highest-quality schools. But another indicator might be the choices made by the children of faculty members. Faculty are among the best-informed consumers of higher education, having committed a career to observing institutions from the inside. Their children tend to value education, to attend elementary and secondary schools that provide good preparation, and to enjoy a home life with reading, conversation, and travel.

A recent survey looked at private liberal arts colleges and research universities that offer, as a fringe benefit, remission of tuition at any school a child of a faculty member chooses to attend.[30] Compared to children of parents with similar incomes and levels of education but other kinds of jobs, children with a faculty parent were much more likely to choose research universities and freestanding liberal arts colleges over other institutions of higher education. And not surprisingly, the children of research university faculty were most likely to choose research universities (even setting aside those who attend the university where a parent works), and the children of faculty who teach at freestanding liberal arts colleges were most likely to attend those kinds of schools.

The cross flows, however, were surprising. The children of research university faculty were decidedly more likely to choose a freestanding liberal arts college than the child of a typical high-income household, while the children of liberal arts college faculty were *less* likely to choose a research university than the child of a typical high-income household. That 23 percent of the children of research university faculty chose freestanding liberal arts colleges while only 14 percent of the children of high-income households did says something about the value faculty members place on the focused undergraduate instruction at liberal arts colleges when it comes to their own children.

Meghan Barnes's question about bargains has many dimensions. The Barneses must first think about where in the pecking order of selectivity Rosemary might land and then try to judge how much quality she wants to buy. Talented, well-prepared, ambitious students are likely to look for more intense, expensive college services. They value a more knowledgeable faculty with whom they can explore ideas in depth. Students with less academic talent, college preparation, or intellectual ambition may find a less intense experience attractive and appropriate, particularly if it is available at a lower price and at a convenient location. For students paying full tuition at private or out-of-state public colleges or universities, the most competitive schools will cost substantially more than much less competitive ones. Among students who qualify for financial aid, however, the cost of attending a more competitive college with high tuition but also a generous financial aid program may be lower than they would pay at a less competitive college.

Rosemary will probably look first at the public school system in Michigan because she is a resident there. Michigan has relatively high enrollment in public higher education, a significant two-year college sector, but also relatively high expenditures per student. Michigan provides ample public support for higher education at every level. In 2005–2006 the University of Michigan was ranked about 25th nationally by *US News*. In-state tuition was $8,910 ($27,129 out-of-state). Room and board was $7,374. The 25,500 undergraduates were enrolled in one of six colleges of the university, and tuition varied among the colleges. Attending college at the University of Michigan at the in-state rate represents a bargain in higher education if there ever was one. The University of Michigan is likely to be Rosemary's first choice for college.

If she isn't ready for the intensity of this highly selective research university, Rosemary might consider her local university, Western Michigan University in Kalamazoo, fifty miles from Benton Harbor. It is in the competitive category as a third-tier national university, with 23,000 undergraduates in six undergraduate colleges. Tuition and fees were $6,152 in-state in 2005–2006 ($15,530 out-of-state), with room and board at $6,821. For in-state students, the difference in tuition between the University of Michigan and Western Michigan is modest, and the size of the undergraduate population is about the same. To discover which is the better value for her, Rosemary will have to dig deeper, using some of the ideas discussed in Chapter 5.

CHAPTER SEVEN

Payment Options: Something for Every Income

Most families need careful financial planning to get their children through college. The total cost of undergraduate education for two students at selective private colleges may exceed the value of a good house in many parts of the country. Houses are often purchased with thirty-year mortgages, and financing college education may involve similar long-range commitments.

There are four ways, in various combinations, to deal with college expenses: working, saving, borrowing, and grants. This chapter describes these four streams of finance in some detail. In each of them, federal, state, and college-sponsored programs can be found in abundance. Every family will have to make its own plan, reflecting its unique financial circumstances. But here's some indication of the range of options.

Bob and Lesley Willis, a schoolteacher and retail worker from Omaha, have after-tax income of $50,000 ($61,000 before federal and state income and payroll taxes) and hold $25,000 in financial assets. The Willises have limited ability to accumulate savings to pay for college for their two daughters, ages fifteen and sixteen, and they face significant constraints on their ability to borrow. When the time comes, the family will use some current earnings and will be eligible for need-based grants at many schools. The Willises will also take full advantage of federal tax credits, especially since their daughters will overlap in college for three of the four years. And they will look carefully at in-state schools such as the University of Nebraska. During the three years of overlap, the Willises will be eligible for higher levels of financial aid than if the daughters were attending sequentially, since colleges, in calculating aid, will split the family's expected contribution between the two children.

Rex and Samantha Bishop, an accountant and a veterinary assistant who live in southern New Jersey, have after-tax income of $80,000 ($106,000 before income and payroll taxes), with $75,000 in net worth. To pay for college for their son, now in middle school, the Bishops are able to save some money, and they will have a larger capacity for borrowing than the Willises. They will also be able to divert more dollars from current earnings to pay tuition. Their son's grant aid will probably be small, unless he lands a merit-based scholarship.

Audrey and Alex Reed, a lawyer and a nurse from Atlanta, have after-tax income of $150,000 ($191,000 before taxes) and $200,000 in net worth. The Reeds' daughter, now three years old, is very unlikely to receive need-based grants, but the family has a high capacity for saving and borrowing and will probably be able to commit more dollars from current earnings than either of the other two families. If Jennifer turns out to be a top student in her Georgia high school, she may have merit-based options to choose from, as we will see.

The U.S. Congress has established a formula for calculating eligibility for need-based federal grants and loans, and it is a useful starting point for thinking about how much college a family can afford. Using information that the family provides about its income, assets, and the number and ages of siblings, the formula calculates the *expected family contribution* (EFC) to the cost of education for each child in college. Federal loan and grant programs and the colleges themselves presume the family will make its calculated contribution. When expected expenditures for college exceed this amount, a financial aid package that includes loans, grants, and earnings from a student job may help fill the gap.[1]

The expected total expenditure at a given college is called the *cost of attendance* (COA), a figure that includes tuition, fees, room, food, books, and an allowance for other typical expenses such as travel. Agnes Scott College, a highly competitive private liberal arts college for women, put its annual cost of attendance at $34,942 in 2005–2006, of which $23,260 is tuition. The cost of attendance minus the expected family contribution is the student's *estimated financial need* (EFN). This represents the upper limit on the amount a student will receive in need-based financial aid. A family with an EFC of $25,000 per year would be eligible for aid up to $10,000 per year at Agnes Scott.[2]

Several websites provide tools that help a family make a detailed estimate of its expected family contribution, based on income, wealth, and family size.[3] In general, the EFC rises with income. The horizontal axis in Figure 2 depicts after-tax income, which is about 80 percent of gross income (the exact amount varies from state to state because of differences in state taxes). With after-tax income under $25,000, a family is expected to contribute little. The Willises, with after-tax income of $50,000 and modest assets, have an EFC of about $7,000 per year. They should expect to pay the full cost of college if the COA of the schools their daughters choose come to

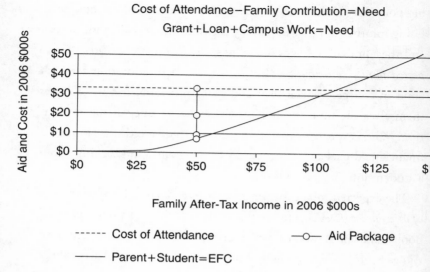

Cost of Attendance – Family Contribution = Need
Grant + Loan + Campus Work = Need

Family After-Tax Income in 2006 $000s

------ Cost of Attendance   —○— Aid Package

——— Parent + Student = EFC

$7,000 per year or less. A local state-sponsored two-year college, for example, would be only a few thousand dollars above the $7,000 per year EFC. A student could earn that amount with a summer job and part-time term employment. But if the Willis sisters want to go to expensive private colleges like Agnes Scott, they will need a huge financial aid package—an additional $28,000 in student work, loans, and grants for one student each year, and $63,000 when the two daughters are in college at the same time ($35,000 × 2 = $70,000; $70,000 − $7,000 = $63,000 per year).

For the Bishops, with after-tax income of $80,000, the EFC will be about $20,000 per year. They should plan to pay the full amount for a school with a COA of $20,000 per year or less. At a university such as Mercer University, where the cost of attendance was $33,000 in 2005–2006, their son would be eligible for a financial aid package up to $13,000. However, at a school that doesn't meet full need for all students—and most don't—he may not receive this amount. In that case, the Bishops would have to make up the difference some-how, with more borrowing and belt-tightening.

The Reeds, with after-tax income of $150,000 ($191,000 before tax), will be expected to pay up to $55,000 per year with one student in college. No college costs this much, at least not yet. Nevertheless, the Reeds may choose to save or borrow, and their daughter may also take a part-time job or win a merit scholarship.

The discussion of financing strategies, below, identifies a variety of ways for families to help their children take advantage of college opportunities. Many public and private philanthropic programs help students complete college. Although some of the programs help the poor, taken together the programs provide assistance to nearly every college student. The assistance is often substantial even for high-income students. A strong reason for such wide support of college education is the recognition that the benefits of a well-edu-cated society extend far beyond the substantial gains in earnings that each student receives. Direct support for colleges and universities, along with a menu of financial aid options for individual students, advances the general welfare as well as benefiting each student.[4]

Working

Most families can provide some support for college from current household income. Funds used for food and clothes while the stu-dent was in high school can be redirected to the same purposes in college. In addition, many families scale back other expenses—they keep the old car going longer, choose a less expensive vacation, and postpone major purchases. Some parents take on overtime or a sec-ond job, or forgo early retirement. Extra parental income is a big part of the financial plan for many college students.

Federal Tax Credits for Higher Education   A suite of recent changes in income tax laws has lowered a household's tax liability when a family member is in college, saving for college, or carrying college loans. Taken together, these tax programs are about as coherent as pick-up-sticks. They require taxpayers to make complex choices, sometimes well in advance of the time when their student enters college. Each new change in federal tax legislation sets off tremors that shift the pile of sticks, upsetting their relative advantages. State income tax laws magnify the changes at the federal level.[5] Here, we'll try to keep it fairly simple.

The Tax Relief Act of 1997 included seven provisions for higher education. The best known of them is the federal Hope Scholarship Tax Credit, an initiative inspired by Georgia's Hope Scholarship program (described below). This credit lowers the income taxes due when a family pays college expenses out of pocket. To receive the credit, a family must make the claim on its income tax form. The federal Hope program offers a full tax credit for the first $1,000 of out-of-pocket tuition and other qualified college expenses for students in each of the first two years of college. It also offers a half tax credit up to $500 for the second $1,000 of qualified expenses. The total maximum credit that any household may claim is $1,500 per year, multiplied by the number of eligible students.[6]

A student is eligible for the Hope credit if she has not yet completed the first two years of college, has been enrolled at least half time, did not have any expenses used for a Hope credit in two earlier years, and has not been convicted of possessing or distributing controlled substances. The Hope Tax Credit is phased out for parents who file jointly and show a modified adjusted gross income (MAGI) between $80,000 and $100,000, and for single filers with a MAGI between $40,000 and $50,000. (The exact dollar limits change over time.) A family cannot receive more credit than its income tax liability, and a household with no income tax liability receives no benefit. The Willises will be eligible for the Hope Tax Credit, but the Bishops and the Reeds will not.

The Lifetime Learning Tax Credit is an alternative to the Hope Tax Credit. The Lifetime program credits 20 percent of qualified tuition expenses up to a maximum credit of $2,000 for each year of postsecondary education, including graduate school. A household with $10,000 of qualified educational expenses would receive the full credit, provided it would otherwise have paid at least $2,000 of taxes. Drug conviction is not a bar to this credit, and a student may be enrolled for less than half time. A family may claim only one $2,000 credit per year, and the phase-out for high incomes is the same as for the Hope credit.

The Willises will use the $2,000 Lifetime credit when their oldest child is in her first year of college, assuming that they have $10,000 in qualified expenses. The following year they'll switch to the Hope credit, for a total of $3,000, because both daughters will be in their first two years of college. After that, for the next three years, they'll switch back to the Lifetime Credit of $2,000. A taxpayer may claim only one of the following in a given tax year: the Hope, the Lifetime, or a withdrawal from a Coverdell Education Savings Account (described below).

Student Employment   As part of their financial aid package, many colleges and universities include a work-study opportunity for students, subsidized by the federal government. The Federal Work-Study Program, which began in 1964, pays a significant fraction of the on-campus wages of students on financial aid, up to an aggregate dollar limit for a given campus. In 2003–2004, 7.5 percent of undergraduates received average earnings of $2,000 for campus jobs performed during the school year, about two-thirds of which was federal subsidy.[7]

Some students choose to work off campus, either to earn higher wages or to pursue different kinds of employment. Nationally, 40 percent of students in higher education are enrolled part-time, usually because work commitments prevent them from taking a full course load. Many of the most intellectually challenging colleges seek only full-time students, however.[8]

Other federal programs provide ways of working for a short period of time to gain assistance for college. AmeriCorps, begun in 1993, offers educational assistance awards of $4,725 for one year of full-time participation in the program. The five federal service academies offer tuition-free education in exchange for a commitment to military service, but admission is highly competitive. ROTC scholarships are available on many campuses, and the military touts educational benefits as an inducement to enlist, with a ceiling of $28,800 for three years of military service and $50,000 for four years. The army also pays one-third or $1,500 of student loan debt for each year of service.[9]

Saving

A second method of financing college involves looking ahead. The Reeds have adopted a college savings plan for their three-year-old, Jennifer. They're planning for a college that costs $25,000 per year in tuition and fees (in today's dollars). They expect to pay room, board, and other expenses from current income and other assets. If Jennifer chooses a more expensive college, the Reeds will meet the extra cost from other sources, possibly by borrowing. If Jennifer chooses a less expensive college or receives merit-based aid, the Reeds will use the funds to pay her room and board or perhaps graduate study.

The Reeds have opened a 529 account, a category of tax-sheltered investment specifically focused on higher education (described more fully below), where they hope to earn 4 percent per year, net of inflation and investment expenses. They will contribute to the account with after-tax dollars, but the interest, dividends, and capital gains earned will not be subject to income tax, as long as the fund is used for approved educational expenses. By putting their money in a 529 account instead of making their customary investments, the Reeds, whose marginal tax rate is 28 percent, will save $20,000 in today's dollars, about $5,000 per year for four years of college. The tax advantages will be even greater if inflation climbs during the next fifteen years.[10]

On the assumption that tuition costs will go up at a rate of 3 percent per year over the next two decades, the Reeds will invest $7,600 in 2006. Every year after that, for the next fifteen years, they will increase the amount they put in the 529 account, based on the Consumer Price Index. This savings rate will build a college fund of $158,000—adequate to cover tuition of roughly $40,000 per year starting in 2021.

Families that save more are likely to have more choices among colleges, and those that save less may have to restrict their sights to schools with lower tuition, higher grant aid, or both. The Willises and Bishops are likely to save at much lower rates than the Reeds, given their lower level of earnings. But they should bear in mind that the most selective colleges and universities, with the highest tuitions, also offer the highest grant aid, based on need and sometimes merit. So a family that has been unable to save should not consider only those schools with a low sticker price. If their student's academic performance and other qualifications are outstanding, they should consider one of the most selective colleges or universities with a reputation for assisting deserving students, whatever the need.

Prepaid 529 Savings Plans   In 1986 the governor of Michigan, James J. Blanchard, established the Michigan Education Trust to allow Michigan residents to prepay tuition at Michigan's public colleges and universities. The idea was that the state could invest the prepaid funds free of federal income taxes and make a greater return than the family would make if it saved the money itself and financed college from its accumulated taxable investments. Since the state was making more money from prepayment, it could give the family a good deal on tuition. The courts upheld Michigan's favorable tax treatment for its prepayment plan, and Congress formalized the tax-exemption for state-managed college prepayment and savings plans in 1996 and 1997 under section 529 of the Internal Revenue Code. Hence the name "529 plans."

Some states, for example Florida, Illinois, and Tennessee, kept their Prepaid Tuition plans, sometimes called Prepaid 529s. In these plans, parents buy units of tuition, for example $36.85 for one one-hundredth of an annual tuition. The price for a unit varies by age group and from state to state.[11] The plans are limited to in-state public colleges and universities, and there is no guarantee that a child will be admitted to any of them. When the economy boomed, the states could fund their campuses from tax dollars, live with modest increases in tuition, and earn handsome returns by investing the prepaid funds. When the stock market tanked, the states' tax funds dried up, public tuition escalated, and the value of investments plummeted. As a consequence, prepaid tuition plans lost financial viability in some states. States that sold these units will, of course, have to make good on their contracts, but some no longer sell them. The prepaid plans are typically attractive only when a family is sure that a student will enroll at an in-state public college—and what family can ever be sure of that?

Investment 529 Savings Plans As of 2002, all fifty states operated at least one 529 tax-exempt college savings plan. (In 2003 a group of private colleges introduced a prepayment program for the private sector as well.) Most references to 529 plans are to the so-called Investment 529s, not the Prepaid 529s. Each state's program is unique, with limits set by state legislatures, but all are designed to provide a tax shelter for earnings on college savings.

The states contract with major investment houses to manage their programs: Fidelity, T. Rowe Price, TIAA-CREF, and Vanguard, for example. After-tax dollars accumulate investment income that is not subject to federal income tax (much like Roth Individual Retirement Accounts), and no federal tax is due at withdrawal as long as funds are spent on qualified educational expenses. The states have set high ceilings on the amount invested; none are less than $100,000 per beneficiary. Households at all levels of income may use the 529 tax shelter to save. But since the tax avoided through a 529 plan is greater the higher a household's marginal tax rate, families like the Reeds will be the greatest beneficiaries of this tax benefit.

The 529s seem somewhat less attractive today than they were in 1997, for a number of reasons. The reduction in income tax rates on dividends and capital gains enacted in 2003 means that sheltering investment income from tax has a lower payoff today than it did in 1997. And the 529 investment plans do not have as much flexibility or choice as many Individual Retirement Accounts and often involve management fees that in some cases are double those in conventional no-load mutual funds.[12]

The 529 plans are more attractive in some states than in others, and a family shopping for a plan is not restricted to the home-state option. Georgia's TIAA plan offers only balanced or equity portfolios, which may be more appropriate for households with a lower marginal tax rate or with few financial assets. A household in the top income tax bracket with a marginal tax rate of 35 percent and substantial wealth may want to find a bond-intensive 529 account, like Nevada's Vanguard plan. The strategy here would be to invest taxable assets in stocks outside the 529 plan (in order to concentrate its capital gains in taxable assets) and tilt 529 investments toward bonds (where interest income will be sheltered from tax).[13]

While many states grant deductions and exclusions from state income taxes for in-state 529 funds, a few states use a stick rather than a carrot: they tax withdrawals from out-of-state 529s. Constructing a plan to save for college that balances this wide and ever-changing array of tax shelters with a family's financial profile and goals is a complex undertaking. For most families, a carefully chosen 529 plan, though not necessarily the home-state plan, will be the first and best choice.

Coverdell Education Savings Accounts (ESA)   The ESAs are modeled on Roth IRAs and are sometimes called Education IRAs. A household may deposit up to $2,000 per year into an ESA and invest the money as they choose. The allowed deposit phases out for households with income over $190,000, and households with an income over $220,000 are ineligible. These accounts are funded with after-tax dollars, but all earnings accumulate free of federal income taxes, and there are no taxes at withdrawal when funds are spent on qualified educational expenses. Significantly for some families, ESAs can be used for elementary, secondary, or postsecondary schooling. The 529 plans apply only to college and postgraduate education.

When a family establishes an ESA, it must designate a beneficiary under the age of eighteen. All the funds must be dispersed by the beneficiary's thirtieth birthday, or the fund may be rolled over to another beneficiary within the same family—a sibling, grandchild, niece or nephew, the spouse of these family members, and so on. Even a first cousin of the beneficiary qualifies. Funds withdrawn and not spent on education are subject to a 10 percent penalty unless the beneficiary dies, becomes disabled, or receives an equivalent amount in other scholarships. Because the tax savings of the ESA apply to the investment income earned in the account, the tax benefits are higher the longer funds stay in the account. For this reason, the ESA is primarily for families who start saving years ahead of need. When maximum tax rates on dividends and capital gains were reduced to 15 percent, the tax advantages of the ESA declined, just as they did for the 529s.

Individual Retirement Accounts   Congress enacted several other tax shelters for college savings in 1997. For example, taxpayers may withdraw funds without penalty from Individual Retirement Accounts (IRAs) to finance qualified higher education expenses, mostly tuition. A number of expenses are excluded from qualified expenses, including insurance, medical care, student health fees, room and board, and transportation. Scholarships, Pell Grants, employer-provided educational assistance, Veterans' educational assistance, and other nontaxable payments received for educational expenses reduce qualified expenses, but student earnings, loans, gifts, inheritances, and personal savings do not.

Expenditure from IRAs undercuts a household's future retirement income and tax advantages. A household that puts the maximum in IRAs each year and then withdraws funds for college cannot later replenish the IRAs. It is usually better to retain the retirement funds and use other tax shelters for college.

Uniform Gifts to Minors Act   Parents, grandparents, or others can transfe
funds to a minor child under the UGMA and serve as custodian o
the investments until the child reaches age eighteen. The funds ca
be invested without restrictions and can be spent for any purpose
The amount transferred in any year without being subject to taxa
tion is subject to the Estate and Gift Tax limit, currently $12,000
per year.

At age eighteen, the beneficiary gains full control of the funds an
need not spend them for college. Funds in a child's name lower eli
gibility for need-based aid significantly. The UGMA option may b
useful for high-income households who do not expect to receiv
need-based aid and who have full confidence that their children wil
make good decisions as they reach maturity. For most families, a 52
plan is a much better choice.

Other Savings   A household can accumulate savings for college outsid
of tax-favored investments. A family with substantial means migh
simply choose to spend for college from its accumulated wealth
However, assets that are tied up in a family business or in long-tern
real estate investments and entrepreneurial ventures, or bound by le
gal restrictions, may be expensive to liquidate for the purpose o
paying tuition. Borrowing, using assets as collateral, is probably
better strategy.

Borrowing

The financial aid package offered by most colleges and universitie
will include at least one federal loan, and schools may offer loan
from their own funds as well. Parents are also encouraged to bor
row, either through federal programs or other mechanisms not spe

cifically designed for college expenses. As more and more students and their families go into heavy debt with both federal and private loans to pay for college, the risk of default and even bankruptcy goes up sharply.

Nevertheless, loans are an important part of college finance at every income level. Students from households with income below $32,000 in 2003–2004 who attended public four-year colleges averaged $12,900 per year in college expenditures, with 49 percent receiving loans that averaged $4,800 per year. If they went to private four-year colleges, their college expenditures averaged $23,800 per year, with 64 percent of them borrowing an average amount of $6,400 per year. Students from households with income over $92,000 who attended public four-year colleges averaged $14,300 in annual expenses, with 35 percent of them borrowing an average of $5,100 per year. Those in this bracket who attended private four-year colleges averaged $30,000 in expenses, with 49 percent of them borrowing an average of $6,800 per year.[14]

If the Bishop family decides that their son should attend a more expensive college than they can pay for from savings and current income, they are likely to borrow the money, through a combination of student and parental loans. The first loan their son will be offered, most likely, will be a Stafford.

Federal Family Education Loans   The Federal Family Education Loans (FFEL), one part of the Federal Stafford Loan program, are placed and collected through financial intermediaries such as banks. The government guarantees repayment to lenders, should the student default on the loan. The loans are applied first to tuition, room, and board, but any residual may be paid to the student for other expenses. After almost a decade of very low variable rates on Stafford

Loans, in 2006–2007 changes in federal rules established a fixed interest rate of 6.8 percent for new loans.[15]

Stafford Loans have been around since the 1960s, and they come in two types: subsidized and unsubsidized. With subsidized loans, the federal government pays the interest while a student is enrolled in college. Subsidized loans are limited by need (COA minus EFC) and are subject to further limits by law. In 2006–2007 Stafford Loans were capped at $3,500 for the first year of study, $4,500 for the second year, and $5,500 per year after two years, including a fifth year if necessary, with a maximum of $23,000 of debt for a dependent student (one whose parents provide support). An undergraduate who is financially independent of his parents has a ceiling of $46,000. Congress changes these specific limits from time to time.[16]

In 1992 Congress created the Unsubsidized Stafford Loan for Middle-Income Borrowers. With unsubsidized Stafford Loans, students are responsible for the interest from the time the loan is disbursed. A student can either pay interest as he goes along or accumulate interest while enrolled and add it to the face amount of the loan when he leaves school. Since the interest is unsubsidized by the government, eligibility is not tied to demonstrated financial need. In 2003–2004, 20.8 percent of undergraduates received unsubsidized Stafford Loans averaging $3,600 per loan. Larger Stafford Loans are available for post-baccalaureate study.[17]

Direct Loans   In addition to the FFEL loans, in 1992 Congress authorized a second channel for distribution of Stafford Loans—this time directly through the colleges instead of through financial intermediaries. Colleges that participate in this Direct Loan option make loans directly to the student, who repays the loan directly to the fed-

ral government after leaving school. The terms of the FFEL and
Direct Loans are basically identical.

PLUS   Parents with a good credit history may borrow from the fed-
ral government to pay for a child's college expenses. The Parents
Loan for Undergraduate Students (PLUS) is a federal program that
began in 1980. Parents must begin repayment within sixty days of
full disbursement. In 2003–2004, parents of 3.4 percent of college
students received PLUS loans with an average amount of $9,000.[18]

In 2006–2007 the rate on PLUS loans was 8.5 percent, higher
than many home mortgages. When mortgage rates are low, some
families will prefer home equity loans to PLUS, particularly given
that mortgage interest is deductible on the income tax. PLUS may
be useful for families who have not built up home equity or who do
not wish to refinance a very low first mortgage or take out a more
expensive second mortgage (such as a home equity line of credit).

Perkins Loans   This federally sponsored program provides loans to the
neediest students. The Carl D. Perkins Loan program (called the
National Defense Student Loan in 1958 and the National Direct
Student Loan in 1972 and Perkins Loan since 1987) provides low-
interest loans up to $4,000 per year under rules defined by individ-
ual campus financial aid offices, with a cumulative borrowing limit
of $20,000 for undergraduates. In 2001 there were 676,000 new
Perkins Loans averaging $1,565 per recipient. Some campuses also
make Perkins Loans available to graduate and professional school
students.[19]

How Much to Borrow?   Two constraints limit a student or parent's capacity to borrow. First, the borrower must have enough income to make

the payments. Since committed, well-prepared students usually se
a good return on investments in higher education, most of them
will earn enough income to repay their loans and still come ou
ahead. Students with lesser preparation and commitment might do
well to consider a less expensive educational strategy rather than
heavy borrowing. Repayment is especially challenging in the earl
years of a career when new employees often take low-paying jobs in
order to gain experience. But even among people in their late twen
ties and early thirties, adulthood often makes other financial de
mands that impinge on loan repayment, for example, setting up
household, providing for children, or returning to school for post
graduate degrees.

The second constraint on borrowing, after income, is wealth
Having wealth in hand that could be used to repay the loan in an
emergency significantly lowers the risk of default and bankruptcy
Illness or unemployment can put a borrower in a financial bind that
makes repayment from current income impossible. If failure to re
pay the loan forces the borrower into bankruptcy, future purchase
of houses, automobiles, and other goods that have to be financed
will become more expensive. Changes in bankruptcy law in 200
make the penalties more severe than in the past.

The old line "Bankers only lend to people who don't need the
money" sends a warning. Lenders will readily make a loan when
they have collateral—cars for car loans and houses for home mort
gages—as long as the borrower can show a regular income and make
a down payment. Loans without collateral are normally made to
people who have sufficient wealth in hand to repay the loan and a
good history of repayment. Since undergraduates who need to bor
row for school typically have limited personal wealth and sparse
credit histories, the federal government stepped in to guarantee the

oans, making them safer for lenders than home mortgages. However, because of the guarantee, lenders offer loans to students without assessing the likelihood of default. The student and her family are left to make their own judgment about the short-term difficulties they might encounter—not earning as much as the student anticipated or borrowing more than the family's wealth can protect if the student can't make her payments. Although families typically bear no direct responsibility for a student's debt, parents often act as a backstop for a student's debt in a crisis.

A student from a family with more wealth may comfortably borrow more, on the assumption that the family will come through for him in dire financial circumstances. A student from a household with few assets runs a greater risk of default and bankruptcy. While the average default rate is 4.5 percent, students from low-income households are about three times more likely to default than students from high-income households, and students from one-parent households are about twice as likely to default as those from two-parent households. Students who do not graduate are more than five times more likely to default than those who do graduate (perhaps reflecting a difference in income). Minority students are more likely to default (perhaps because minority families have less wealth).[20]

In 1998, 11.5 percent of those at all levels of income who began repayment on a Perkins Loan defaulted in the next year, and 6.9 percent of those who began repayment on a Direct Loan or a FFEL defaulted in 1999. The overall national default rate on federal Stafford Loans in 2003 was 4.5 percent, with much higher rates among low-income students. Students face significant penalties if loans are not repaid in a timely manner. Their credit rating is adversely affected, and the government may take legal action, or apply a tax refund to the outstanding debt, or have an employer deduct up to 15 percent from the student's future paychecks. If a loan in default is assigned to an agency for collection, any expenses incurred in collecting the defaulted loan become the responsibility of the student.[21]

Student loan programs are inherently an ineffective mechanism for supporting college study for students from low-income households. They are most relevant for middle- and upper-income households with financial assets. The Willises, with financial assets of $25,000, ought to limit borrowing to a modest fraction of their assets, perhaps $5,000. The Bishops, with $75,000 of nonretirement financial assets, might borrow $40,000, and the Reeds might borrow up to $100,000 with little risk of default. These limits are conservative. Millions of students borrow more than their family's net worth. In doing so, they run a considerable risk.

Loan Consolidation and Repayment   Most students require many years—sometimes decades—to pay off their college loans. Ten years is the standard payoff period, but there are options for longer periods that allow lower payments in the early years. In 1999–2000, 65 percent of four-year graduates had borrowed to pay for their education, with an average amount of $19,300, up from $12,100 in 1992–1993 (measured in 1999 purchasing power). Paradoxically, much of the growth in borrowing occurred among families with higher incomes. In 1992–1993 only 8.2 percent of students with family income over $100,000 borrowed for college, but by 2003–2004 that percentage had risen to over 38 percent. The median amount they borrowed during this period grew over twice as much as the median amount borrowed by students with family incomes under $30,000.[22]

Much of the growth in loans among higher income students can be attributed to the unsubsidized Stafford Loan program. Between 1998 and 2006 Stafford Loans had attractive interest rates, and more students borrowed more for college than ever before. Consequently, they graduated with more debt.

All Perkins, Stafford, Direct, and PLUS Loans may be consolidated under a separate federal consolidation loan program. FFELs are consolidated through private lenders, and consolidated Direct Loans go to the federal government. These loans are available during the grace period at the end of college or graduate study or while the loans are being repaid. In 2006 Congress fixed the rate on consolidated loans at 6.8 percent. In some cases, students with consolidated loans may pay a lower interest rate than they were already paying through some of their individual loans. Up to 4 percent of the face amount of the loan is charged as a one-time fee to insure the government against default and to pay for the operation of the program.[23]

Grants

Grants or gift aid is money that does not have to be paid back. This is the most desirable kind of financial aid, and it comes in two forms: merit-based and need-based. The largest federal grants are tied to need, as are a number of state programs (though not all). While most institutional grants are also need-based, merit scholarships have a prominent place in the admission strategies of many wealthy colleges and universities. The line between need and merit aid is fuzzy. Some merit programs have income ceilings, while some need-based aid treats more talented students more generously.

Federal Pell Grants   The largest source of federal grant support for higher education is the need-based Pell Grant program. These grants, the successor to college aid for World War II veterans under the GI Bill, became a uniform national college grant program in the 1960s. In 2004, $13 billion of grants went to 5.3 million students, with an average award of $2,420 per recipient. Thirty-two percent of undergraduates received Pell Grants in 2003–2004. The program is not available for post-baccalaureate study.[24]

Pell Grants are based on the FAFSA application (see below), but the Department of Education applies a unique eligibility formula for Pell Grants, based on a federally defined EFC and a cost of attendance (COA) specifically defined for federal programs. The goal is to assign the maximum grant ($4,050 in 2005–2006) to those with the lowest income. The grant falls as income goes up, in $100 increments. For household incomes over $42,000, no grant money is awarded. Even the Willises, with two children headed to college and a low capacity for saving or borrowing, would not be eligible for a Pell Grant.[25]

Pell Grants flow to the student through the college attended and may be credited to a student's college bill or paid directly to the student. They are pro-rated for part-time students. The specifics of the program depend on annual congressional appropriations. In 2006 Congress created Academic Competitiveness grants that provide extra grants to first and second year Pell-eligible students with strong academic records ($750 for the first year, $1,300 for the second) and National SMART grants to juniors and seniors who major in math, science, or engineering (grants up to $4,000).[26]

For students of modest means at low-tuition colleges, the Pell Grant can meet much of a student's need. For a student from a family with relatively low income at a more expensive college, the Pell Grant may be the first, but modest, component of a larger financial aid package. When Congress funds a higher level of Pell Grants, current recipients receive larger grants up to the maximum for Pell awards or to their need, whichever is lower. But students may then see some reduction in other sources of aid if costs have remained constant, particularly on campuses committed to meeting full need. Federal rules require that total aid not exceed identified need.

Smaller-scale federal grant programs include the Robert C. Byrd Honors Scholarship Program, which awards grants of $1,500 to 27,000 high school seniors. The states define their own allocation and eligibility rules.[27] The Federal Supplemental Educational Opportunity Grants (SEOG) provide up to $4,000 per year, based on need, through college financial aid offices. The Veterans Administration offers some support for veterans and for the survivors and dependents of veterans.

State Grants   State-sponsored financial aid programs for college students have grown significantly over the last decade. In 2003–2004, 39 percent of full-time undergraduates with family income under $32,000 received state grant aid, with an average award of $2,800 per year. Among undergraduates from families with income over $92,000, 9 percent received state grants, with average awards of $2,300. Some states tilt their scholarship programs toward in-state public colleges and universities. But in many states the grants may be used on any in-state campus, public or private. Paradoxically, a $3,000 scholarship to a private college costs a state less than a $2,000 scholarship to a public college because the state pays a considerable additional amount per student in direct support to its public colleges but little or no direct support to private colleges.

Need-based state grants remain more important nationally than merit-based aid. In 2003–2004, 12 percent of undergraduates received state need-based grants, while only 3 percent received merit-only awards. Need-based grants averaged $1,943, only modestly more than the $1,819 average merit-only award. State grants were just under half of the average total grant aid of $4,019 per student. Need-based awards tilted slightly toward private colleges, particularly the proprietaries. Ten percent of students at the for-profit colleges received state need-based grants, while less than 1 percent received merit-only grants. While need-based grants concentrate support on middle- and lower-income households, merit grants provide assistance to higher-income students.[28]

Merit-based programs differ from state to state. Some states set higher minimum grade-point averages in high school and in college than other states. Some states require threshold scores on SAT or ACT tests. Some reduce the state's merit grant by the amount of Pell or other grants, and some do not make merit awards to households with income over a certain ceiling. The states change the details from time to time, but the State Departments of Education typically have websites that describe the details of their current programs. The discussion here will focus on Georgia, California, and New York as examples of the range of grant programs from state to state.[29]

In 1993 the Helping Outstanding Pupils Educationally (HOPE) program began to use Georgia State Lottery funds to finance college scholarships for qualified state residents. Students with a high school grade-point average of 3.0 and above on a 4.0 scale (or an 80 on a 100-point scale) are eligible for a HOPE scholarship if they complete 16 units of academic work: four in English, four in math, three in social studies, three in science, and two in a foreign language. Once in college, students must maintain a grade-point average of B (3.0) or above to continue to receive support.[30]

Qualified Georgia high school graduates receive full tuition at in-state public colleges plus an allowance per semester for books. Residents who attend in-state private colleges receive up to $3,000 per academic year. HOPE supported 77.9 percent of full-time undergraduates in Georgia's postsecondary institutions in 2000.[31] If the Reeds continue to reside in the Atlanta area while Jennifer is in college, she will most likely be eligible for tuition-free attendance at a public in-state college or a $3,000 grant per year to a private in-state college, assuming her grades qualify. With such highly respected in-state public schools as Georgia Tech, the University of Georgia, and Georgia State, along with such outstanding private schools as Agnes Scott, Emory, Mercer, Morehouse, Spelman, and Savannah College of Art and Design, the state of Georgia, through its merit-based HOPE scholarship program, offers an excellent value for its promising high school graduates who choose to attend college close to home.

The state of California awards grants to about 75,000 students per year. Although its grant program dates to 1956, its four series of grants took their current form in 2000. We'll look at just one series, the CalGrant A. To disperse these grants, the California Student Aid Commission computes a score for each student that considers family income, parents' education, the student's high school grade-point average, time out of high school, and number of parents in the household. Based on the score, the program assigns tuition awards to graduates of California high schools. For students attending California State University campuses, the top of the range was $2,520 in 2005–2006; for students attending University of California campuses, it was $6,141; and for students attending in-state private colleges it was $8,322.[32]

Applicants for a CalGrant A must have a high school grade-point average of 3.0, and the ceiling on income for a family of four was $72,300 in 2005–2006. The commission takes the money made available by the state and disperses awards starting with the highest scores and continuing down the list until all funds are committed.

In 1974 New York replaced a small merit-based college grant program with its Tuition Assistance Program (TAP), one of the largest need-based state college aid programs in the country. The average award for undergraduates in 2004–2005 was about $2,200, with the size of the award based on the year of first enrollment, the tuition and type of school, family financial status, and the number of siblings in college. The amount of the grant decreased as family income rose from $7,000 to $80,000. The maximum award in 2005–2006 was $5,000, and students were required to maintain a grade-point average of at least C to retain support.

Institutional Grants   A third source of grant aid is the colleges and universities themselves. Grants based on academic merit are sometimes called academic scholarships or honors scholarships. But athletes, debaters, musicians, and actors, among others, may also receive institutional grants based on their achievements rather than on demonstrated financial need. The private four-year colleges, which accounted for only 14 percent of enrollments nationally in 2003–2004, awarded nearly half of all merit-based scholarships that year. (In this calculation, merit aid includes aid not based on need, some of which goes to students with need.) These grants averaged $5,800 per recipient. Often a student need not apply for an institutional scholarship but will be considered simply on the basis of information in the regular admission dossier, though this varies from school to school. Financial information is usually not required.[33]

Many leading colleges and universities use merit scholarships to attract outstanding students who might otherwise enroll at schools with a higher national profile. Emory, for example, awards ninety scholarships based on academic merit to approximately 5 percent of its entering class. The University of Arizona provides an extra $3,000 merit award to NMS Finalists on top of its Murphey Scholarships. The total covers nearly all of the cost of attendance at the university. Although Northwestern University employs need-blind admission and all aid is based on need, it awards two Hardy Scholarships to members of its nationally ranked debate team. These grants replace campus work requirements. Whitman College offers $2,500 in merit scholarships plus need-based awards to its debaters. Though many wealthy and very selective schools have added merit grants to their list of enticements, the less wealthy private colleges in the less competitive categories tend to offer relatively more merit aid to attract able students to their campuses. For many middle-class students with respectable high school records, this is a place where some true bargains may be found.[34]

Scholarships at some schools induce musicians to participate in marching bands and other performance groups that bring recognition to the school. Idaho State and Jacksonville State are examples. Departmental scholarships may be awarded by faculty to students who enroll in the department's programs. Theatre students at Western Michigan University, for example, may qualify for this kind of scholarship.[35]

The Ivy League and a few elite liberal arts colleges do not award merit-based aid, out of concern that high-performing students from wealthy families will flourish in the competition, at the expense of talented students from lower income families. What most of these colleges offer instead is need-blind admission (admission without regard to a student's ability to pay) and a commitment to meeting the full need of every student they admit. In 2001 and 2002, Yale and Williams extended their need-blind admission policy to international students, and more schools may do so in the future. Most other colleges limit need-blind admission to students from the United States (and sometimes Canada).

A group of very competitive, well-endowed research universities and colleges offer a mix of all three strategies: need-blind admission, aid that meets full need, and merit scholarships for outstanding applicants who do not qualify for need-based grants. The result is that grant money gets spread around to all income brackets. Among full-time undergraduates from families with income under $32,000, 33 percent received institutional grants in 2003–2004, with an average award of $4,700. But 28 percent of those from families with income over $92,000 also received institutional grants in 2003–2004, with an average award of $6,100 per year. The difference in the dollar value of awards probably reflects the fact that students from needier families are more likely to attend low-tuition schools.

Outside Grants   Merit-based aid also comes from private organizations like the Elks and from high schools and civic groups. Coca-Cola, for example, runs one of the most competitive scholarship programs in the country, awarding 50 National Scholarships of $20,000 each and 200 Regional Scholarships of $4,000 each. The competition is open to students who have a minimum grade-point average of 3.0, and more than 90,000 students apply. Some 1,500 to 2,000 applicants are selected to submit biographical data, recommendations, high school reports, and an essay. The 250 finalists are invited to Coke's headquarters in Atlanta for interviews. Approximately 5 out of every 10,000 applicants receive the $20,000 award, and 27 out of every 10,000 applicants receive a $4,000 award. The probability of success is not a whole lot better than the chance of winning the lottery.[36]

Students have a better shot at landing scholarships that are more closely tailored to their own strengths or targeted at a specific group to which they belong. Princeton Review and FastWeb maintain websites that allow students to enter their characteristics (grades, home state, and so on) in order to identify scholarships for which they might apply. In 2003–2004, 14 percent of full-time undergraduates with family incomes under $32,000 received grants from outside organizations, with awards averaging $2,100. Of students from families with incomes over $92,000, 16 percent received merit-based grants from outside organizations, with average awards of $2,500.

Determining Need

To qualify for federal and most state aid programs, a family must first submit the Free Application for Federal Student Aid (FAFSA) between January 1 and June 30. Based on the family's income, assets, number and ages of children, and so on, the Department of Education computes an expected family contribution (EFC), and this figure becomes the basis for deciding eligibility for federal aid. The DoE passes the EFC along to colleges when requested to do so by the student. Most colleges require students to apply for federal aid every year by completing the FAFSA, before they can be considered eligible for institutional grants. Some colleges rely solely on the federal government's assessment of need in computing their financial aid package. As its name suggests, FAFSA is a free service.[37]

In addition to the FAFSA, more than three hundred colleges and universities use the College Scholarship Service's Financial Aid Profile as a way to assess need. To receive offers of aid from these schools, a family must complete the CSS Profile in January or February of the year of entry. CSS charges $5 for each online application and $18 for each college to which the application materials are sent.[38]

A large number of colleges have their own financial aid applications and use their own formulas in determining need. Some colleges require submission of copies of income tax returns and other financial records, including the financial status of the noncustodial parent when parents are not married.

Both the federal and institutional methodologies define the EFC in terms of the family's earnings and financial assets. With more earnings and savings, the EFC is greater and therefore the defined need is less. However, the details matter. The federal definition of the EFC begins with an *adjusted available income* (AAI). This number is arrived at by setting aside roughly $20,000 from parental income, net of state and local taxes, for basic consumption and then adjusting that figure to take account of the number of children in the household and the number of working parents. When the AAI falls between $20,000 and $32,000, approximately 22 percent is assumed to be available to support college. The marginal percentage contribution rises to 47 percent when the AAI passes the $45,000 mark. For a family in this last bracket, of every extra $100 of income earned, $47 is assumed to be available for college, and the student's need is reduced by that amount.[39]

Contributions from a parent's assets also have a set-aside, depending on the age of the older parent. A parent of age 45 would have an asset allowance of about $38,000. A share of the value of assets over the set-aside allowance, a maximum of 5.64 percent, is assumed to be available to support the student's college expenses.[40]

Since 1992 home equity has been excluded from the calculation of the EFC in the federal methodology, but it factors in different ways in the various institutional methodologies. Princeton follows the federal example in not counting home equity. Yale sets aside the first $150,000 of assets, including savings and home equity. Stanford sets aside home equity of $165,000 for households earning less than $55,000.[41]

Institutions also differ in how they consider the income and assets of divorced parents. Tulane and many other schools require the noncustodial parent to fill out the CSS's Noncustodial Parent's Statement. The University of Rochester requires information from just two parents: either the parent and step-parent the student most recently lived with or both birth parents (or, in the case of adoption, both adoptive parents).[42]

Colleges and universities treat outside scholarships differently. When an institution pledges to meet full need, it views outside support as lowering need and therefore lowering the required aid from the college. Some colleges—Middlebury and Vanderbilt, for example—first lower need-based loans and work requirements before reducing the college grant. Some schools lower their grants by $0.50 for each dollar of outside support. Some colleges take into account elementary and secondary private school tuitions for siblings in defining the expected family contribution, while others do not.[43]

From 1954 to 1991, financial aid officers from twenty-three private colleges in the northeast met annually to compare notes on individual applicants, in order to diminish differentials in the way the schools calculated the EFC. This Overlap Group sought to eliminate bidding wars for the most desired students, including athletes, and thereby to concentrate financial aid on meeting the full need of all admitted students. The Department of Justice initiated anti-trust action and ended the practice. Congress then enacted a law to allow colleges to coordinate their aid policies and devise common formulas but not to discuss individual students.[44]

In 2001 a larger national group of twenty-eight colleges that commit to meeting full financial need for all U.S. students—the 568 President's Working Group (named for the section of the law authorizing such groups)—proposed a more detailed formula to reduce variation in institutional aid methodologies. The proposed formula would account for all biological and step-parents, provide for regional cost-of-living differentials, consider savings in Coverdell ESA, 529, and other programs as parental assets, reduce EFC by 40 percent if a family has two children in college, reduce EFC by the cost of elementary and secondary education of siblings, exclude all nonrecurring income, and collect the most recent tax returns. One of the widely noted features of the 568 plan is a proposal to limit the inclusion of home equity to 2.4 times income. Five percent of home equity, that is, market value less mortgage debt, is taken as available to support college expenses each year. A family with $60,000 of income would have a ceiling of $144,000 of equity and a maximum contribution from home equity of $7,200 per year. The 568 group of colleges and universities with need-blind admission continue to promote refinements in the definition of need.[45]

Some observers view the federal financial aid formula as discouraging household savings. And by this same logic, it might also reduce the incentive of families to improve their household income. These concerns must be bracketed in three ways. First, students from families with high incomes have little expectation of need-based financial aid, regardless of the family's savings or lack thereof. Second, families with incomes at or below the set-asides have EFCs near zero, and therefore their defined need will not change with modest changes in earnings or savings. Third, at colleges that do not meet full need, an increase in EFC because of more earnings and savings would probably have a smaller effect on aid than the official formula indicates. The bottom line is this: families with more earnings and savings have, on average, more choices in higher education. A tactical decision to restrain family earnings and savings to gain more need-based aid may prove to be shortsighted in the long run.[46]

A student's own income and assets may have dramatic effects on defined need, however. A student had a set-aside of only $2,550 for earnings in 2006–2007. Fifty percent of income over that amount was assumed to be available for college. As of 2007–2008, 20 percent of a student's savings, investments, and other assets are also assumed to be available to pay for college. Of course, need-based aid programs assume that a student's income and savings will be focused on college, and they include work-study earnings as part of the aid package. While some students may limit their income and savings in order to avoid reductions in aid, the desire for a higher standard of living pushes many students into a part-time job.

Meeting Less than Full-Need   When a college cannot afford to meet the full need of all the students it admits—the case for most colleges—it must ration its available aid. One policy is to meet full need for most of the students admitted but to fill the last 5 or 10 percent of spaces in an entering class with students who pay full tuition. This policy lowers the academic threshold for some students who are able to pay their own way. In 2002 Brown moved away from this practice, toward a need-blind policy for all admitted students. In the same year, Mount Holyoke abandoned its eighteen-year-old need-blind policy to move toward a need-aware policy. The college meets full need for most of its admitted class but denies admission to some students with high need and marginal (but admissible) academic records.[47]

Some schools admit needy students but offer them little or no aid. Others distribute their available funds over more students by offering to meet a fraction of full-need, a policy called "gapping." Agnes Scott College reports meeting 86 percent of the full need of admitted students. Some colleges and universities make a need-aware second review, choosing from their wait lists only students who do not need aid. (The wait list is a subject for Chapter 8.) Colleges do not always announce these policies, but a student might well ask whether need is a factor in the admission decision and what fraction of students on financial aid have their full need met by grants, loans, and work. A college that chooses to meet full need with loans has a dramatically less generous financial aid policy than a college that meets full need with grants. Students who choose to finance their education with loans are not limited to those in the school's financial aid package; they may wish to shop around for a better rate.[48]

The fact that most colleges do not meet full need will lead some households to choose lower-priced schools. But it is worth emphasizing that a student from a low-income household may attend a high-tuition college at lower cost to him or his family than he would incur at a low-tuition college. One study put the net price for poor students at expensive colleges at $400 below the net price at low-tuition colleges. Since quality as measured by total expenditure per student is much higher at the expensive colleges, a low-income student with an outstanding high school record should seriously consider reaching for the best school that will admit him, regardless of sticker price.[49]

Negotiating Aid   Some colleges are willing to review aid offers from similar colleges and may increase their own award in order to compete for desired students. Carnegie Mellon University invites admitted students who have offers of aid from CMU to tell the financial aid office about any better offers from competing schools. In 2001 about 13 percent of admitted students (675 applicants) asked CMU to reconsider their aid offer. CMU increased 314 awards, and 171 of these students enrolled. More than one-fourth of the students who received aid negotiated higher awards. This strategy may allow CMU to offer slightly lower initial aid awards on average and to increase awards on demand, as better offers elsewhere emerge for specific highly desirable students. By managing its scarce aid funds carefully, CMU met 80 percent of the demonstrated need of its entering class in 2005–2006.[50]

Most colleges do not encourage such negotiation, but financial aid offices will usually listen to appeals based on new information about a family's circumstances. Needy students should think especially hard before applying for early admission (discussed in Chapter 8) because it takes away the opportunity to compare offers of financial aid in deciding where to attend.

How Much Will College Really Cost?

In thinking about the expense of having a student in college, a family will find itself in one of four situations. In the first case, a family simply pays the full cost of attendance from its own resources, without need-based financial aid. The Reeds are in this situation, though perhaps they will take advantage of Georgia's HOPE scholarship, and they will certainly use a 529 plan to shelter their college savings from the taxman. Whatever college Jennifer may choose, they will probably be able to afford it. Not so the Willises. If they wind up paying their own way, their daughters will have to look for a college with a COA (tuition, room and board, and ancillary costs) around $7,000 per year. And even this will require some changes in the family's lifestyle and some borrowing.

In the second case, a student might be accepted at a college that meets full financial need. These are usually the most selective colleges, where the cost of attendance is well above the expected contribution for most families. Financial aid, in some combination of grants, loans, and student employment, fills the gap. Since grants are a substantially more attractive offer than loans and employment, a family that gets a financial aid package from several schools will want to look very carefully at the mix. A family's willingness to accept loans will depend on both its confidence in the earning power of a college degree and its concern that the debt incurred might push the family into financial crisis.

In a third case, families get some aid but not enough to meet full need. A family's financial resources determine how much colleges will expect a family to pay. A college with a COA of $33,000 per year might offer admission to a student whose EFC is $9,000 but provide less than the $24,000 of grants, loans, and work-study needed to fill the gap. In choosing such a college, a family will take on an even larger financial burden than that defined by the EFC. A less expensive college might be a better—indeed, the only practical—choice.

In a fourth scenario, some students will be offered merit-based aid. But access to such scholarships can be idiosyncratic, and families should not count on them as part of their financial plan. If the Bishops' son wins a small scholarship for playing the tuba, they should think of it as icing, not the whole cake.

The price a student pays for college, net of financial aid, varies in large measure because financial aid from federal and state governments and from the colleges themselves varies in many ways. But in general, households with more income and assets will pay higher net prices. Average students from low-income households will have to look for lower tuition, Pell Grants, and part-time employment. For good students from middle-income families, institutional grants, federal loans, education tax credits, and tax-sheltered savings will allow them to choose a more selective college with somewhat higher tuition. Upper-income households are more likely to finance college from accumulated savings using tax-sheltered plans, reductions in current consumption, and borrowing.

Comparing Financial Aid Offers   Offers of aid are not uniform, and they can be difficult to compare. To interpret an offer, begin by computing the cost of attendance: tuition, fees, room, board, books, supplies, transportation, and incidentals (the last four differ little across colleges). College websites often define a COA for their campuses. Next, use one of the financial aid calculator websites to identify the expected family contribution under the federal methodology. The difference between these two amounts is the estimated need.

With the offer of aid in hand, add up the outright grants, bearing in mind that there may be more than one. Then add up the loans offered, noting those that are subsidized and those that are not. Then, note the opportunity for income from campus employment. The sum of grants, loans, and income from campus employment is the total aid package. Compare it to the estimate of need at that particular college. If the total aid package equals the estimate, the college is offering to meet full need. If the total aid package is less than need, the college isn't offering to meet full need.

To find the net price, subtract the total amount of grants from the cost of attendance. This amount is the student and family's responsibility. *Comparing net price across colleges is the simplest way to compare the cost of different colleges to a household.* The larger the share of need met by grants, the more generous the financial aid award.

Subsidized loans are more attractive than unsubsidized loans. Compare the interest rates on the loans offered against other possible sources of finance, for example, refinancing a home mortgage, taking into account the tax advantages of each.

The net price will differ from state to state and across otherwise similar private colleges. Talented students at any level of income will find appropriate support at many selective colleges. Students with outstanding talent and preparation are likely to win acceptance at some excellent colleges, get higher financial aid offers, and receive more grant money and fewer loans in the financial aid award. Even schools that claim not to offer merit awards will frequently adjust this mix to attract a highly desirable student.

A family's plan for paying for college will have three phases. First are decisions about accumulating savings, which require setting up a 529 plan or an ESA years in advance so that tax-sheltered earnings can grow. More saving will increase a student's range of choices of college and reduce pressure on family finances while the student is in college. But parents with children in middle school or the first years of high school may still benefit from setting up a 529 account. For example, a family with ample home equity and earned income may want to refinance their mortgage when rates are low. If they cash out, say, $75,000 and put it into a 529 account at a guaranteed rate of 5 percent, by the time their eighth grader starts college the fund will be worth $91,000, and they will have received two tax benefits: a higher mortgage interest deduction and a tax shelter for their college savings.

The second phase involves decisions about where to apply and enroll, since applications for financial aid are part of the admission process. The student's accomplishments and career prospects are important factors in deciding how much college the family can afford, since grant aid is higher for more talented students at more expensive colleges. A family's liquid financial assets, particularly its savings for college, will influence its choices, as will its current income and prospects for borrowing. The tuition policies of home-state public colleges and the state's financial aid programs are highly relevant as well. With acceptances and financial aid offers in hand, a student can compare net prices against differences in the quality of services.

The third phase is making good on the commitment to adjust current family spending, to liquidate assets, to borrow funds as needed, to claim tax credits, and to repay loans. A good plan for investing in college will yield high returns on the funds spent, will take advantage of available public and private financial aid programs, and will support an effective college experience without paying too much.

CHAPTER EIGHT

The Admission Game: Strategies for Success

Elaine and Miles Hyde want to give sensible advice to their son, Tim, as he navigates his way toward college. Elaine graduated from a liberal arts school in the upper Midwest and is enjoying her career as an editor. Miles completed bachelors and masters degrees at an in-state public university and works as a sales manager for a medical devices company. Tim just finished his sophomore year in high school. He's a good student whose academic strength seems to be history. He also plays drums in several musical groups, is the principal timpanist in the school orchestra, and has performed in theatrical productions. The suburb where the Hyde family lives supports its schools very well.

Elaine and Miles recognize that the process of choosing a college has two sides. As parents, they have to help their son weigh the costs, benefits, and likelihood of admission at the various schools that interest him, and they want to make sure that he considers a range of choices. Tim's task is to gain a sense of the commitment needed, both now and later, to succeed in college. Elaine and Miles want to know how to counsel their son and what milestones to look for as Tim heads into his junior year.

The undergraduate admission process has three steps. First is the student's choice of where to apply. Second is the colleges' decision about whom to accept. Third is the student's decision about where to attend. This chapter concentrates on steps one and two: choosing where to apply and maximizing the chances of acceptance. We'll look at twelve critical points in the admission process and at key components of the college application. We'll also consider some special angles in playing the "admission game," and then try to assess realistically the odds of acceptance at top-ranked schools. Step three—deciding where to attend once a student is accepted—will be taken up in Chapter 9.

Where to Apply?

In taking this first step on the path to college—deciding where to apply—Tim will talk with his parents, teachers, and counselors, of course. But he will also be heavily influenced by the opinions, behavior, information, and misinformation of his peers. As he sorts and re-sorts his options, real or imagined, Tim will gradually take into account his academic potential and career goals, at the same time that he grapples with such practical questions as how far away from home he really wants to go, what kind of campus setting appeals to him (urban, rural, or suburban), and how big or small his ideal college or university would be.

Academic Potential   A student who has thrived in a challenging high school and succeeded in AP or other accelerated courses shows clear evidence of intellectual intensity, and that makes him attractive to selective colleges. Tim Hyde's high school offers an array of AP and honors courses, and his prospects for college will be shaped in part by his grades in these classes and his scores on SAT II and AP tests. If he does well, he should consider applying to some of the most selective schools in the country.

Students who find AP and honors courses too difficult or uninteresting would be wise to concentrate their efforts on less selective schools. And if a student's academic accomplishments are limited or her commitment is uncertain, she might want to start out in a community college. Students who complete a two-year program often see substantial returns on the time and money invested (see Chapter 2).

When a high school does not offer intensive courses, its graduates have less information about their own academic potential, and teachers and counselors have to look for other ways to judge the capacity of their students to succeed in college. Certainly, students who read widely, enjoy classroom discussion and writing, and excel in whatever academic environment they find themselves should consider applying to selective schools. Even the most competitive colleges and universities keep an eye out for valedictorians from rural and inner-city high schools and, increasingly, home-schooled students who can demonstrate convincingly that they have something unique to contribute to campus intellectual life.

Career Goals   Students with specific careers in mind frequently apply to colleges or universities with programs that will move them toward their goal. Social workers, engineers, composers, nurses, graphic designers, teachers, farmers, filmmakers, financial managers, artists, actors, and clergy (just to name a few) often get their undergraduate education in schools devoted to career preparation.

A student who wants to be an architect, for example, may wish to apply to schools such as Virginia Tech or Ball State in Indiana that offer an undergraduate program in architecture. Maine Maritime Academy is one of several accredited four-year colleges that focus exclusively on the maritime industry and related careers in transportation, shipping, engineering, and the military. Parsons in Manhattan, a four-year design school within New University, produces design professionals ranging from fashion and product designers to interior and landscape designers. Northeastern University's College of Criminal Justice in Boston prepares students for such careers as policing, national security, youth intervention, and international intelligence. Auburn University's School of Forestry and Wildlife Services offers four undergraduate majors, including a prevet program.

Career goals frequently shift in college, as students discover new interests or find success in unexpected arenas. A budding biology major who gets swept away by his geology course may switch from medicine to a career in mining, oil, or water resources. One of my students—a violinist with enough skill to make a career in music—developed carpal tunnel syndrome and could no longer play. So he redirected his energy in his junior year and became an accomplished economics major. About 40 percent of students who enter four-year colleges and begin a natural science or mathematics major switch to a major outside the natural sciences before graduating. About 20 percent of students who begin in other areas (business, humanities, or education) switch to a different major, including the natural sciences. Many students solve their dilemma by double-majoring. The advantage of general education classes during the first two years of a liberal arts program is the opportunity they offer to discover and explore many fields of interest before career goals harden.[1]

Campus Visits   Many students start visiting college campuses during their junior year, particularly in the spring. Most colleges extend invitations for visits on specific days and offer extensive talks by admission staff, faculty, and others. Tim will visit while school is in session in order to attend a class and encounter students on campus.

A prospective student who can afford it should visit a number of colleges before applying, including a few that are not initially the most appealing. Some visits will cause a student to drop a college from her candidate list, and other visits will raise her opinion of a school. A campus visit serves to make the idea of college concrete. The unique chemistry of an institution can be discovered only by putting "boots on the ground." Prospective students make quick and personal judgments about a campus during a visit, drawing inferences from the manner of the tour guide, the priorities of the admission officer leading the information session, and even overheard conversations at lunch. Such emotional reactions are certainly not infallible, but having a good feeling about a place can help a student narrow down her options and make it through her admission essays with a positive attitude.

Some colleges and universities count the number of contacts an applicant has with the school, including letters of inquiry, meetings with a campus representative at the high school, visits to campus, and follow-up notes. The cumulative pattern of contact allows an admission office to get a sense of the student and to assess the seriousness of his interest. When two comparable students are under consideration, the student who has shown sustained enthusiasm and asked serious questions about the college experience is likely to get a more favorable reading.

How Many Applications?   A typical student who has some possibility of entering a competitive college or university will apply to several schools. Students who place great value on entering the most selective college they possibly can may average eight or more applications.[2]

Experienced counselors will point a student toward three or four "matches" (schools where the probability of acceptance is about fifty-fifty) and one or two "safeties" (schools where the probability of acceptance is high). The safeties should be places where the student can imagine being happy if she winds up there. Counselors also encourage most students to apply to one or two "reaches" (schools where the probability of acceptance is less than 50 percent). But assessing the probability of acceptance is not easy, as we'll see near the end of this chapter. If an outstanding student can present substantial evidence of academic potential, her counselor may advise her to apply to colleges within a narrower band of competitiveness. A bright student with less evidence of academic achievement might do better to apply to a range of colleges with a wide spread of selectivity, just in case.[3]

Applying to many colleges is costly in terms of application and test fees and, most importantly, essays to be written and contacts to initiate and maintain. A prospective student will want to plan carefully the time and cost needed to complete the application process at each school. It is a much better investment of time to send thoughtful applications to fewer colleges than perfunctory applications to many.[4]

The Admission Process

About a third of students in four-year colleges enroll at colleges that are selective in admission—that admit less than 75 percent of their applicants. However, only 7 percent are enrolled in the *most* selective colleges—those that accept less than one-third of their applicants. So for the majority of students, selective pressures are modest. But for those seeking spots in the most competitive group of colleges, the details of the admission process are important. Here's a twelve-point summary of critical events in the admission process at selective colleges and universities.

National Tests   Applicants take the SAT I or ACT, usually in early spring of their junior year. If the results are not satisfactory, they will have time to take the test again in late spring or the following fall. If schools of interest require two or three SAT IIs, or if students wish to submit these scores even if not required, they should plan to take them in their junior and even sophomore year when possible. This leaves time to repeat a test if necessary.

AP testing usually occurs in the spring. Students who want the option of including their AP scores in their college application should plan to take AP courses in their junior and even sophomore year and should take each test as soon as possible after the course is finished. Students are not required to report all AP scores; they can be selective. So a student scoring a 5 in biology and a 4 in chemistry would want to report these scores, but certainly not the 2 in U.S. history and maybe not the 3 in French.

Pre-Application and Fee   In the fall of their senior year, applicants file a pre-application form with an application fee (approximately $50)

This is a formal notice of intention to apply and establishes the student's identity with the college admission office. These forms can often be filled out online, and application fees can usually be paid by credit card. The admission office will open a dossier and initiate follow-up mailings.

Early Decision and Early Action   Applicants may apply early to their first-choice college for a decision about admission. A student admitted under an "early decision" program is honor-bound to enroll, unless the financial aid package falls short of meeting need. The deadline for application is in October or early November. At the same time, applicants may apply to other colleges through the regular decision process. Colleges make their early decisions known in December, and if a student is admitted, she must withdraw her application at any other colleges to which she applied.

If admission is deferred, a student will be put in the regular admission queue, where her chances of acceptance are much lower. At that point, she also has the option of going into a second round of early decision at a different school. Dozens of colleges and universities offer this option in January, with decisions rendered in February. The rules of early decision II are the same as early decision I: if a student is accepted, she must withdraw applications at all other colleges.

"Early action" is different from "early decision." Early action allows a student to apply to just one college in October or November, but he need not enroll if admitted. The student may then apply to as many places as he likes during the regular admission cycle, and he may accept any offer by May 1. Harvard followed this policy for many years before ending it for students applying in fall 2007. Yale and Stanford adopted it in 2004; that year, early applications at Harvard fell by nearly half and increased at Yale and Stanford, making the volume of early applications similar at the three colleges.[5]

Of 378 colleges reporting an early program in 2006, 197 offered early action, 149 offered early decision (some offered two rounds), and 37 offered both early decision and early action (though the student has to choose one program or the other).[6]

Regular Decision   The deadline for regular admission is typically in early January but may be as late as March on some campuses. A complete application form, along with essays, high school transcripts through the fall term, national test scores, and letters of recommendation, must be sent in before the deadline. Some selective colleges, for example, the University of Michigan and Seton Hill, have rolling admission: they advise students of the admission decision as the process unfolds and may continue to accept applications for admission into the spring.

Academic Score   College admission offices compile complete dossiers on each applicant in January and February. The admission office builds a computer database of the quantifiable information they have, using various formulas for weighting high school grades, class rank, and tests scores. An applicant's academic record is typically then summarized in a single number, the academic score.

Reader Scores   Next, various admission officers read the dossiers and assign reader scores. Michele Hernandez, who was an admission officer at Dartmouth College for several years, emphasizes that readers look for a consistent pattern across high school record, test scores, letters, and essays.[7]

Triage   On the basis of the academic score and reader scores, the admission office assigns applications to one of three groups. The top applicants are clear admits. The bottom applicants are clear denies. Those in the middle group are deemed admissible but are largely indistinguishable from one another. Consequently, this middle group gets the closest scrutiny.

At this point, the process becomes highly variable from school to school. Sometimes a second reader goes through the full dossiers of the middle group and assigns an independent second reader score. On some campuses a committee of admission officers considers the applicants in the middle group carefully and votes on each one, assigning the applicant to the admit, deny, or wait list stack. At many colleges the director of admission reviews the dossiers and the recommendations of the committee and renders a final decision.[8]

The Yield Rate   Selective colleges have target enrollment numbers, tied to the number of faculty, classrooms, and residences they have available. The admission office's goal is to meet the target without going over. Since every student they admit through early decision is honor-bound to enroll, admission offices tend to fill a large fraction of their freshman class from early decision candidates. These are students they can count on. A much smaller proportion of applicants in the regular admission cycle in March are accepted, and the ones who are admitted may choose not to enroll.

The proportion of students who are admitted and who also enroll is called the yield rate. This number is always less than 100 percent. At Harvard in recent years it has approached 80 percent, but at many selective schools it may be 40 percent or even lower. Rarely, the yield rate is much greater than the admission office anticipates, and then the college has to scramble to find additional housing and hire extra faculty to meet the crunch. In 2001, for example, Dartmouth College admitted 2,220 of 9,720 applicants, only to discover that 1,135 freshmen were on their way, exceeding the target enrollment of 1,075. The school had to erect six temporary dorms, called "Tree Houses," to accommodate the overflow. Such is the price of underestimating one's own popularity.

If the yield rate is near 50 percent, as it has been at Dartmouth for some time, then the admission office must admit about twice as many applicants as it has spaces in the class. A strategically minded student might want to compare yield rates and consider applying to selective colleges with a lower yield rate, on the theory that they have to accept more students initially in order to fill their class. To fill a freshman class of 2,000 students, a school with an 80 percent yield rate will accept only 2,500 students, while a school with a 40 percent yield rate will accept 5,000—twice as many fat envelopes. On average, a student's chances of acceptance would double, given the same number of applications.

The Wait List   To hedge their bets further against a lower than expected yield, admission offices notify some applicants that they are not admitted but have been put on the wait list. They will receive consideration if places remain available after the first batch of admitted students decide which offer of admission to accept. The meaning of being wait-listed is highly variable from school to school and year to year. But in general, most students on most wait lists have little hope of admission.

The Envelopes   At a pre-announced date in late March, the admission office notifies regular decision applicants of their status. In the old days, admitted students received an envelope thick with materials about orientation, registration, and housing. Students who were denied admission or put on the wait list received a thin envelope with a carefully worded letter of regret. A peak into the mailbox was all that was needed to learn one's fate. Today, most colleges notify applicants of their admission decision on a website or by email. Some colleges send encouraging notes to top applicants a few weeks earlier, tipping their hand. The fat or thin envelope that eventually straggles in through snail mail is an anticlimax.

Deposit   With a postmark of May 1 or earlier, admitted students send a nonrefundable deposit to the college of their choice, reserving a place in the class. The typical matriculation fee is $400. The admission office counts these students as paid and coming. If this total number is less than the target, the admission office trolls through its wait list to find the most likely candidates.

Summer Melt   When a student on the wait list accepts an offer of admission, he has to forfeit his deposit elsewhere. This lowers the paid-and-coming count on the other campus, and that school may then have to go into its own wait list, and so on down the line. A few students ask to defer admission for a year to deal with health problems, to travel, to pursue some other activity, or to address an unexpected family circumstance. A small number of admitted students have such significant drops in their final high school grades or commit such egregious acts (a felony, or a lie on their application) that the college rescinds its offer of admission. By whatever means it occurs, the loss of paid-and-coming students—called "summer melt"—happens almost every year, and astute admission offices take it into account, so as to land softly on target as classes begin.

The Application

The college admission process is elaborate but it is not precise. Consequently, applicants can take a number of steps to enhance their prospects at schools of interest. To start with, a student should try to find out if a given admission office is number-driven or word-driven. If the former, admission officers will spend less time reading dossiers and place more emphasis on the quantitative academic score. But the most selective colleges are word-driven: they place less emphasis on academic score in favor of a more careful reading of a student's dossier. By trying to understand the logic and controversies associated with each element in the application, parents may be able to help their student individualize his strategy.

The Common Application   Nearly three hundred colleges that are committed to a word-driven application process invite students to use a form that is common to all. This "common app" can be completed online at www.commonapp.org and sent directly to participating colleges of the student's choice with just a few clicks of the mouse. The common application initiative began in 1975 to reduce the tedium and expense imposed on students of completing several similar but slightly different applications. Stanford, Chicago, and Brown don't participate, but many distinguished research universities and liberal arts colleges do.

The 2006–2007 common form invites an applicant to choose among five essay topics or to make up her own. The colleges who participate in the common application treat it as essentially equivalent to their customized form, though they may supplement it with some additional questions. A few use only the common app. A student has many opportunities to explain his interests, preparation, and ambition on the common application, just as he does on forms created by individual colleges.

The downside of the common app is that it encourages students to apply to colleges where they have demonstrated little interest otherwise—schools they've never visited, never discussed with an alum or admission representative, and never corresponded with directly. Colleges and universities are happy to receive these applications (and fees) because their selectivity rating goes up. But at the most selective colleges and universities, a common app arriving out of the blue, with no other contacts, will probably be viewed less favorably than one from a comparable student who has demonstrated a strong and sustained interest in the school.

The Quantitative Academic Score   An applicant's dossier normally includes grade-point average, rank in high school class, test scores, number of AP courses attempted and completed, and average test scores for the high school attended or other indicators of the quality of the high school. The admission office typically summarizes this quantitative evidence by assigning a weight to each item.

One way to assign the weights is to use a statistical procedure (a multiple regression) to compute the correlation between the quantitative elements in application dossiers and students' subsequent grades in the first year of college. Statistics from recent classes—correlating the numbers in their application with their grade-point averages at the end of freshman year—are used to create a weight for each quantitative element in the dossier. This weighting system then allows the admission office to forecast a predicted grade-point average for each applicant's first year of college at their institution. Predicted grade-point averages play a significant role in the admission process at many colleges and universities.[9]

One goal of the quantitative academic score in admission is to keep nonstudents off the playing fields. In the Ivy League, the mean quantitative academic score for players in a sport may not be more than one standard deviation below the mean for all students on campus. Quantitative rules as defined by conferences and the NCAA often play a formal role in the admission of athletes.[10]

Some people erroneously assume that a number-driven admission strategy is more meritocratic and fair. But in practice, it doesn't yield a more talented class than a word-driven strategy. The central problem with the quantitative academic score is that a student's predicted grade-point average forecasts her college grades only very roughly. Some students with relatively high predicted grade-point averages perform poorly, while many with relatively low predicted grade-point averages perform well. This forecasting difficulty arises both because high school records and standardized test scores are difficult to interpret and because of the fundamental randomness in human nature.

High School Record   Generally, the high school record is the best evidence of a student's likelihood to succeed in college and beyond. Teachers award good grades in order to recognize talent, industry, and ambition. The challenge for the admission officer is to interpret that evidence, along with other less formal comments teachers provide in their letters of recommendation.

High schools differ in their grading policies just as colleges do. A cumulative GPA of 3.9 on a four-point scale with a top grade of A = 4.0 may mean quite different things in different settings. For example, some high schools that offer Advanced Placement or other honors classes add an automatic "bonus" amount to each AP or honors course grade, say, 0.5. In an ordinary four-point grade scale, an A counts as 4, a B as 3, and so on. With the honors bump, an A counts as 4.5 and a B as 3.5. It frequently happens that a good student with a number of AP or honors classes will have a grade-point average exceeding 4.0 on a four-point scale. At high schools that weight their honors courses but also put a ceiling of 4.0 on the grade-point average, a number of students may hold a 4.0 and share the title of class valedictorian.

Some high schools use a 100-point numeric grading system rather than letter grades. Although admission offices routinely map 100 points to letters, they have no way to be sure that they are looking at equivalent practices across high schools. Without careful statistical exploration, such mapping is nearly meaningless and illustrates the fuzziness of both letter and numerical grades. Making the only A in a class of two hundred means something quite different than making one of the twenty-five As in a class of fifty.

Another problem in interpreting high school grades is that some high schools and teachers prepare students more effectively than others. Capable, challenging, inspiring teachers draw out students and help them develop critical reading, careful writing, and insightful mathematical problem-solving skills. High school students in such a setting may have grade-point averages that are well below grades in less demanding high schools, but these applicants may be better prepared for college nevertheless. At less sophisticated high schools with limited academic opportunities, some students are self-starters who read widely on their own and have considerable talent, and they make outstanding college students. But their grade-point average may be no higher than that of others with limited intellectual potential but who complete routine assignments on time. High school grades and rank in such settings reveal little.

For all these reasons, class rank in high school is more informative than grades. However, many of the most challenging schools in the nation do not report class rank to students or to colleges, or they do so only in broad groups, for example, deciles. Their stated reason is that reporting class rank fosters an unhealthy atmosphere of competition in the school. The real goal may be to give the impression that all their students are above average. Colleges, on the other hand, do not view all students from a given high school as above average (except maybe those from Lake Wobegon). When high schools suppress information about their students, the remaining information in the application dossier, particularly standardized test scores, inevitably carries more weight.[11]

Because the high school record is not necessarily a clear, unambiguous measure of preparation, talent, industry, and ambition, it is a limited basis for forecasting success in college. Nevertheless, a college must act on whatever information it can get. A student who takes the most challenging courses at a well-regarded high school and accumulates an outstanding record that is readily apparent in the transcript gives the strongest available evidence of likely future success. For other students, the more information a high school can provide about the strength of its curriculum and the success of its students in college, the more readily a college admission office can interpret its graduates' performance.

Many high schools send academic profiles of their graduating classes to colleges, along with their students' transcripts. These profiles are available to parents as well. They describe the grading system, the distribution of grades, the size of the graduating class and high school, and the proportion of graduates who entered postsecondary education in recent years, including a list of the colleges where graduates enrolled. The average SAT I and ACT scores, the extent of AP offerings and test success, and an overview of the curriculum, including honors classes, rounds out the picture.

Colleges assign staff members from their admission offices to particular regions. The regional officers visit the best high schools, build relationships with counselors, and talk with students who have contacted their college. Students from less sophisticated high schools and those that choose to provide limited information about student performance may want to find other ways to distinguish their applications. Parents of outstanding students will prefer high schools that provide complete information to colleges.

National Test Scores   SAT I and ACT tests provide only a broad indication of likely success in college and add little to the applications of students who fall into the admission office's middle pile. Admission officers know that a difference of as much as 100 points on the SAT I makes no statistically significant difference in college performance, given the student's high school record. On the other hand, if a school is working hard to raise its national ranking, the admission office may be under some pressure from the administration to favor students with marginally higher test scores.

Essays   Writing an essay for college admission allows a student to reveal personality, enthusiasm, and introspection even as it showcases mastery of the writer's craft. Where admission decisions are word-driven, an effective personal essay can carry the day.

Well-written essays allow the reader to discover a part of the individual behind the application. Effective essays evoke a specific time, a place, an emotion, often with the applicant herself as an important character. Admission officers read hundreds of essays, and at some point understandably their eyes glaze over. But they are drawn to good stories well told, to anecdotes with deeper implications, in short, to memorable essays. Yawn-inducing essays include my summer in Outward Bound, my vacation trip to France, or my recovery from an injury. I have read many forgettable essays along the lines of "The most difficult event in my life was making friends when I moved to a new high school." On the other hand, the most memorable college essay I have ever read began: "I dissected a chicken in the workroom over our garage." Good essays take some risks.

Websites and professional admission counselors can be found who will edit essays for a fee. Indeed, some sell whole essays. Tim Hyde will be better off keeping others at arms' length from the creative process. An essay written by a committee, incorporating suggestions from parents, teachers, and counselors, is likely to have too many legs and not enough teeth. Good writing is more personal and distinctive than handwriting. Attempting to adopt a persona different from one's own will probably be detected as counterfeit.

Of course, having conversations about possible themes, trying out several in draft, and seeking reactions can be helpful. But in the end, the essay should be the student's own, and its demonstration of creativity, organization, and basic technique should be in character with what he produces in the SAT I or ACT writing section. Remember, the writing section is not just scored but is made available to admission committees for comparison with the essays on the application. A huge discrepancy will send up a red flag.

Letters of Recommendation   Most colleges expect to receive two or three letters of recommendation from people who know a student's academic work well. Unfortunately, not all letter writers are effective. The qualities of a persuasive letter are similar to those of an imaginative essay. Better letters are specific, they draw inferences from details, they describe a student's imagination and motivation as well as his accomplishments, and they are adept in the use of telling metaphors and other literary devices. Unfortunately, letter writers seldom get feedback on their recommendations. I have written hundreds of letters for college students and gotten comments from evaluators exactly once, and that was from a friend. There's no built-in process leading to improvement.

Applicants should choose letter writers who know them well and who are likely to take the time to write insightful, well-supported letters. It is appropriate to provide a letter writer with a resume and a statement of goals for college so that the writer will not confuse the captain of the cheerleading squad with a recluse in the same class, or mention how much a student wants to go to law school when medical school is the goal. Indeed, if each applicant had an interview with a prospective letter writer to discuss the resume and goals, the quality of recommendations might improve.

Rachel Toor, who spent three years as an admission officer at Duke, notes that teachers' recommendations are the components of the dossier least subject to packaging by admission counselors and parents and therefore often carry great weight, especially when well written. Perhaps the best an anxious parent can do is ask around at the PTA meeting and find out which teachers have reputations as sparkling letter writers.[12]

Extracurricular Achievement   Note that this does not say "Extracurricular Activities." The sheer number of extracurricular activities matters little to an admission committee. A student who concentrates on a few accomplishments—perhaps playing in a regional wind ensemble or winning a regional competition on the debate team—is much more impressive than one who lists a dozen activities without distinction. Many colleges recruit students for specific extracurricular activities in the same way that they recruit athletes. An oboist or even a bagpiper who auditions for the music department might win an offer of admission (and perhaps a merit scholarship) ahead of students with stronger quantitative scores because the campus needs to fill an opening.

In recent years, service trips abroad have become a popular way to fulfill a high school's community service requirement and burnish college applications while seeing a bit of the world. On these trips, adult counselors accompany groups of teenagers to foreign countries, where they assist local agencies in building houses and meeting other needs. Students (or their parents) pay a tuition of $4,000 or more for this experience, which covers all expenses. But as Marlyn McGrath Lewis, admission director at Harvard, points out, "We are very sophisticated in telling the difference between students who are genuinely ambitious and motivated and those who do things just for their applications." Jim Stoll, who directs one of these programs, has this to say: "I think colleges, quite frankly, are more impressed by someone who went out and made cool things happen on his own and didn't come to a prepared experience such as we are."[13]

Participation in a few serious activities over a number of years and playing a leadership role are signs of industry, talent, maturity, and ability to work with others. This kind of extracurricular achievement adds weight to an application and helps admission officers choose among applicants whose quantitative information is statistically indistinguishable.

Supplements   A dossier may be enhanced by supplementary material such as a poem or a CD of a musical performance, so long as the material is central to an applicant's academic record and goals. The admission office will send sophisticated items to a relevant faculty member with a request for comment. A painter who submits slides of her portfolio should assume that an art professor will evaluate it.

Because supplementary material imposes an additional burden on the admission staff, it is welcome only when it is of sufficient relevance and quality to be persuasive. A second-string cellist who wants to enter nursing school gains little by submitting a tape of her cello recital. On the other hand, a woodworker who wants to get into an undergraduate architecture program might consider sending slides of his cabinetwork.

Whenever possible, art students should ask to present their portfolios in person to the art department, so that individual items can be discussed, and musicians should request a live audition, especially if they are competing for merit scholarships. Many schools encourage students with special skills to establish contact with professors who can evaluate their work with insight and influence. This relationship may be initiated during a campus visit or by email.

Interview   Standard interviews with admission officers and alums have little influence over the decision to accept or deny an applicant. One might think that an interview would give an admission officer a more personal sense of the applicant. However, interviews are idiosyncratic. A quiet interviewee may stimulate little conversation but be an outstanding student and a forceful person in class and other settings. A charming interviewee may be a poor student. Interviewing is not a good way to judge students, and they are time-consuming and therefore expensive for an admission office. Alumni interviews are even more variable because the admission staff must decide how much confidence to place in the alum's judgment.

The real beneficiary of an interview is the student who's trying to choose a college, not the college that's trying to choose a student. Talks with recent alumni or current students can provide information about classes, the dining hall, fraternities and sororities, the library, intramurals, weekends, Wi-Fi, residences, religious life, cars on campus, studying, hazing, drinking, security, political organizations, dress code, rock concerts, and much more—the inside scoop that's difficult to get in other ways.

Alternate Strategies

The best way to influence the probability of acceptance at a selective college is to be an able, energetic student and prepare an effective application. But membership in certain groups—legacies, recruited athletes, and under-represented minorities—adds an undeniable advantage, when all other things are equal. And the biggest leg up in college admission—and one available to almost every student—comes from applying through early decision or early action.

Early Admission   By my estimate, in 2006 nearly 20,000 students applied early to the eight Ivies, and 40,000 applied early at other colleges and universities. Some selective colleges admit nearly 50 percent of their freshman class early via this process. For example, 48 percent of the entering class of 2009 at Princeton was admitted through early decision, and 52 percent of the class at Stanford was admitted in early action. Some schools give early financial aid information to early admits as well.[14]

An early application gets a more favorable reading, equivalent to about 100 extra points on the combined SAT I (on the old 1600-point scale), even when the colleges' admission literature and admission officers claim that early applicants have no advantage. Why do colleges value the early application process so much that they will admit students early whom they would not accept in regular admission?[15]

First, the higher the number of early decision admits, the lower the variation in yield rate because yield rate on early decision admits is nearly 100 percent. With lower variation, the admission office has a better chance of meeting without exceeding its target class size. A second consideration is that early decision allows a college to populate the lower quartile of its class with "happy" students—admissible students who really want to be at the school. At a highly competitive college or university, someone has to be in the bottom quartile of admits—and it might as well be students who are just glad to be there at all. Third, early admits in every quartile are more likely to graduate, and completion rates are a factor in a school's national ranking. And finally, the admission office likes to spread its workload over more months rather than concentrate all decisions in February.[16]

Critics of early decision point to the pressure on high school students to make a binding decision about where to go to college in October rather than April. Six months is a long time in the life of a seventeen-year-old. Younger people are less likely to understand themselves well enough to judge what kind of college environment is a good choice. Students with no clear first choice feel pushed into applying to only one college, and this distorts the admission process. Some students who are doubtful about getting into their first-choice school may try to game the system by applying early decision to their second-choice college, where the probability of acceptance is greater (or so they think). If indeed they are accepted, they will have forgone the opportunity to know if they would have been admitted to their first-choice school and if they would have been happy there.

Fortunately, the details of how students sort themselves out among generally similar colleges probably have no discernable effects on life prospects in the long run. Although those attending the most selective colleges gain a lifetime advantage relative to those attending much less selective colleges, it makes little difference whether one chooses Berkeley over Yale, or Bucknell over Washington and Lee, or any other school in a wide band of very selective institutions.

The big exceptions here are students requiring financial aid. A student who applies for early decision has selected a school without knowing the amount of the financial aid award or how it will break down between loans and grants. Although an applicant may walk away from an otherwise binding admission offer when the financial aid award is inadequate, she will have no other aid offers for comparison. And since aid awards based on merit are not usually announced at the time of acceptance but come later, in March or April, the student has no way to factor this possibility into the equation. Students who apply in the regular cycle receive offers of aid at the time of admission, and they may weigh them carefully in considering where to attend.

Early decision II is useful for seniors who want to include their fall grades in their application for early acceptance or who need more time to decide on a first-choice college. The strategy is also favored by many selective schools as a way to scoop up desirable students who were denied admission or deferred in the first round of early decision at another school. The proportion of students admitted by early decision I and II declines with falling selectivity. Aggressive use of early decision seems to be a game played primarily among the most selective colleges, though it may become important in other selective colleges as time goes on.[17]

In September 2006 Harvard University made headlines by announcing that as of 2007 it will no longer offer an early application program—neither early action nor early decision. All applications will be due by January 1, with all decisions made in its regular cycle.[18] Princeton very quickly followed suit. These two distinguished universities expressed the hope that this dramatic change of policy would make them more accessible to low-income and minority students, who have been much less likely to use the early process. Instead of gaming the system, students would be able to make a more deliberate, less stressful choice in April, with all of the facts and financial aid information in hand. They expressed the hope that other colleges and universities would do the same.

Paradoxically, if most early application programs ended tomorrow, the selectivity of the top-tier colleges, as measured by yield rate, would go up, not down, because a substantial number of students who now apply early to just one school would apply to many colleges on their wish list, on the chance that one "reach" school would look favorably on their application.

Wait List   Applicants who are notified that they are on the wait list in March have an opportunity to express continuing interest or to decline. A simple, sincere note to the admission office will enhance a student's prospect of being drawn from the wait list should the opportunity arise; the notice should be repeated periodically. There may be a separate wait list for each admission queue, that is, for each program in a university. So aggregate information about the likelihood of getting in can be misleading.

Colleges vary widely in their use of wait lists. Some use a shorter wait list when the likelihood of admitting applicants from it is low. But others routinely assign hundreds of applicants to the wait list without regard to the likelihood that any of them will be admitted. In 2006 Tufts University, having offered admission to 4,073 of its 15,280 applicants, put an additional 1,800 students on its wait list, even though the school had offered admission to none of the 1,800 hopefuls on the previous year's list. In 2005 George Washington University notified 2,082 students that they were on the wait list and then admitted only 97 of them.

College admission officers use the wait list for their own strategic advantage in another way. Every selective college wants to increase the number of students who apply, because more applications make them look more selective, and selectivity improves ranking. Since high school guidance counselors have a lot of influence over where students apply, admission officers want to maintain good relations with them. Guidance counselors are not happy when their students are denied admission to schools they have recommended. In order to limit the number of outright rejections at a given prestigious high school, admission officers recommend that some students be put on the wait list instead of being rejected outright. A similar tactic is used for legacies that the school has no intention of admitting but no desire to offend.[19]

For all these reasons, the wait list may be a less promising strategy than it seems. The National Association for College Admission Counseling requires its members to tell students on a wait list how many applicants were wait-listed the preceding year and how many were admitted from the list. Rather than stay on a wait list, most students sensibly choose among the schools where they have been admitted and quickly become emotionally attached to their choice.

Athletics   For an athlete, a key question is whether to seek college admission based on athletic success in high school. A student with significant athletic skill and academic qualifications sufficient to graduate from a selective college certainly enhances his prospects for admission by playing the sports card. Coaches in every division of intercollegiate athletics are constantly on the lookout for promising recruits, and colleges typically give preference to them in admission.

Good athletes sometimes need not apply through regular channels but are recruited in a special process through the athletic department. At one quite selective college, the probability of admission for "promising" athletes whose combined SAT I exceeded 1150 (in the old 1600-point system) was 84 percent. Coaches from Division I and II colleges in the National Collegiate Athletic Association (NCAA) are allowed to travel to recruit top athletes and to offer them scholarships. Although football, basketball, and baseball come to mind, essentially the same process and opportunities apply in less popular sports.[20]

Ironically, at small highly selective colleges such as Amherst and Williams, which field teams in dozens of sports, recruited athletes comprise a much greater fraction of an entering class than is found at larger schools such as the Big Ten. The athletic department is much more influential in defining the freshman class in these schools than at large public flagship universities. Although NCAA rules forbid Division III schools from offering athletic scholarships, these schools do offer need-based grants (as opposed to loans) to promising athletes, and they give preference to recruits in admission. DIII coaches are not allowed to travel to recruit, but they make extensive use of telephone calls, emails, informational sessions, campus overnights, and summer camps to identify able players and sway them to play on the college team. Other team members participate in this elaborate, highly competitive recruiting system.[21]

If a coach has little experience with the general admission procedure, a prospective student may get confusing or misleading signals. One of my students considered transferring to another college as a junior in order to play soccer. The coach at the candidate school encouraged the student and helped him navigate the transfer process. But eventually the student learned that he had earned too many college credits to be eligible for transfer as a junior. If an offer of admission isn't in writing, it may not be reliable. The same can be said for promises of playing time. Some athletic conferences require that the team's average SAT I scores and grade-point average meet a certain threshold. This has led some coaches to sign up athletes with high academic promise simply to raise the team's academic profile rather than contribute anything on the field. Playing time, if any, is limited to when the team is either far ahead or far behind.[22]

If a high school athlete concludes that she wants to participate in intercollegiate sports, she should make her interest known to college coaches by spring semester of her junior year. Many schools have a form on their website that prospective recruits can fill out online. College coaches typically ask for a video showing footage of games or matches played, and putting it together may require the cooperation of a student's high school athletic department.

Legacies   Children of alumni, called legacies, frequently receive preference in admission, and the number of legacies on a given campus may be quite noticeable. Some schools even give some preference to siblings and grandchildren of alumni. Among applicants to five selective colleges, 22 percent of legacies with SATs in the 1100 to 1199 range were offered admission, compared with 18 percent for other white students in this range. But when SATs passed 1300, legacies had a 60 percent probability of acceptance, compared with 24 percent for other white applicants. Of course, the SAT score does not reflect high school grades or other attributes of applicants. It is likely that, at a given SAT score, legacy applicants offer better high school grades and other attributes that enhance their prospects.[23]

In 2001–2002 the acceptance rate for legacies at Harvard was 40 percent (compared with 11 percent overall); at Notre Dame it was 57 percent (31 percent overall); at the University of Virginia it was 52 percent (36 percent overall); and at the University of Pennsylvania it was 41 percent (21 percent overall). Children of substantial donors and children of celebrities (including prominent politicians) are also likely to receive preference, but the donations and celebrity must be quite large and therefore the number of students affected is very small.[24]

Under-represented Minorities   An admission process that depended exclusively on the SAT I would tilt heavily toward students from affluent communities, those who take the test multiple times with extensive test preparation, and those who quickly jump to the conventional answer. Even when the high school record bears significant weight, a number-driven process selects a relatively homogeneous group and reinforces the affluence of the affluent. "Ivy begets Ivy," it has been said.

When a college has the goal of serving social advancement, of educating the next generation's leaders from many groups, and of creating a livelier, more diverse social context for all its students, it will adopt a less number-driven admission process. If the goal is to attract students who will make the greatest gains from college, the students with the highest numbers are not the only ones to include.

For these reasons, since the 1960s many selective colleges have actively solicited applications from African American, Latino, Native American, and sometimes Asian students, as well as students of different religions, regions, countries, and economic circumstances. At ten quite selective colleges in 2005, 11 percent of the entering class was African American, 12 percent was Latino, 21 percent was Asian, and 56 percent was white or other groups. The probability of admission for black applicants with SATs in the 1100 to 1199 range (on the old 1600-point scale) was 40 percent (much higher than for legacies), and at SAT ranges over 1300 the probability of admission was 70 percent for African American applicants. Different colleges put emphasis on different minority groups: for example, since 1970 when Dartmouth established its Native American Program, over 500 Indians from over 120 tribes have attended the school. Colleges also define their minorities differently: students from Spain or Portugal may or may not count as Latino for the purposes of affirmative action.[25]

Affirmative action for minorities does not mean quotas. It means taking extra measures to invite applications and to consider carefully all of the attributes of applicants from under-represented groups. In a world where race and ethnicity bring stereotypes to mind, taking extra measures to overcome them is essential for fairness. Moreover, as the racial and ethnic composition of the nation continues to change, college experiences that build a sense of community across boundaries have a value that benefits the nation as a whole, not just individual graduates.

Gauging the Chance of Admission

Most college guides report a gross rate of admission for each college they describe. This number is the percentage of students offered admission, compared with the total number of applications received. While the admission rate gives an overall sense of the selectivity of the college, it should not be interpreted as the probability of admission for a typical student. Oberlin College admitted 34 percent of its applicants in 2005, but that did not mean that one out of three applicants in each category of applicant was accepted. Because athletes, legacies, minorities, students of high academic achievement, and students who apply early decision have much higher probabilities of admission, the typical student who applies through the regular admission channel has a lower chance of acceptance than the published figure. At Oberlin, the probability for this kind of student dropped to about 29 percent.

To approximate the probability of admission for a regular applicant, let's begin with the total number of applicants and the total number of admits and, by subtracting out students in the special categories, calculate a net admission rate. For the sake of simplicity, let's assume that legacies and athletes, on average, are in the early admit group; so we'll subtract the number of early applicants from the total applicants and the number of early admits from the total admits.

Next, let's assume, again for simplicity, that targeted minorities—African Americans, Hispanics, and Native Americans—are not in the early applicant pool because they are more likely to need financial aid and may want to compare offers. Data on the number of minorities in the applicant and admitted pools are not available, but colleges do report the number of targeted minorities who enroll. So we'll subtract that number from the total applicants and the total admitted, bearing in mind that because more minorities were admitted than actually enrolled, our final approximation of the net admission rate will be somewhat high.

Finally, we know that applicants with very high academic qualifications are much more likely to be admitted than the typical student, but we cannot measure academic qualifications with complete accuracy. Also, schools do not report data on the total number of high academic achievers admitted. So to simplify, let's look at the number of *enrolled* students with verbal or math SAT I scores over 700 and subtract two-thirds of them from the total number of applicants and from the total number admitted.

After making these adjustments and assumptions, we can calculate the ratio of those remaining in the regularly admitted group to those in the regular applicant pool. The number we come up with is the net admission rate—an approximation (probably on the high side) of the probability that a regular applicant will be admitted. The calculations here are limited to private schools, because in-state and out-of-state applicants to public colleges and universities have dramatically different rates of application, admission, and enrollment.

The approximate net admission rate differs most dramatically from the gross admission rate at the top ten research universities in the 2006 *US News* ranking. The average net admission rate among these schools is 4 percent for a regular applicant—about one student accepted for each twenty-one not accepted (see Table 6). Yet these schools report a gross admission rate of 12 percent—suggesting that one in eight applicants will be admitted. Among the top three universities, the odds of admission for a regular applicant are minuscule: for every one student admitted, thirty students are turned away. Yet a majority of these rejected students are qualified for admission on the basis of a "match" between their high school record/test scores and the numbers published by the universities themselves. So just because a prospective student's numbers fall within the overall range of a school's numbers, that doesn't mean the regular applicant has a reasonable chance of admission.

The picture gets a little brighter when we move away from the top ten and look at the research universities ranked 15 to 25. There, the gap between gross and net admission rates is much narrower. The gross admit rate averaged 42 percent for a sample in this set, while the approximate net rate was 38 percent. So a student in the regular admission pool with, on average, a 4 percent chance of get-ing into a prestigious school like Stanford or Columbia would have a 38 percent chance, on average, of getting into a highly respected research university like Rice, Notre Dame, Tulane, or Georgetown. These campuses lock in a much smaller share of their entering class through early admission programs, make smaller commitments to targeted minorities, and capture a smaller share of the very top tier of academic talent. As a result, their net admission rate is not far from their gross rate.

The top liberal arts colleges fall about half way between the top ten research universities and those universities ranked 15 to 25. The average gross admission rate of the top ten liberal arts colleges is 23 percent, while the approximate net admission rate is 17 percent. These colleges capture somewhat fewer students through early application, they are between the two groups of research universities in attracting top academic talent, and they do less well than the universities in attracting targeted minorities. The second group of liberal arts colleges, those generally in the 15 to 25 rank, show gross and net rates that are similar to the second group of research universities, though their enrollment of minorities is quite low.

It is important to bear in mind that the approximate net admission rate for liberal arts colleges in both groups may be too high because these schools make a large commitment to recruited athletes—much larger than the research universities do, when the total size of the class is taken into account. In other words, student athletes who do not apply for early admission at a liberal arts college may nevertheless have a much greater chance of admission there than a nonathlete going through the regular admission channel. Colleges do not systematically report these numbers, but at Williams, for example, 12 percent of each freshman class since 2003 has consisted of athletes given special treatment in admission, some of whom did not apply for early admission. That's more than a third of all student athletes at Williams (who make up about a third of the entire student body).[26]

The lesson here for regular applicants—students who do not apply for early admission and who find themselves in that middle pile of difficult-to-distinguish students—is to discount heavily the chance of success at the very top colleges and universities. The odds are long indeed. Colleges and universities in the next group provide excellent educational services for undergraduates (though the details matter), provide much better odds of admission for regular applicants, and may even offer generous financial aid packages, including possibly merit scholarships, for desirable students who wouldn't win the lottery at the top ten schools.

So to sum up: Most colleges fill most of the seats in their freshman class with students from that difficult-to-distinguish middle pile—not with Westinghouse scholars, fourth-generation legacies, wide receivers, registered Cherokees, kids from Idaho, or nationally ranked tuba players. These good-enough teenagers have a great chance of academic success on campus, but their records are difficult to differentiate from others in the group. Colleges try to make fine distinctions by looking carefully at extracurricular achievements, essays, and recommendations. But at the end of the day, a large element of chance enters into admission decisions, even (or especially) at the most discerning schools.

The only way students can offset this randomness is by applying to several schools and giving each application their best shot. If they have a clear first-choice school with an early admission program, and if they can afford to forgo comparing any financial aid award to offers from other schools, then applying in the early admission program will give them an undeniable advantage.

CHAPTER NINE

The Choice: Comparing Offers

In April of 2005, Ellen Adderley, a high school senior in Shawnee Mission, Kansas (a suburb of Kansas City), had offers of admission in hand from three very good schools: Northwestern University in nearby Evanston, the College of William and Mary in Virginia, and Haverford College in Pennsylvania. All three undergraduate programs were listed in Barron's "most competitive" category, but they differed in other important ways that Ellen was trying hard to sort out before making a commitment. She had enjoyed her visits to the campuses but felt no personal ties to any one of them.

Northwestern (ranked 12th among national research universities by *US News* in 2006) is a leading private research university in Evanston, Illinois, with a distinguished faculty who are internationally recognized for the originality of their intellectual work and who lead well-regarded graduate and professional programs. Its PhD programs in economics and sociology and its professional schools in law and business are in the top dozen in their fields nationally. William and Mary (ranked 31st by *US News*) is a public university in Williamsburg, Virginia, with a very select student body and a central focus on quality undergraduate instruction, although it has ten graduate programs in arts and sciences as well. Haverford (ranked 8th among liberal arts colleges by *US News*) is a small, classic free-standing liberal arts college in Haverford, Pennsylvania, with an able faculty and a carefully chosen student body. Each of these campuses promises Ellen a significant intellectual challenge and an ample reward for her efforts and her financial investment.

The cost of attendance for the upcoming fall was pegged at about $43,081 at Northwestern, $42,726 at Haverford, and $30,453 at William and Mary (the out-of-state rate). Ellen received offers of work, grants, and modest loans from Northwestern and Haverford that made the costs at these two private colleges similar. William and Mary offered no financial aid. Solely on the basis of objective financial information, Ellen should have enrolled at the college with the lowest net price, William and Mary. The financial aid packages at the other two schools did not make the net price comparable, from a strictly dollars-and-cents perspective. Fortunately, Ellen's family viewed all three schools as affordable, so price was only one factor among many she was considering.

In the previous year, admission statistics at the schools were comparable, with Northwestern and William and Mary admitting about 30 percent of applicants, while Haverford admitted about 26 percent. About 40 percent of admitted students at each school chose to enroll there. Northwestern's new students had somewhat higher SAT scores, particularly in math. Haverford's freshmen had somewhat higher rank in their high school class. Ellen expected to be in the middle third of freshmen. She knew that her own commitment, talent, and luck would have considerable influence on her class rank at graduation. Completion rates at the three schools show that 90 percent of entering students earned a degree within six years of enering. The colleges also showed success in placing their graduates in medical school—an option Ellen wanted to keep open.[1]

Ellen played field hockey in high school but not with the kind of success that attracts college coaches. She had made a decision not to fill out the schools' recruiting forms online or initiate any other contact with athletic departments, and she was pleased that she had gained admission on the basis of her academic standing alone. She was looking for differences in campus life and the intellectual character of the educational programs to guide her final decision.

Broad Choices

Ellen's choices were narrower than those many students face. Often applicants are admitted to schools that range across wide categories. In thinking about such broad choices, a main question to ask is: What is the likelihood that I will complete a four-year degree if I go to this school?

This question does not imply that students seeking a bachelor's degree should avoid two-year colleges or that they should never transfer. Forty-two percent of college students begin at a two-year school, and slightly over one-fourth of them transfer to four-year colleges. Many students who enter two-year colleges pursue certificate or associate degrees that are not designed to feed into four-year programs. But those who enter two-year programs designed to prepare students to move on to four-year schools are often successful. Among students who make the transition to four-year programs, about 60 percent earn bachelor's degrees within eight or so years. This rate of completion is about the same as the rate for all students who enroll in four-year programs initially and earn at least ten credits.[2]

An academic program at a two-year college is an important and inexpensive first step toward a bachelor's degree for many students. Of course, the quality of the specific educational services matters and the ease with which credits can be transferred toward a four year degree should be taken into account. Some states require their two-year public colleges to meet the expectations of their four-year public colleges. In 2004, 26 percent of all undergraduates were enrolled in two-year public colleges, while another 46 percent were enrolled in four-year public colleges. (The remaining 28 percent of full-time undergraduates were enrolled in private colleges, including proprietaries.) About 88 percent of first-time students at public four year colleges were residents of the state where they go to school.[3]

The arts and science disciplines—the core of a liberal arts education—accounted for about 37 percent of all bachelor's degrees in 2003–2004. Professional programs accounted for the remainder: business at 22 percent; engineering, computer science, and technology at 10 percent; education at 8 percent; communications/journalism, health professions, and visual/performing arts at 5 percent each; several other small fields at 8 percent. A bachelor's degree from one of the top specialty programs is among the most prized degrees in higher education. Examples include Caltech and MIT, Julliard and the New England Conservatory of Music, the Rhode Island School of Design and the Art Institute of Chicago. These schools, and many others like them, are excellent choices for undergraduates who have already chosen a professional direction while in high school.[4]

But before enrolling in a specialty school, students might want to consider how easy or difficult it would be to change course if their career interests don't work out. A big advantage of a liberal arts program even on a large campus is that transition among disciplines is usually easy. In fact, colleges encourage students to experiment with

ntroductory courses in several fields before committing to a major
ometime in the sophomore year. By contrast, students who choose
he College of Design at Iowa State may face hurdles in switching
nto business, engineering, or music on the same campus. The ISU
College of Business requires students to complete a year's worth of
pecified courses with a minimum grade-point average before being
dmitted to the business program in sophomore year. A student
vho spent his first year in core courses at the College of Design
vould be unlikely to meet the requirements for transfer to the business program. Movement in the opposite direction would be no eas-
er. Moreover, neither program's first year provides a base of experi-
nce for choosing between the two. Switching between professional
programs, even on the same campus, can be difficult and costly.
Usually it will mean extending undergraduate education beyond
our years.

Many students transfer, sometimes to a less demanding or less expensive school, sometimes to a program that is not available at their
irst school, sometimes to a more challenging (and likely more expensive) college. Sixty percent of all undergraduates ultimately at-
end more than one school before graduating, and 35 percent of
hose who enroll in a second college do so in a different state. Many
tudents use a local public university as a launching point for their
tudies and then transfer to other campuses farther from home, as
heir goals become clearer and their interests mature.

Contrary to what parents might assume, students who transfer
rom one school to another have a high probability of complet-
ng their bachelor's degree. On the other hand, students who take
courses on several campuses without formally transferring their
primary enrollment have a lower probability of graduating, other
hings being equal. Delay between high school and college, inter-

rupted study, and part-time enrollment are other factors associate
with lower rates of graduation, especially for students who start ou
in four-year colleges with very little selectivity.[5]

By considering the full range of choices in American higher edu
cation, almost any student can find an affordable path to colleg
graduation and beyond. What counts is the personal commitmen
of the student and the quality of educational services. Taking cha
lenging courses and doing well in them is the best way to open th
next door.

Narrow Choices

Ellen Adderley's goal was more than simply completing a bachelor
degree. She was looking for a college with significant intellectu
challenge, in hopes of improving her prospects for admission to pro
fessional school and a career beyond. She was particularly intereste
in the sciences, along with other things.

Her three options fell within the category of quite selective four
year colleges, a group where costs are high. The expense would b
justified, Ellen's family believed, because she was prepared for
more intense program than she could find in less selective schools
Still, choosing among these three similarly selective colleges in
volved subtle tradeoffs. Each of them offered a liberal arts program
had female enrollment of 53 to 55 percent, and was located in a met
ropolitan area. But the schools differed in size and focus, in th
tenor of student life, and in specific academic programs.

To begin with, the three campuses operate on vastly differen
scales and give different emphasis to undergraduates.[6] Northwester
is a large research university with many graduate and professiona
programs and a major research enterprise. Its 8,031 undergraduate

make up about 60 percent of enrollment on its Evanston campus and 44 percent of total enrollment, including the law and medical programs in Chicago. Although Northwestern has a $1.8 billion endowment, it is unclear how much of the endowment serves undergraduates. Dividing total endowment by total enrollment shows about $100,000 per student, a figure likely to provide about $5,000 per year per student in operating funds. Northwestern University's undergraduate schools include engineering, music, communication, and journalism in addition to arts and sciences.[7]

The College of William and Mary's undergraduate enrollment of 5,540 is nearly three-fourths of its total enrollment of 7,544, and the only substantial post-baccalaureate professional program is the law school. William and Mary is primarily an undergraduate college. The $355 million endowment amounts to about $50,000 per student, enough to support about $2,500 of annual operating budget per student. In addition to the liberal arts, William and Mary serves undergraduates in schools of business administration and education.

Haverford College is tiny by comparison with the other two. It has only 1,172 students, all of whom are undergraduates in the liberal arts. Students can also take courses for credit at nearby Bryn Mawr College, a school for women. Haverford's endowment of $350 million approaches $300,000 per student, enough to support about $15,000 of operating expenditures per student each year.

Student life differs dramatically on the three campuses. Northwestern and Haverford are in the suburbs of Chicago and Philadelphia, respectively; William and Mary is in the center of Williamsburg, a tourist destination of considerable charm. Two thirds of William and Mary's students are from Virginia; about a quarter of Northwestern's undergraduates are from Illinois; only about one seventh of Haverford's students are from Pennsylvania. The student body differs in race and ethnicity from school to school. The per centage of entering students who are black or Hispanic is 12 percent each at Northwestern, 11 percent at William and Mary, and 15 percent at Haverford. The percentage of entering students who are of Asian or Pacific Islander ancestry is 7 percent at William and Mary, 12 per cent at Haverford, and 16 percent at Northwestern. The percentage of students from abroad is 2 percent at William and Mary, 4 percent at Haverford, and 5 percent at Northwestern. William and Mary's student body is a little less diverse than Haverford's or Northwest ern's, primarily because it draws so heavily on residents of Virginia.

About 65 percent of Northwestern's 8,031 undergraduates live in university housing, creating a campus with a significant residen tial character. Thirty percent of male undergraduates belong to fra ternities, and a larger share of women belong to sororities, making Greeks an important part of campus social life. Northwestern is the only private university that competes in the Big Ten athletic conference with Michigan, Wisconsin, and Illinois, among others. Northwestern fields twenty athletic teams, including cheerleading. In 2006 Northwestern's field hockey coach announced seven new scholarship students, a typical annual inflow to the team of twenty three players. There's virtually no chance that Ellen could walk on as a field hockey player at Northwestern. But sports might be a big fac tor in social life on campus.[9]

About 75 percent of William and Mary's 5,540 undergraduates live in campus housing. Greek life attracts about 25 percent of un dergraduates, slightly below the rate at Northwestern. William and Mary competes in the Colonial Athletic Conference (Division I of the NCAA) with Delaware, Towson, and George Mason, among others. Fewer than 10 percent of undergraduates participate in the twenty-three varsity sports the college supports. William and Mary's

ield hockey program offers about six scholarships to recruited ath-
etes each year; only one unrecruited freshman has walked on in the
ast twenty years.[10]

All Haverford students live on campus, and there are no Greek
organizations. A whopping 40 percent of Haverford students partic-
pate in NCAA Division III varsity athletics, with ten teams for men
and eleven for women. Another 10 to 15 percent of students play
club sports, ranging from rugby and golf to ultimate Frisbee. Haverford
competes in the Centennial Conference with Swarthmore, Johns
Hopkins, and Gettysburg, among others. Participation in intercollegiate athletics is a much more important part of student life at
Haverford than at William and Mary or Northwestern, even though
the school does not offer athletic scholarships. Ellen views her prospects for participating in athletics either in field hockey or a club
sport as higher at Haverford than at the other two colleges. On the
other hand, if she chooses not to play sports, she worries that she
might be in the minority of students.

The academic programs differ in both instructors and class sizes.
Although about 80 percent of the faculty are tenured or tenure-track
(outside the law and medical programs) on each of the three campuses (with the other 20 percent being lecturers), the role of graduate students differs. William and Mary had 796 graduate assistants
among its 1,334 graduate student population serving its 5,594 undergraduates. Northwestern has 2,079 doctoral students in the schools
offering undergraduate instruction. A substantial number of these
(the exact number is not reported) serve as teaching assistants.
Clearly, graduate students play important roles in instruction on
both campuses, while also requiring instruction themselves. In contrast, Haverford has no graduate students. All instruction is by faculty, and the faculty do not offer courses for graduate students.

William and Mary lists 1,112 class sections for its undergraduates. Middle-sized classes predominate. Fewer than 3 percent of the student seats are in sections with under ten students, 35 percent are in sections with forty or more students. The average section size from the student's point of view is forty-one.[11] In contrast, at Northwestern, 11 percent of student seats are in class sections with fewer than ten students and 42 percent of student seats are in class groups with forty or more students. The average class section size is about forty-four students. Northwestern, then, offers a welcome combination of small and large classes, rather than emphasizing middle-sized classes, and it conducts a larger share of undergraduate instruction in small sections than does William and Mary.[12]

At Haverford, 11 percent of student seats are in sections with fewer than ten students, a rate similar to Northwestern's, but only 14 percent of student seats are in classes with forty or more students. The average class section size from the student's point of view is about twenty-four students. None of Haverford's classes have more than ninety-nine students. Haverford's instructional program concentrates on small sections, taught by tenured and tenure-track faculty.[13]

Differences in the intellectual focus of the three campuses are apparent from the pattern of degrees granted across fields. At Northwestern, 22 percent of graduates complete majors in communication, journalism, or English language and literature, compared with just 9 percent at both William and Mary and Haverford. At William and Mary, 14 percent of graduates complete majors in business and 13 percent in education, compared to 1 percent in each at Northwestern and no majors in business or education at Haverford. There, 12 percent of majors are in biology, compared with 8 percent at William and Mary and 4 percent at Northwestern. Mathematics and physics account for 17 percent of majors at Haverford, 7 percent at William and Mary, and 20 percent at Northwestern (many in the engineering program). At Haverford, 36 percent of majors are in social sciences and history, compared with 28 percent at William and Mary and 21 percent at Northwestern. Five percent of Haverford students complete majors in a foreign language, and 7 percent major in philosophy and religion. The other two campuses draw 2 or 3 percent to each of these fields. Nearly 50 percent of William and Mary and Haverford's graduates will study abroad at some point during their careers, but only about 35 percent of Northwestern's graduates will do so.[14]

All three colleges have writing centers and require at least one small-scale writing-intensive course in the first year; Northwestern requires two. All three offer the possibility of a senior thesis or sizable student research project. Haverford requires significant independent work in a senior project, with a thesis in some disciplines and a research essay developed in a seminar in other disciplines, including biology. Haverford offers a more writing-intensive curriculum overall.[15]

The calculus curricula differ across the three colleges. The math program at Haverford makes extensive use of computers and varied instructional methods, including student projects. Among the four faculty teaching the first course in the basic calculus sequence, one is tenure track, one is a long-term lecturer, and two are temporary.[16] Northwestern also offers a weekly recitation section in its basic calculus courses but does not use a laboratory philosophy. Calculators are not allowed in exams. Of the six faculty members teaching in the first two terms of the basic calculus sequence, one is a long-term lecturer, four are temporary, one is a graduate student, and none are tenure-track faculty. Northwestern offers an accelerated math curriculum for students who enter college having completed a year's study of calculus.

For the majority of students who will use basic calculus as a tool in the sciences and social sciences, William and Mary has the strongest math program, with a heavier commitment of permanent faculty and an instructional philosophy that emphasizes developing deep thinking skills. The first two semesters of basic calculus include a weekly lab that uses a graphing calculator. The calculus sequence shows significant influence from the calculus reform movement mentioned in Chapter 5. Of the seven faculty members involved in teaching the first two terms of the calculus sequence in 2005–2006, five are tenure track faculty, the sixth is a long-term lecturer, and only one is temporary.

The three schools also show a range in their respective efforts to discourage cheating and plagiarism. A national survey comparing the rate of cheating on campuses with different kinds of honor codes has shown that student-led efforts to promote ethical behavior reduce cheating, even on large campuses where many students are part-time and have relatively weak ties to the campus. Cheating is also much lower, on average, on smaller campuses with a strong sense of community. Students like Ellen who want to work hard and be rewarded for their efforts are demoralized by cheating. The student body at Haverford votes annually to renew its honor code, requiring a two-thirds majority to agree. William and Mary also has an active student judiciary to address cheating. Northwestern relies solely on a dean to address the issue. Cheating is likely to be lower at William and Mary than at Northwestern, and lowest of all at Haverford.[17]

Although the three campuses are similar in selectivity, the differences in scale, focus, the character of student life, and the intensity of the instructional program for undergraduates, as well as price, will cause different students to make different choices. Northwestern's prominence as a major research university and role in big-time athletics sets it apart. William and Mary has a stronger focus on undergraduates with a lower net price and a predominance of middle-sized classes. Haverford is a liberal arts college with small classes taught by regular faculty and a high rate of participation in intercollegiate athletics by both men and women. It also has the highest percentage of biology majors, suggesting that this department is strong on campus. This turned out to be an important factor in Ellen Adderley's decision.

Big Fish, Small Pond

Frequently, students face a choice of being just another student at a more selective college versus being one of the best students at a less selective college. Students on wait lists at more selective colleges may be marginal admits, in the eyes of the admission office. Yet the same academic and personal record might attract a merit scholarship at a less selective campus where, in the eyes of that admission staff, the student is a top prospect. Admission officers are only moderately effective at forecasting academic performance, and when students look a lot alike and the stakes are relatively low, the personal tastes of particular admission officers may tip the balance.

Some students come into their own by being in a less competitive environment, where their potential and achievements are recognized and encouraged—a big fish in a smaller pond. Others may want a more competitive environment and are content to be a small fry there. It can be a wrenching experience for students who were first in high school to discover they are below the middle of a distinguished class in college. If the quality of a student's performance improves with the quality of the competition, and if better performance in college improves one's life prospects, then on average students will lean toward being a small fish in a more competitive pond. This phenomenon fuels the positional race. Yet, as noted in Chapter 2, class rank in college has a positive effect on earnings, other things being equal, and a student's class rank may go up at a less competitive school. The effect may not be enough to overcome large differences in the intellectual intensity of a college, however.

Statistically speaking, Ellen is likely to rank near the middle of the class at the colleges she is considering. The chemistry and biology courses required for admission to medical schools are particularly competitive arenas on all three campuses, with grades taken as important signals of likely future success in medical school. Pre-med students in the top quartile of their class will have excellent life prospects. To move into that group, Ellen will need energy, focus, excellent mentoring, and a measure of good luck.

Well-Rounded Students versus Well-Rounded Classes

Over the last several decades, the college admission process has moved to a goal of building a well-rounded class, as opposed to building a class of well-rounded individuals. Although the well-rounded class will include primarily well-rounded individuals, it will have students who excel in specific roles but are undistinguished in other ways.

In the 1950s in the Ivy League, the captain of the football team might also have been active in student government and in other venues outside of class and off the field. Today, the demands of athletics and the methods used to recruit players make campus athletes little known outside their role in sports. Similarly, musicians, artists, and debaters may give boffo performances but add less than average otherwise. Colleges that look for strong niche players like these have become so common that some parents make their eight-year-old drop soccer on Saturday so that he can concentrate on his violin lessons. Sustained distinction in one area is much better than lesser achievements in several activities, they've been told.[18]

Success in a niche can unduly influence where a student applies, gets accepted, and chooses to enroll. Of course, the majority of students do quite well in a variety of roles and gain nothing by forgoing activities they enjoy, even if their performance is mediocre. Limiting a student to a niche is risky because the pool of opportunities is smaller and more variable. A slot for a premier bassoonist may open only once every four years at Colgate, and the able student with her heart set on both Colgate and the bassoon may be flat out of luck.

Most undergraduates at most selective colleges are well-rounded people who study hard, participate in a range of campus activities, enjoy a satisfying social life, and seek intellectual challenge. They know that to learn they must take some risks, experience some reversals, and cope with stress. They pursue several channels of learning, in order to develop richer, more flexible capabilities and to function in many different domains, among people who are not like themselves. These are the common goals of college students, and most are fulfilled at most good colleges most of the time. The initial competition for a spot on a highly selective campus ought not to distort this fact of college life. During their four years of undergraduate study, students grow into new roles, often in ways that they could never have predicted in advance, and they will meet people they would never have met at any other place or time. The college admission process—an arduous experience that can tie whole families up in knots for a decade—quickly pales in comparison to the college experience itself and the work life that follows.

After much indecision, Ellen chose to enroll in the small, intensive program at Haverford, despite its extra cost and despite some initial qualms about choosing a school that was smaller than her high school. She knew that to get into medical school, she'd need all the one-on-one attention from professors she could get. She looked forward to an engaging intellectual experience, with many intense classes and an accessible faculty who serve their undergraduates well. Although her prospects in field hockey were unclear, the club sports program offered an appealing alternative. Relieved at finally making a choice, Ellen went online and ordered sweatshirts for her parents from the Haverford College Bookstore.

Table 1 Financial Returns to Higher Education.

Degree earned	Comparison levels of education	Years of school added	Annual tuition ($)	Present value of increased net earnings @ r = 0.10		Internal rate of return (%)		Earnings over $150K (%)	
				Men	Women	Men	Women	Men	Women
High school	—	0	0	257,217	141,901			0.6	0.1
All AA	HS to AA	2	3,936	16,595	15,587	15	16	1.0	0.3
Baccalaureate	HS to BA	4	8,599	58,744	18,536	16	13	4.2	0.7
Master's	BA to MA	2	8,026	−10,741	1,143	8	10	6.3	1.4
Professional	BA to Pro	3	16,534	74,864	55,971	14	15	25.0	7.8
PhD	BA to PhD	6	−13,565	−23,768	82,017	7	115	12.6	4.8

Source: Author's calculation from reported earnings of adult workers in the Bureau of the Census, *Current Population Survey 1996–2002*, with earnings inflated to 2002 values by the Consumer Price Index. Tuition is the average in-state tuition for public and private colleges. The tuition for professionals is a weighted average of tuition at law and medical schools with degrees awarded as the weights. The negative "tuition" shown for Ph.D. is the average stipend paid to graduate students as reported in a survey of six disciplines from forty-five universities by the *Chronicle of Higher Education*, September 21, 2001. Students in graduate programs are assumed to have earned a BA at the BA rates of tuition. The present value shown for those with a high school education is the present value of expected lifetime earnings. It appears as a point of comparison. The internal rate of return is comparable to the annual rates of return on financial assets. It is the interest rate at which the present value of the gain in earnings equals the present value of the cost of the education. HS is high school, AA is Associate's degree, BA is baccalaureate, MA is master's degree, Pro is professional degrees, and PhD is Doctor of Philosophy.

2 Mean Earnings in Thirteen Selected Occupations, 1996–2002 (in 2002 dollars).

pation	Men ($)	Women ($)	Jobs (thousands)	Percent women
y	29,730	26,816	369	14
ers other than college & university	35,822	30,830	5,353	75
rters & editors	41,003	33,363	288	56
tered nurses	44,963	40,504	2,111	93
e, detectives, & supervisors	45,241	38,106	676	13
untants & auditors	49,042	33,275	1,592	57
ance sales	49,555	31,550	577	43
ge & university teachers	51,164	38,501	961	44
cial managers	59,871	39,795	784	50
eers, all types	59,094	48,547	2,093	10
eting, advertising, & PR managers	65,155	45,154	755	38
ers & judges	83,530	62,635	926	30
cians	93,740	69,303	719	28

e: Author's calculations from the *Current Population Survey 1996–2002*. The means are computed in thms and reported as anti-logs. They refer to annual earnings of full-time workers (including nment and self-employed workers) who earned more than $400 at the longest job held in the ding year, regardless of the level of education attained. To protect the confidentiality of individuals, ensus does not report individual earnings over certain thresholds it sets. For these respondents, the us replaces the individual earnings with an average (called a top code) of the high-income group vary by demographic group and over time. Jobs and percent female are for 2000 from the tical Abstract of the United States 2002, Table 593, "Employed Civilians by Occupation, Sex, Race, Hispanic Origin."

Table 3 Average Earnings of Adult Workers by Level of Education and Sex, 2002.

Highest level of education completed	Sex	Number of people in survey	Percentage women	Mean earnings ($)	Top sixth ($)	Bottom sixth ($)	Mea (ye
High school	Men	69,506		29,152	53,714	15,821	3ξ
	Women	49,948	41.8	20,669	37,017	11,540	4.
Some college	Men	39,688		33,298	63,018	17,594	3ξ
	Women	31,164	44.0	23,712	43,396	12,957	3ξ
Associate vocational	Men	10,162		35,130	62,953	19,604	3ξ
	Women	8,213	44.7	25,731	45,894	14,426	4C
Associate academic	Men	7,843		37,469	67,555	20,782	4C
	Women	7,767	49.8	27,669	49,185	15,565	4C
Baccalaureate	Men	42,247		47,086	88,773	24,975	4I
	Women	29,883	41.4	33,780	60,716	18,794	38
Master's	Men	13,607		57,392	104,697	31,461	44
	Women	10,231	42.9	42,770	72,778	25,135	4ξ
Professional degree	Men	4,898		78,871	148,003	42,031	4ξ
	Women	1,799	26.9	54,710	109,953	27,222	4I
PhD	Men	3,834		68,378	125,024	37,397	47
	Women	1,338	25.9	52,525	101,265	27,244	44
Total	Men	191,785		37,201	73,034	18,949	40
	Women	140,343	42.3	26,234	49,739	13,837	40

Source: Author's calculations from the *Current Population Survey 1996–2002*, inflated to 2002 values ▮ the Consumer Price Index. Earnings over 150,000 are top-coded to an average value by demographic group by the Bureau of the Census. For this reason, the actual average is somewhat above the value shown in the table. Average earnings are the antilog of the mean of the log of earnings. The threshc for the top and bottom sixths are the antilog of the mean of the log of earnings plus and minus one standard deviation and denoted 15.9 percent of the distribution in the tails, approximately one-sixth

Table 4 Internal Rates of Return to Education in Thirteen Selected Occupations.

Add	Occupation	Men	Women
BA	Clergy	Low	0.13
BA	Teachers, not college	0.01	0.09
MA	Teachers, not college	0.05	0.10
BA	Reporters & editors	0.16	0.12
AA	Registered nurses		0.39
BA	Registered nurses		0.15
MA	Registered nurses		0.18
Some college	Police, detectives, & supervisors	0.20	0.32
BA	Police, detectives, & supervisors	0.12	0.16
BA	Accountants & auditors	0.16	0.15
BA	Insurance sales	0.23	0.16
PhD	College & university teachers	Low	0.91
BA	Financial managers	0.19	0.22
BA	Engineers, all types	0.20	0.24
BA	Marketing, advertising, & PR managers	0.09	0.19
JD	Lawyers & judges	0.18	0.26
MD	Physicians	0.16	0.12

Source: Author's calculation from *Current Population Survey 1996–2002* data. Base is the comparison set, is the level of education evaluated. HS = high school, BA = four-year degree, MA is masters. The nal rate of return is comparable to the annual rates of return on financial assets. Low indicates the ns are too low to calculate an internal rate of return. Blanks indicate too few observations to make sible calculation.

Table 5 Enrollment by Category for Four-year Colleges Listed in Barron's
2007.

Admissions competitiveness	Proportion of applicants accepted (%)	Number of colleges	First-time undergraduates (thousands)	National first-year enrollment (%)
Most competitive	Less than 33	74	86	7
Highly competitive	33 to 50	109	179	15
Very competitive	50 to 75	279	316	26
Competitive	75 to 85	613	499	41
Less competitive	85 to 98	193	115	9
Noncompetitive	98 or more	99	24	2
Special (art, music, etc.)	(n.a.)	71	11	1
Total		1,438	1,230	100

Source: Selectivity rank by Barron's Educational Services, *Profiles of American Colleges,* 27th
edition (Hauppauge, NY: Barron's 2006), 239–250. Barron's selectivity class is based on
more than just the admissions ratio. The admissions ratio is an easy but not definitive
indicator. Enrollment is from National Center for Education Statistics, IPEDS data 2004.
The count of institutions varies from the full list because it excludes Puerto Rico, and
some campuses under common control are not counted separately. Some institutions are
not matched in IPEDS.

le 6 Gross Admission Rate and Approximate Net Admission Rate for the Most
      Selective Private Colleges, as ranked by *US News* 2006.

io	Research universities		Liberal arts colleges	
	Top 10	15 to 25	Top 10	15 to 25
ss rate: total admitted / all applied	12	42	23	42
ly enrolled / all admitted	30	10	15	11
geted minorities enrolled / all admitted	12	9	7	3
high SAT enrolled / all admitted	31	6	16	8
t admission rate	4	38	17	37

rce: Author's calculation using the common data sets of a sample of four to seven colleges in each
gory. Targeted minorities are black non-Hispanic plus Hispanic plus American Indian or Alaska
ive.

Notes

1. Introduction: The High Cost of Higher Education

1. "America's Best Colleges 2005," *US News & World Report,* 2005
(www.usnews.com). National Center for Education Statistics, "Digest of Education Statistics 2004" (Washington, DC: US Department of Education, 2004).

2. Barron's, *Profiles of American Colleges 2005* (Hauppauge, NY: Barron's, 2004). "America's Best Colleges 2005," *US News & World Report,* 2005 (www.usnews.com).

3. Frank Levy and Richard J. Murnane, "U.S. Earnings Levels and Earnings Inequality: A Review of Recent Trends and Proposed Explanations," *Journal of Economic Literature* 30, no. 3 (1992): 1333–1381. Lisa Barrow and Cecilia Elena Rouse, "Does College Still Pay?" *The Economists' Voice* 2, no. 4 (2005). Moohoun Song and Peter F. Orazem, "Returns to Graduate and Professional Education: The Role of Mathematical and Verbal Skills by Major," work in progress, Department of Economics, Iowa State University, 2005.

4. John G. Riley, "Silver Signals: Twenty-Five Years of Screening and Signaling," *Journal of Economic Literature* 39, no. 2 (2001): 432–478.

5. Caroline M. Hoxby, "The Return to Attending a More Selective College: 1960 to the Present," Department of Economics, Harvard University, 1998. Stacy B. Dale and Alan B. Krueger, "Estimating the Payoff to Attending a More Selective College," *Quarterly Journal of Economics* 117, no. 4 (2002): 1491–1527.

6. Because the lender of a home mortgage can sell the house if the borrower fails to repay the loan, the lender's risk of a large loss is less than with an unsecured personal loan where prospects for making claims on the borrower's other assets are much lower. The house is collateral on the home mortgage, causing home mortgage rates to be much lower than rates on personal loans. Rates on guaranteed student loans are close to rates on home mortgages.

7. National Center for Education Statistics, "Digest of Education Statistics 2004." Table 175 reports total enrollment in higher education in 2001 at 15.9 million students, with 9.4 million full-time and 6.3 million part-time.

8. Economists continue to explore how families make decisions. Ted Bergstrom

provides a thoughtful review that integrates ideas from evolutionary biology with economists' ideas about bargaining behavior. Ted Bergstrom, "Economics in the Family Way," *Journal of Economic Literature* 34, no. 4 (1996).

2. Financial Returns: Does College Pay Off?

1. Jacob Mincer, "The Production of Human Capital and Life Cycle Earnings: Variations on a Theme," *Journal of Labor Economics* 15, no.1 (1997): 526–547.

2. Demand for higher education rises in recessions as unemployment rates rise (that is, when jobs are hard to find). Demand falls in booms when jobs are readily available. In contrast, investment in physical capital falls in a recession and rises during booms.

3. Lisa Barrow and Cecilia Elena Rouse, "Does College Still Pay?" *The Economists' Voice* 2, no. 4 (2005).

4. Thomas J. Kane and Cecilia Elena Rouse, "Labor-Market Returns to Two- and Four-Year College," *American Economic Review* 85, no.3 (1995): 600–614. Kane and Rouse estimate that about 20 percent of the observed differential is due to background rather than the education itself. Alan B. Krueger and Mikael Lindahl, "Education for Growth: Why and for Whom?" NBER Working Papers (2000), suggest that the overestimate of returns when background isn't accounted for is offset by underestimated returns due to reporting errors.

5. The predicted earnings are from a regression of the log of earnings on years of experience as a quartic (fourth order polynomial) with marriage, non-government employment, white, not self-employed, and living in a metropolitan area. The average values reported in the text, and shown in the charts, are the anti-log of the predicted values from the regression.

6. U.S. Bureau of the Census (Washington, DC: US Government Printing Office, 2001).

7. Although the internal rate of return is the most common method of comparing investments, it cannot be computed in every case. For example, payment streams with stretches of ups and downs may have more than one internal rate of return. The present value can be computed in every case and, because it is a dollar amount, can be readily compared to tuition. Both methods are useful.

8. Kane and Rouse, "Labor-Market Returns," 600–614.

9. Moohoun Song and Peter F. Orazem, "Returns to Graduate and Professional Education: The Role of Mathematical and Verbal Skills by Major," work in progress, Department of Economics, Iowa State University, 2005. This paper estimates returns to post-baccalaureate education with controls for background characteristics.

10. Orley Ashenfelter and Alan B. Krueger, "Estimates of the Economic Return

to Schooling from a New Sample of Twins," *American Economic Review* 84, no.5 (1994): 1157–1173; Jere R. Behrman et al., "The Impact of College Quality Choices on Wages: Are There Differences among Demographic Groups?" Williams Project on the Economics of Higher Education Discussion Paper, 1996. The authors estimate the return to education using data for identical twins but do not attempt to measure the effect of different attributes of colleges.

11. Domonic Brewer, Eric Eide, and Ronald G. Ehrenberg, "Does It Pay to Attend an Elite Private College? Cross Cohort Evidence on the Effects of College Quality on Earnings," *Journal of Human Resources* 34, no.1 (1999): 104–123. Caroline M. Hoxby, "The Return to Attending a More Selective College: 1960 to the Present," Department of Economics, Harvard University, 1998.

12. Stacy Berg Dale and Alan B. Krueger, "Estimating the Payoff to Attending a More Selective College," *Quarterly Journal of Economics* 117, no.4 (2002): 1491–1527.

13. William G. Bowen and Derek Bok, *The Shape of the River* (Princeton: Princeton University Press, 1998).

14. About 42 percent of students entering higher education begin in two-year colleges, and 26 percent of those continued their studies in four-year programs. More than half of the 2.5 million students who entered two- and four-year colleges in 2002 completed a four-year degree. "Digest of Education Statistics 2004," National Center for Education Statistics (Washington, DC: US Department of Education, 2004). Ellen M. Bradburn, Stephanie Nevill, and Emily Forest Cataldi, "1992–93 Bachelor's Degree Recipients and Their Opinions about Education 2003," *Baccalaureate and Beyond* (Washington, DC: National Center for Education Statistics, 2005).

3. Career Opportunities: The Choices that Matter

1. Education, sex, age, occupation, and the few attributes mentioned just above account for only modest amounts of the variation in earnings. The Census's Current Population Survey does not report other background information (for example, a parent's income), the quality of education, or other details about educational programs, or give more detail about the jobs (for example, how many people a person supervises). To explore each of these issues in detail is beyond the scope of this book. The discussion here offers broad contours rather than complete explanations. The analysis estimates an age-earnings profile for workers of each sex, by highest level of education completed, for benchmark occupations using responses from the Current Population Survey from 1996 to 2002. All values are inflated to dollars of 2002 purchasing power and allow the estimation of the profiles to account for changes by

year so that the profiles apply to 2002. The reported profiles are for white, non-Hispanic persons, who are married, are living in a metropolitan area, and are not self-employed. For teachers and police, the earnings are for government employees. For the other occupations, the pattern of earnings is for private employees.

2. The financial returns on investment in education reported in Table 3 reflect only patterns in earnings. To get a more accurate picture of the relationship between earnings and education, other characteristics of people and other differences in occupations would have to be taken into account.

3. Sean Flynt, "Alabama Teacher of the Year, Betsy Rogers, Continues Grandmother's Samford Legacy," *Seasons* 19, no. 2 (2002).

4. Frederick Flyer and Sherwin Rosen, "The New Economics of Teachers and Education," *Journal of Labor Economics* 15, no. 1, part 2 (1997): S104–139.

5. Tom Loveless, ed., *Conflicting Missions?: Teachers Unions and Educational Reform* (Washington, DC: The Brookings Institution Press, 2000). Lorraine M. McDonnell, *Encyclopedia of Education Research* (New York: Macmillan, 1992), 1444. J. Protsik, "History of Teacher Pay and Incentive Reform" (Madison: Consortium for Policy Research in Education, 1995).

6. Flyer and Rosen, "The New Economics of Teachers and Education," S104–139.

7. Charles F. Manski, "Academic Ability, Earnings, and the Decision to Become a Teacher: Evidence from a Longitudinal Study of the High School Class of 1972," National Bureau of Economic Research Working Paper, 1985.

8. Daniel Goldin, "Colleges Ease Way for Teachers to Get Advanced Degrees," *Wall Street Journal,* September 22, 2003, 1.

9. The coefficient on "non-government employment" in the analysis of female baccalaureate teachers is −0.255; for men, −0.170.

10. William M. Boal and Michael R. Ransom, "Monopsony in the Labor Market," *Journal of Economic Literature* 35, no. 1 (1997): 86–112. Douglas Staiger, Joanne Spetz, and Ciaran Phibbs, "Is There Monopsony in the Labor Market? Evidence from a Natural Experiment," National Bureau of Economic Research Working Paper, 1999. Edward J. Schumacher, "The Earnings and Employment of Nurses in an Era of Cost Containment," *Industrial and Labor Relations Review* 55, no. 1 (2001): 116–132.

11. Peter I. Buerhaus, Douglas Staiger, and David I. Auerbach, "Implications of an Aging Registered Nurse Workforce," *Journal of the American Medical Association* 283, no. 2 (2000): 3948–3954.

12. Schumacher, "Earnings and Employment of Nurses," 116–132.

13. American Institute of Certified Public Accountants, *AICPA Annual Report 2001–2002* (New York: American Institute of Certified Public Accountants, 2002), 7, puts the number of CPAs at 350,000.

14. Tantatape Brahmastrene and Donna Whitten, "Assessing Success on the Uniform Exam: A Logit Approach," *Journal of Education for Business* 77 (2001): 45–46. Charles W. Wootono and Barbara E. Kemmerer, "The Changing Genderization of the Accounting Workforce, 1930–1990," *Accounting, Business & Financial History* 10, no. 2 (2000): 169–190.

15. Bureau of Labor Statistics, *Occupational Outlook Handbook* (Washington, DC: U.S. Government Printing Office, 2002), 24, reports the average starting salary for accountants with the BA was $39,397 in 2001 (both men and women) and $43,272 with the masters. National Association of Colleges and Employers salary survey.

16. Bureau of Labor Statistics, *Occupational Outlook Handbook* (Washington, DC: U.S. Government Printing Office, 2002).

17. Beatrice Sanders, *The Supply of Accounting Graduates and the Demand for Public Accounting Recruits—2000 for Academic Year 1998–99* (New York: American Institute of Certified Public Accountants, 2000). Brahmastrene and Whitten, "Assessing Success on the Uniform Exam," 45–46.

18. "Controller's Compensation," *The Controller's Report, 1997,* 4–5.

19. It is only an estimate because licensure is by state and a person may be licensed in several states. Taking the number of people who are licensed as a ratio to the total count of engineers in the Survey indicates that between 10 and 20 percent of engineers are PEs. The pass rate on the "Principles and Practices of Professional Engineering Exam" is about 66 percent for first-time test takers across fifteen fields in which exams are offered. See National Council of Examiners for Engineering and Survey, "Council Releases October 2002 Pass Rates," *Licensure Exchange* (2002): 5. Eleanor Babco and Jane Prive, *Salaries of Scientists, Engineers, and Technicians,* 19th ed. (Washington, DC: Commission on Professionals in Science and Technology, 2001).

20. Jeff Biddle and Karen Roberts, "Private Sector Scientists and Engineers and the Transition to Management," *Journal of Human Resources* 29, no.1 (1994): 82–107.

21. Richard Freeman, "A Cobweb Model of the Supply and Starting Salary of New Engineers," *Industrial and Labor Relations Review* 29 (1976): 236–248. Sherwin Rosen and Jaewoo Ryoo, "The Market for Engineers," George J. Stigler Center for the Study of the Economy and the State working paper, University of Chicago, 1992.

22. Domonic Basulto, "Forget the Philosopher-King, Now It's the Lawyer-CEO," *Corante* (www.corante.com), 2004.

23. Joe G. Baker, "The Influx of Women into Legal Professions: An Economic Analysis," *Monthly Labor Review* (2002): 14–24. Baker estimates an internal

rate of return in law for the holder of a baccalaureate degree using the 1993 National Survey of College Graduates. Baker reports a 15.8 percent return for men and a 14.8 percent return for women, well above the 10 percent cost of capital used here.

24. Susan Saab Fortney, "Soul for Sale: An Empirical Study of Associate Satisfaction, Law Firm Culture, and the Effects of Billable Hour Requirements," *University of Missouri at Kansas City Law Review* 69 (2000): 239–309. Median billable hours have increased from 1,500 per year in the 1960s to nearly 2,000. A 1990 study noted that 16 percent of attorneys in private practice billed more than 2,400 hours per year.

25. Robert C. Clark, "Why So Many Lawyers? Are They Good or Bad?" *Fordham Law Review* 61 (1992): 275–302.

26. "ABA-Approved Law Schools," American Bar Association Section of Legal Education and Admission to the Bar, 2004. A number of law schools are not accredited by the ABA. Eight states allow persons to sit for their state bar exams without having graduated from an ABA accredited law school. Career options for graduates of unaccredited law schools may be limited. The nonprofit professional association sets standards for law schools to be recognized by the association. Many states only allow graduates of ABA approved law schools to be licensed as lawyers to practice in the state. Ken Myers, "Complaint of Accreditation Draws Federal Antitrust Inquiry," *National Law Journal* (1994): A6. Henry J. Reske, "ABA Settles Antitrust Suit on Accreditation: Justice Department Says Review Process Inflated Law School Faculty Salaries," *ABA Journal* 81, no. 24 (1995). Robert C. Reuben, "An Alternative Law School Sues ABA," *ABA Journal* 80, no. 24 (1994). Marina L. Lao, "Discrediting Accreditation? Antitrust and Legal Education," *Washington Law Quarterly* 79 (2001): 1035–1102. Robert H. Frank, "Winner-Take-All Markets and Wage Discrimination," *The New Institutionalism in Sociology*, ed. Mary C. Brinton and Victor Nee (New York: Russell-Sage Foundation, 1998), 208–223. R. H. Frank and P. J. Cook, *The Winner-Take-All Society* (New York: Free Press, 1995).

27. David Hechler, "The NLJ 250 Survey Shows the Pace Has Slowed by Half to 3.7%," *National Law Journal* 25, no. 61 (2002): A1. Kimberley Blanton, "Associates' Bonuses Up at Top Hub Law Firms," *Boston Globe*, December 22, 2004, C1. Jonathan Glater, "West Coast Law Firm Closing after Dot-Com Collapse," *New York Times*, January 31, 2003, C1.

28. Dentistry and veterinary medicine showed a similar expansion in the 1970s. Dentistry saw earnings fall and enrollment in dental schools dropped. Veterinary medicine also saw earnings stagnate, but the veterinary medical colleges maintained enrollments even in the face of considerable decline in demand. Malcolm Getz, *Veterinary Medicine in Economic Transition* (Ames: Iowa State

University Press, 1997), 48–63. Audrey Williams June, "Accreditation Is Near for Medical School," *Chronicle of Higher Education* 48, no. 11 (2002): A29, announces provisional accreditation.

29. John D. Wassanaar and Sara L. Thran, *Physician Socioeconomic Statistics 2003* (Chicago: American Medical Association, 2003).

30. Some observers point to rising malpractice insurance premiums as one cause of increased costs of physician services, but this phenomenon is of short duration and concentrated in a few states. Professional liability premiums per physician fell from 1988 to 1997. Recent increases have not returned the rates to historic highs.

31. Eric D. Gould, "Rising Wage Inequality, Comparative Advantage, and the Growing Importance of General Skills in the United States," *Journal of Labor Economics* 20, no. 1 (2002): 105–147.

32. Ofer Malamud, "Breadth and Depth: The Effect of Specialization on Labor Market Outcomes," work in progress, Graduate School of Public Policy Studies, University of Chicago, 2005.

33. Carter J. Brown, "The Art of Creating Culture, an Interview, in Academy of Achievement 2005" (www.achievement.org), Academy of Achievement, 2005.

4. College Rank: The Pitfalls of Prestige

1. Rebecca Zwick, *Fair Game? The Use of Standardized Admissions Tests in Higher Education* (New York: Routledge Falmer, 2002), 85. Zwick reports regressions that explain college grade point average. High GPA alone gives a correlation of 0.39 (r-square of 0.152); SAT alone gives correlation of 0.36 (r-square of 0.130); and high school grades with SAT gives a correlation of 0.48 (r-square of 0.230).

2. Jesse M. Rothstein, "College Performance Predictions and the SAT," *Journal of Econometrics* 121, no. 1–2 (2004): 297–317.

3. William G. Bowen and Derek Bok, *The Shape of the River* (Princeton: Princeton University Press, 1998), 122–142.

4. Proposition 209 amended the State Constitution prohibiting discrimination or preferential treatment based on race, sex, color, ethnicity, or national origin. In November 2006 voters in Michigan adopted a similar referendum banning preference in college admission for the same categories.

5. Clarence Thomas, *Barbara Grutter, Petitioner v. Lee Bollinger et al.,* Supreme Court of the United States, 2003. Justice Sandra Day O'Connor's opinion in the Michigan Law School case said: "In order to cultivate a set of leaders with legitimacy in the eyes of the citizenry, it is necessary that the path to leadership be visibly open to talented and qualified individuals of every race and ethnicity." See Linda Greenhouse, "U. of Michigan Ruling Endorses the Value of Campus Diversity," *New York Times,* June 24, 2003, A1, A25.

6. The legal issue is how the 14th Amendment to the Constitution that guarantees equal protection of the laws to each person should apply to college and graduate school admission. The Supreme Court has evolved a doctrine that equal protection means that individuals may not be treated differently in government action on the basis of five categories (sex, race, age, religion, or national origin) without a compelling state interest that would dictate otherwise. An admission decision may take account of any background factors other than these without running counter to the 14th Amendment. Public colleges are part of the state and their actions are ruled by the 14th Amendment. The Court forced the Virginia Military Academy to admit women under this doctrine. The principle could also apply to private colleges that accept federal funds. The few remaining men's colleges eschew federal funds in order to retain their single sex identity. Title IX of the Higher Education Act requires both public and private colleges to move toward equality in athletics for women under the 14th Amendment doctrine.

7. Bowen and Bok, *The Shape of the River,* 395–402.

8. Suggs Welch, "New Grades on Academic Progress Show Widespread Failings among Teams," *Chronicle of Higher Education* 51, no. 27 (2005): A40.

9. In 2006 the College Board announced that it had reported SAT I scores to colleges for more than 4,000 students that had been incorrectly scored. Some reports had been more than 100 points below the actual scores. The College Board makes available for extra fees back-up scoring services. The erroneous scores caused some students to apply only to colleges they viewed as less attractive because their SATs were unexpectedly low. Anne Marie Chaker and John Hechinger, "SAT Takers Advised to Pay for Test Reviews," *Wall Street Journal,* March 15, 2006, D1.

10. Educational Research Service Inc., *Testing for College Admissions: Trends and Issues* (Arlington, VA: Educational Research Service, 1981), gives values that imply the following values for the standard deviations: SAT-Verbal 43, SAT-Math 46, SAT II American History, 45, SAT II Biology 42, with similar values for other subject tests. The mean SAT score for the nation tends to drift over time, in part, because the population of people taking the test shifts. When only a few hundred thousand students intent on admission to highly selective schools took the test the mean national score was higher than when millions of students with widely varying intentions took the test. The SAT recentered its score range in 1994 so as to restore the mean to 500 on the quantitative and on the verbal tests. Scores prior to 1994 are not directly comparable to scores after that year.

11. To be distinguished statistically, two individual scores would need to differ by more than 1.96×2 standard deviations in order to have less than 5 percent probability of a false negative and less than a 5 percent probability of a false

positive: $1.96 \times 2 \times 30 = 117.6$. Therefore, scores as close together as 450 and 550 could occur with probability of 5 percent or more when two students of identical skills each take the test for the first time, due to randomness found among test takers.

12. Jacob L. Vigdor and Charles T. Clotfelter, "Retaking the SAT," *Journal of Human Resources* 38 (Winter 2003): 1–33.

13. Andrew Allen, *Admissions Trade Secrets* (New York: Writer's Club Press, 2001), 167. The estimate of 29 (= 13 + 16) total points gained on second taking uses ETS data that provides no indication of how a student may have prepared for the test. It is an average of those who crammed and those who did not pursue extra preparation.

14. Rothstein, "College Performance Predictions," 297–317.

15. George H. Hanford, *Life with the SAT* (New York: College Entrance Examination Board, 1991), 33–35. William H. Angroff, *The College Board Admissions Test Program: A Technical Report on Research and Development Activities Relating to the Scholastic Aptitude Test and Achievement Tests* (New York: College Entrance and Examination Board, 1971).

16. David Owen and Marilyn Doerr, *None of the Above: The Truth Behind the SATs* (Lanham, MD: Rowman and Littlefield, 1999), 41–64, reports several questions with considerable ambiguity.

17. Hanford, *Life with the SAT,* 8–15.

18. ACT, "The Test" (Iowa City: ACT, 2004). Formerly known as American College Testing, the firm is now known as ACT. The ACT test includes four broad areas: English, reading, math, and science reasoning, and seven subareas. Scores range from 1 (low) to 36 (high). The subject scores have a standard error of 2; the standard error of the composite is one. The mean ACT score in 2002 was 20.8. ACT views scores of 17 or below as an indication that a student is not ready for college work. Jeffrey R. Young, "Average SAT Scores Hold Steady, While ACT Scores Slip," *Chronicle of Higher Education* 49, no. 2 (2002): A50. Illinois and Colorado required the test of all eleventh graders. Nationally, 13 percent scored 27 or higher, a score typical of students entering highly selective colleges, 42 percent scored 22 or above, scores typical of selective colleges, 73 percent scored 18 or higher.

19. Hanford, *Life with the SAT,* 92; William C. Hiss, "Optional SAT's at Bates: 17 Years and Not Counting," *Chronicle of Higher Education* 47, no. 10 (2001): B10. Bates stopped requiring SAT IIs in 1990. "Schools That Do Not Use SAT I or ACT Scores for Admitting Substantial Numbers of Students into Bachelor Degree Programs," The National Center for Fair & Open Testing, 2003.

20. "College Class of 2010 the Most Diverse in Harvard History," *Harvard Uni-*

versity Gazette, April 6, 2006. Harvard admitted 2,109 students out of 22,753 applications (9.3 percent overall). Nearly 2,600 candidates scored a perfect 800 on their SAT verbal test; 2,700 scored 800 on the SAT math; and nearly 3,000 were valedictorians of their high school classes.

21. In 2005 the Educational Testing Service made significant changes in the SAT, in part to make it more like its main competitor, the ACT. Tamar Lewin, "New SAT Writing Test Planned," *New York Times,* June 23, 2002, 23.

22. Ona Wu, "The Nobel Prize Internet Archive" (www.almaz.com), 2004. There are six Nobel Prize categories including peace and economics, with usually one or two winners per year, worldwide. For example, of 26 people winning the prize in physics from 1993 to 2002, eighteen were affiliated with ten universities in the United States, three were with government or industry in the US, and five were foreign. The National Academy of Sciences identifies a very small set of all faculty.

23. An Internet search of "rank of physics departments" or any other discipline will point to many such rankings, using various methods.

24. The most recent, widely used ranking, National Research Council, *Research-Doctorate Programs, 1995,* is based on a 1993 survey. This ranking is to be updated in 2007. Jerry G. Thursby, "What Do We Say about Ourselves and What Does It Mean? Yet Another Look at Economics Department Research," *Journal of Economic Literature* 38, no. 2 (2000): 383–404. National Research Council, *Research-Doctorate Programs in the United States: Continuity and Change* (Washington, DC: National Academy Press, 1995), provides information about the study. Ronald G. Ehrenberg and Peter J. Hurst, "The 1995 NRC Ratings of Doctoral Programs: A Hedonic Model," *Economics of Education Review* 17, no. 2 (1998): 137–148.

25. Charles T. Clotfelter, *Buying the Best: Cost Escalation in Elite Higher Education* (Princeton: Princeton University Press, 1996).

26. Brian Leiter, "The Philosophical Gourmet Report" (www.philosophicalgourmet.com).

27. Monir H. Sharobeam and Keith Howard, "Teaching Demands Versus Research Productivity," *Journal of College Science Teaching* 31, no. 7 (2002): 436–441. J. Scott Armstrong, "Business School Prestige-Research Versus Teaching," *Interfaces* 24, no. 2 (1994): 13–43.

28. National Center for Education Statistics, "National Study of Postsecondary Faculty: 1999," US Department of Education, 2001.

29. Ronald Ehrenberg in Eliot Applestein, "Style Plus: Applications, Admissions & College Rankings," *Washington Post,* August 24, 2000, C4.

30. *US News* conducts an opinion survey of college administrators to ask them to assess other colleges and assigns (circa 2003) a 25 percent weight to the

administrators' opinions. It assigns a 20 percent weight to faculty characteristics, where class size, faculty salaries, percent with PhD, percent full-time, and student-faculty ratio are the components. It also assigns a 20 percent weight to retention and graduation rates (that is, of the students entering college X, what proportion persist at X beyond the first year and what proportion graduate from X within six years), and 15 percent weight to the selectivity of the admissions (mean national test score, percent of students in the top ten percent of their high school classes, and the ratio of admitted students to applicants). Financial resources (spending per student) count 10 percent; alumni giving (percent of alumni who gave to their college) 5 percent; and 5 percent is for meeting or exceeding predicted graduation rates based on student characteristics. Jacques Steinberg, "College Rating by U.S. News Drops Factor in Admissions," *New York Times,* July 10, 2003, A14, reports that *US News* dropped the use of the yield rate, the ratio of enrollees to acceptances, in 2003.

31. Amy Graham and Nicholas Thompson, "Broken Ranks," *The Washington Monthly* 33, no. 9 (2001): 9–13.

32. Christopher Avery, Mark Glickman, Caroline M. Hoxby, and Andrew Metrick, "A Revealed Preference Ranking of U.S. Colleges and Universities," National Bureau of Economic Research Working Papers, 2004.

33. A more complex analogy puts the college as the brand and the program within the college as the flavor. In any case, just because more consumers prefer Breyers doesn't mean that those who prefer Ben & Jerry's are less satisfied.

34. Merrill Goozner, "Cram Schools Chain Japanese Kids to Their Desks," *Chicago Tribune,* September 6, 1992, 23. "SIS WHO Mortality Table 1 Numbers and Rates of Registered Deaths," World Health Organization, 2005. Ben Gose, "If at First They Don't Succeed . . . " *Chronicle of Higher Education* 51, no. 48 (2005): A30.

5. The Learning Environment: What Your Money Really Buys

1. Susan M. Donovan, John D. Bransford, and James W. Pellegrino, eds. *How People Learn: Bridging Research and Practice* (Washington, DC: National Academy Press, 1999).

2. For example, Davidson College requires three semesters of a second language and a composition course as skills, plus nine courses for breadth and about ten courses (maximum of twelve) in a major (some may double count as skills and breadth), for a total of thirty-two courses required for graduation. Davidson also requires four credits in physical education. ROTC students must take courses in military science that often do not carry credit toward graduation. See Davidson College's website for details.

3. The writing as process approach evolved as research on the process of teaching writing began to develop. There are now journals with essays devoted to the study of how to teach writing.

4. David A. Smith at Duke University is one of the leaders of the movement. David A. Smith, "Trends in Calculus Reform," *Preparing for a New Calculus,* ed. Anita Solow (Washington, DC: Mathematical Association of America, 1994), 3–13.

5. Uri Triesman, "Studying Students Studying Calculus: A Look at the Lives of Minority Mathematics Students in College," *The College Mathematics Journal* 23, no. 5 (1992): 362–372. Triesman found that black students who failed calculus at a high rate tended to work alone. When they worked in study groups, they outperformed white students. The investigation took place at the University of California Berkeley.

6. Smith, "Trends in Calculus Reform."

7. Richard D. Lambert, *International Studies and the Undergraduate* (Washington, DC: American Council on Education, 1989), 72.

8. Richard J. Light, *The Harvard Assessment Seminars Second Report 1992* (Cambridge: Graduate School of Education, Harvard University, 1992), 69–72.

9. Some foundations have supported pedagogical initiatives, notably the Carnegie Foundation for the Advancement of Teaching and the Pew Charitable Trusts.

10. "Basic Program Celebrates 50 Years of Great Books," The University of Chicago News Office, September 30, 1996.

11. See, for example, GenEd requirements at Carleton College.

12. See websites for Marquette and Brown universities.

13. Derek Bok, *Our Underachieving Colleges: A Candid Look at How Much Students Learn and Why They Should Be Learning More* (Princeton: Princeton University Press, 2006), 101–108.

14. See, for example, Centre College, University of Nebraska at Lincoln, and University of Chicago websites.

15. Kathleen Andre, Harper Andre, David B. May, and Keith W. Oliver, "Using Undergraduate Students as Physics Lab Teaching Assistants," *The Physics Teacher* 40, no. 4 (2002): 226–228.

16. The Chemical Engineering specimen curriculum at Vanderbilt provides for nine electives over four years, five from the humanities or social sciences, two from technical fields, and two unconstrained. Bok, *Our Underachieving Colleges,* 297–300, also comments on the lack of breadth in the engineering curriculum.

17. See for example Vanderbilt University, Yale University, and Williams College websites.

18. See Colorado College website.

19. Peter E. Kennedy and John J. Siegfried, "On the Optimality of Unequal Class Sizes," *Economics Letters* 50 (1996): 299–304. The effect of class size on learning, other things held constant, has been a major controversy among social scientists over the last twenty years. Alan B. Krueger, "Economic Considerations and Class Size," *The Economic Journal* 113, no. 485 (2003): 34–63, provides a critical review and concludes that the most careful studies show a statistically significant effect for class size but does not show a wide enough range of class sizes to test the idea that the relationship is nonlinear. The non-linear effect of class size assumed here reflects earlier work that has not been refuted but will be subject to more study.

20. Richard J. Light, *The Harvard Assessment Seminars First Report* (Cambridge: Graduate School of Education, Harvard University, 1990), 70–76.

21. See Williams College, Vanderbilt University, Oberlin College, and Colorado College websites.

22. Common Data Set (CDS) Advisory Board, "Common Data Set Initiative" (www.commondataset.org), Washington, DC, American Council on Education, 2006.

23. Many colleges report their distribution of class sizes in a section of their websites called the "common data set." Colleges have agreed to use standard definitions of data elements collaboratively with the College Board and other publishers. CDS, "Common Data Set Initiative," 2006. Part I3 of the common data set reports the distribution of class sizes.

24. William E. Becker, "Teaching Economics to Undergraduates," *Journal of Economic Literature* 35, no. 3 (1997): 1347–1373.

25. For example, Kenneth G. Elzinga, Robert C. Taylor Professor of Economics at the University of Virginia, held the Cavaliers' Distinguished Teaching Professorship, University of Virginia, 1992–1997, an honor reflecting his skill in giving large lectures in introductory economics. For another example, Harvey C. Mansfield, William R. Kenan, Jr., Professor of Government at Harvard, offers a large political philosophy course that is extremely popular.

26. Catherine E. Shoichet, "Reports of Grade Inflation May Be Inflated," *Chronicle of Higher Education* 47, no. 44 (2002): A37. Eric Hoover, "Princeton Proposes Limit on the Number of A's," *Chronicle of Higher Education* 50, no. 33 (2004): A40. "Harvard Raises the Bar to Curtail Grade Inflation," *Chronicle of Higher Education* 47, no. 39 (2002): A39.

27. For details see the Emory University website.

28. Robert M. Schmidt, "Who Maximizes What? A Study in Student Time Allocation," *American Economic Review* 73, no. 2 (1983): 23–28. Peter Dolton, Oscar D. Marcenaro, and Lucia Navarro, "The Effective Use of Student Time:

A Stochastic Frontier Production Function Case Study," *Economics of Education Review* 22, no. 6 (2003): 547–560.

29. George A. Akerlof and Rachel E. Kranton, "Identity and Schooling: Some Lessons for the Economics of Education," *Journal of Economic Literature* 40, no. 4 (2002): 1167–1201. Garey C. Durden and Larry V. Ellis, "The Effects of Attendance on Student Learning in Principles of Economics," *American Economic Review* 85, no. 2 (1995): 343–346, shows lower test scores for students skipping more than four classes in a course.

30. Light, *Harvard Assessment Seminars First Report*, 41–60.

31. 1957 remark picked up by *Time* and *Playboy* as reported in "Former UC President Clark Kerr, a National Leader in Higher Education, Dies at 92," *UC Berkeley News*, December 2, 2003.

32. James L. Shulman and William G. Bowen, *The Game of Life* (Princeton: Princeton University Press, 2001), 227–257. James J. Duderstadt, *Intercollegiate Athletics and the American University* (Ann Arbor: University of Michigan Press, 2000), 126–146.

33. The NCAA (see website) includes 977 colleges in 2002. Other national athletic sanctioning boards are the National Association on Intercollegiate Athletics with 332 colleges, the National Junior College Athletic Association with 523 colleges, and the National Christian College Athletic Association with 119 colleges.

34. "Small Colleges, Short of Men, Embrace Football," *New York Times*, July 10, 2006. "Swarthmore Cuts Football Program," *New York Times*, December 4, 2000. See Reed College website.

35. Shulman and Bowen, *The Game of Life*, 40–50.

36. William G. Bowen and Sarah A. Levin, *Reclaiming the Game: College Sports and Educational Values* (Princeton: Princeton University Press, 2003), 127–144.

37. Ibid., 109–115. Shulman and Bowen, *The Game of Life*, 94–112.

38. Shulman and Bowen, *The Game of Life*, 101.

39. http://d3football.com/notables/swat.html.

40. Charles T. Clotfelter, Ronald G. Ehrenberg, Malcolm Getz, and John J. Siegfried, *Economic Challenges in Higher Education* (Chicago: University of Chicago Press, 1991).

41. Most universities publish the dissertations of their PhD graduates through UMI (formerly called University Microfilm). Many libraries provide an index called "Dissertation Abstracts" that allows anyone to identify dissertations from nearly all universities by author, title, or topic and order a copy for a fee. Better dissertations are published as conventional books or may lead to essays published in standard academic journals, the primary vehicle for pro-

mulgating new ideas in many disciplines. A search of Ulrich's Periodicals Directory (www.ulrichsweb.com) for active, refereed (scholars review the articles), academic/scholarly serials gave a worldwide count of 18,468 in July 2003. A worldwide perspective is important because the best journals in some disciplines are published abroad.

42. Not all doctoral degrees are PhDs. Some doctoral degrees involve extensive course work but do not require creation of an original book-length work. National Center for Education Statistics, "National Study of Postsecondary Faculty: 1999," US Department of Education, 2001.

43. Joshua S. Gans and George B. Sheperd, "How Are the Mighty Fallen: Rejected Classic Articles by Leading Economists," *Journal of Economic Perspectives* 8, no. 1 (1994): 165–179. For example, in 1962, the editor of the *Journal of Finance* declined to publish William Sharpe's essay on capital asset prices. It appeared under new editors two years later: William F. Sharpe, "Capital Asset Prices: A Theory of Equilibrium under Conditions of Risk," *Journal of Finance* 19, no. 3 (1964): 425–442. It has had more than 2,000 citations and was a key factor in Sharpe's winning the Nobel Prize in 1990.

44. Michael S. McPherson and Gordon C. Winston, "The Economics of Academic Tenure: A Relational Respective," in *Paying the Piper: Productivity, Incentives, and Financing in U.S. Higher Education,* ed. M. S. McPherson, M. O. Shapiro, and G. C. Winston (Ann Arbor: University of Michigan Press, 1993), 109–131.

45. Ibid.

46. National Center for Education Statistics, "Digest of Education Statistics 2004," US Department of Education, 2004.

47. Xianfei Chen, "Teaching Undergraduates in U.S. Postsecondary Institutions Fall 1998," National Center for Education Statistics, August 2002.

48. Author's calculations from National Center for Education Statistics, "National Study of Postsecondary Faculty: 2004," May 6, 2005.

49. From Yale University's website in 2002.

50. Author's estimates from National Center for Education Statistics, "National Study of Postsecondary Faculty: 1999," US Department of Education, 2001.

6. Sticker Shock: Will You Pay Too Much?

1. Margaret Allen, "Operating Expenses, Endowment Market Value & Voluntary Support," Bowdoin College, Office of Institutional Research, 2004.

2. National Center for Education Statistics, "Digest of Education Statistics 2001," U.S. Department of Education, 2002.

3. Cathy McGonigle, "Regents Adopt University Tuition and Fees for 2004–05," Arizona Board of Regents News Release, March 11, 2004.

4. Gordon C. Winston and Ivan C. Yen, "Costs, Prices, Subsidies, and Aid in

U.S. Higher Education," Williams Project on the Economics of Higher Education Discussion Paper (32), 1995. These estimates include the current operating budget and an evaluation of the physical capital stock in annual terms.

5. Ibid. Winston and Yen's expenditure per student is net of dollars of revenue the college receives for sponsored research, treating them as a measure of both research inputs and outputs. It also excludes the institution's own scholarship funds, treating them as a price discount. It includes an estimate of the annual rental value of buildings and equipment.

6. Author's calculation using data from ibid.

7. University of Virginia, Darden Graduate School of Business, website.

8. In 2000 with extension in 2002, Congress enacted a law that gives recent high school graduates from the District of Columbia credits of up to $10,000 per year for five years for the difference between in-state and out-of-state tuition at any public college in the country. It also provides a smaller grant for attendance at private colleges in neighboring counties of Virginia and Maryland and at historically black colleges. Stephen Burd and Sara Hebel, "In Pre-Recess Flurry, Congress Acts on Visas, Student Loans, and Tax Credits," *Chronicle of Higher Education* 47, no. 18 (2002): A30. The University of the District of Columbia offers two-year programs as well as four-year and some graduate programs.

9. Sandy Baum and Kathleen Payea, "Education Pays 2004: The Benefits of Higher Education for Individuals and Society," *Trends in Higher Education* (New York: The College Board), 2004.

10. A simple regression across states gives the following result. Expenditure = 7664.59 + 0.4858 Tuition + error. R-square = 0.047. The t-ratio on the coefficient is 8.08.

11. The estimates of the financial aid award at in-state public colleges involve knowing how aid varies with income and assets. The estimates used in the text rely on the National Education Longitudinal Survey of 1988 with information for 1992 concerning payment for college and financial aid received. Forecasting the probability that an enrolled student receives aid is not the same as forecasting the probability that an applicant will receive an offer of aid.

12. Digest of Education Statistics, US Department of Education, 2005, table 197.

13. See Emory University website for its "Kosher Supplemental Meal Plan."

14. "The Hobsons Guide to Historically Black Colleges and Universities," www.collegeview.com/product/hbcu, 2003.

15. Bill Pennington, "Small Colleges, Short of Men, Embrace Football," *New York Times,* July 10, 2006.

16. Susan E. Lennon, "The Compelling Imperative of and for Women's Colleges," Women's College Coalition: The College of Saint Catherine Com-

mencement Address (www.womenscolleges.org), 2005. Tamar Lewin, "At Colleges, Women Are Leaving Men in the Dust," *New York Times,* July 9, 2006.

17. Goldie Blumenstyk, "For-Profit Education Companies Brace Themselves for '60 Minutes' Expose," *Chronicle of Higher Education* 51, no. 22 (2005): A28. Stephen Burd, "Promises and Profits: A For-Profit College Is under Investigation for Pumping Up Enrollment While Skimping on Education," *Chronicle of Higher Education* 52, no. 19 (2005): A21.

18. Elizabeth F. Farrell, "For-Profit Colleges Rush to Fill Nursing Gap," *Chronicle of Higher Education* 50, no. 19 (2004): A29.

19. Florence Olsen, "Phoenix Rises," *Chronicle of Higher Education* 49, no. 10 (2002): A29.

20. Michele A. Hernandez, *A is for Admission: The Insider's Guide to Getting into the Ivy League and Other Top Colleges* (New York: Warner Books, 1997).

21. Barron's, *Profiles of American Colleges 2007* (Hauppauge, NY: Barron's, 2007). Simple measures of selectivity can be misleading. A college might discourage applications by raising its application fee. Because processing applications is costly, a college may not want to attract applications from students to whom it is unlikely to offer admission.

22. Author's average of undergraduate tuition at four-year institutions in 2004 from National Center of Education Statistics, "Integrated Postsecondary Education Data System," US Department of Education.

23. Robert H. Frank and Philip J. Cook, *The Winner-Take-All Society* (New York: Free Press, 1995).

24. Elizabeth Bernstein, "Want to Go to Harvard Law?" *Wall Street Journal,* September 26, 2003, W1, W12. The top medical schools in the analysis were Columbia, Harvard, Johns Hopkins, The University of California San Francisco, and Yale. The top law schools were Chicago, Columbia, Harvard, Michigan, and Yale. The top MBA programs were Chicago, Dartmouth, Harvard, MIT, and Penn.

25. Some universities have special admissions arrangements for their undergraduates in entering their professional schools. For example, Washington University and Vanderbilt admit some students simultaneously to their undergraduate program and their professional schools.

26. Bruce Sacerdote, "Peer Effects with Random Assignment: Results from Dartmouth Roommates," *Quarterly Journal of Economics* 116, no. 2 (2001): 681–704. John J. Siegfried and Michael A. Gleason, "Academic Roommate Peer Effects," work in progress, Vanderbilt University, 2003. David J. Zimmerman, "Peer Effects in Higher Education: Evidence from a Natural Experiment," *Review of Economics and Statistics* 85, no. 1 (2003): 9–23.

27. Sacerdote, "Peer Effects with Random Assignment," 681–704. Zimmerman, "Peer Effects in Higher Education," 9–23.

28. Michael Kremer and Dan M. Levy, "Peer Effects from Alcohol Use Among College Students," National Bureau of Economic Research, working paper, 2003.

29. "Trends in College Pricing 2006," The College Board, Trends in Higher Education Series (www.collegeboard.com).

30. Malcolm Getz and John J. Siegfried, "Where Do the Children of College Faculty Attend College?" *Economics of Education Review* 25, no. 2 (2003): 201–210.

7. Payment Options: Something for Every Income

1. The federal methodology is described in detail at US Department of Education, "Federal Student Aid Handbook," Information for Financial Aid Professionals Library (http://ifap.ed.gov), US Department of Education.

2. From Agnes Scott College website.

3. Two websites with calculators: The College Board, "College Financing Calculator" (www.collegeboard.com) and ACT, "Financial Aid Need Estimator" (www.act.org).

4. Darin Acemoglu and Joshua Angrist, "How Large Are Human Capital Externalities? Evidence from Compulsory Schooling Laws," *NBER/Macroeconomic Annual* 15, no. 1 (2000): 9–59.

5. Forty-two states including the District of Columbia tax income including earnings. Two more tax dividends and interest. In Vermont and some other states, the state tax is a simple added percentage of the federal income tax liability. Joseph Llobrera and Robert Zahradnik, "The Impact of State Income Taxes on Low-Income Families in 2004," Center on Budget and Policy Priorities, 2005.

6. Thomas J. Kane, "Student Aid after Tax Reform: Risks and Opportunities," *Financing a College Education: How It Works, How It's Changing,* ed. Jacqueline E. King (Phoenix, AZ: Oryx Press, 1999), 137–140.

7. Lutz Berkner et al., "2003–04 National Postsecondary Student Aid Study," NCFE Statistics, US Department of Education, 2005, 10–11.

8. National Center for Education Statistics, "Digest of Education Statistics 2004," US Department of Education, 2004, table 178.

9. For more information about application to a service academy, go to the academy website and contact a member of Congress.

10. Alan J. Auerbach, "The Bush Tax Cut and National Savings," *The National Tax Journal* 55, no. 3 (2002): 387–407.

11. See for example www.collegeillinois.com.

12. Jonathan Clements, "Clearing Up Confusion Over 529 Savings Plans," *Wall Street Journal,* January 5, 2006.

13. Vanguard's website provides a comparison of 529 plans across all states.

14. National Center for Education Statistics, "Undergraduate Financial Aid Estimates for 2003–04 by Type of Institution," US Department of Education, 2005.

15. Chief Operating Officer of Federal Student Aid, "Federal Family Education Loan Program," *Federal Register* 70, no. 216 (2005): 67997–67999, announces the interest rates on student loans for 2005–2006.

16. The US Department of Education defines dependency status for the purpose of determining financial aid awards.

17. Michael Mumper, *Removing College Price Barriers* (Albany: State University of New York, 1996).

18. National Center for Education Statistics, "2003–2004 National Postsecondary Student Aid Study," Student Financial Aid Estimates for 2003–2004, February 2005.

19. US Department of Education, "Federal Student Aid Handbook," Information for Financial Aid Professionals Library, US Department of Education, 2005.

20. Laura G. Knapp and Terry G. Seaks, "An Analysis of the Probability of Default on Federally Guaranteed Student Loans," *Review of Economics and Statistics* 74, no. 3 (1992): 404–411. Mark Dynarski, "Who Defaults on Student Loans? Findings from the National Postsecondary Student Aid Study," *Economics of Education Review* 13, no. 1 (1994): 55–58.

21. U.S. Bureau of the Census, *Statistical Abstract of the United States 2000.* Margaret Spellings, "Secretary Spellings Announced New Low Student Loan Default Rate," US Department of Education, 2005. "The Student Guide to Financial Aid for the U.S. Department of Education 2002–2003," US Department of Education, 2004. Direct Loan Servicing, "Welcome to Direct Loan Servicing," US Department of Education, 2004.

22. National Center for Education Statistics, "Debt Burden of College Graduates," US Department of Education.

23. Kelly Field, "Congress Cuts $12.7 Billion from Student-Loan Program," *Chronicle of Higher Education* 52, no. 18 (2006): A1. The fee is to decline over five years beginning in 2006.

24. US Bureau of the Census, *Statistical Abstract of the United States,* US Government Printing Office.

25. Office of Management and Budget, "Budget Department of Education," The White House, 2004.

26. The Federal Supplemental Education Opportunity Grant (FSEOG) is of-

fered through the colleges. A college may elect to participate in the FSEOG. The US Department of Education assigns a fund to each campus to make grants intended primarily to supplement Pell Grants for students with a demonstrated need. The individual grants, varying from $100 to $4,000 annually, must be assigned to the most needy undergraduates. Field, "Congress Cuts $12.7 Billion."

27. "Robert C. Byrd Honors Scholarship Program," U.S. Department of Education (www.ed.gov/programs/iduesbyrd).

28. National Center for Education Statistics, "National Postsecondary Student Aid Survey, 2003–2004," U.S. Department of Education.

29. Susan Dynarski, "The New Merit Aid," *College Choices: The Economics of Where to Go, When to Go, and How to Pay for It,* ed. Caroline M. Hoxby (Chicago: University of Chicago Press, 1994). "State Fin Aid Offices & Guaranty Agencies" (www.fastaid.com), FASTaiD, 2004, gives address, telephone number, and hyperlink financial aid offices for all fifty states, the District of Columbia, and Puerto Rico.

30. Georgia's HOPE Scholarship Program (www.gsfc.org/HOPE), Georgia Student Finance Commission, 2004.

31. Susan Dynarski, "The Consequences of Merit Aid," National Bureau of Economic Research working paper, December, 2002, 63–97.

32. Jeffrey Selingo, "How California's Ambitious Aid Program Stumbled Badly and Disappointed Many," *Chronicle of Higher Education* 47, no. 27 (2002): 23. The California Student Aid Commission and EdFund, "Fund Your Future 2002–2003," The California Student Aid Commission and EdFund, 2001. California Student Aid Commission, "California Student Aid Commission Applauds Governor's Proposals for College-Going Students," press release, January 10, 2006.

33. National Center for Education Statistics, "National Postsecondary Student Aid Study: Student Financial Aid Estimates for 1999–2000," ed. Andrew G. Malizio, U.S. Department of Education, 2001, 8. In 2006 the federal rules made clear that 529 and other prepaid assets would count as savings rather than as a reduction in tuition and thereby lower eligibility for need-based aid only modestly. Karin Fischer, "Congress Votes to Remove Penalty on Some Families That Invest in Pre-Paid Tuition Plans," *Chronicle of Higher Education,* February 3, 2006.

34. See University of Arizona, Vanderbilt University, Northwestern University, and Whitman College websites. Eric Hoover, "Who's Up and Who's Down in National Merit Scholarship Competition," *Chronicle of Higher Education* 47, no. 26 (2002): A36.

35. See Idaho State, Jacksonville State, and Western Michigan websites.

36. The Coca-Cola Scholars Foundation (www.coca-colascholars.org).

37. Families may apply after January 1 of the year of matriculation in a postsecondary institution, but before July 1 of the following year, without exceptions. The FAFSA form is available online at www.fafsa.ed.gov or may be obtained in most high school guidance and college financial aid offices, public libraries, or by calling the Student Aid Information Center at the Department of Education (1–800–4-FED-AID). One to four weeks after submission of the FAFSA form, the Department of Education returns a Student Aid Report (SAR). The SAR will reiterate all of the information on the FAFSA form and report the Expected Family Contribution (EFC). Using the information on the FAFSA and a congressionally approved aid formula, the Department of Education calculates the EFC, which is the amount that a family should be able to contribute to a student's college costs. This process and formula is called the Federal Methodology. It is important to review the SAR for mistakes to ensure that the correct amount of aid is awarded.

38. Elizabeth A. Duffy and Idana Goldberg, *Crafting a Class* (Princeton: Princeton University Press, 1998), 172. Michael S. McPherson and Morton Owen Schapiro, *The Student Aid Game* (Princeton: Princeton University Press, 1999), 6–7. The College Board's online PROFILE can be found at profileonline.collegeboard.com.

39. For a student of divorced parents, some aid calculations count only the income of the custodial parent. Some count the income of both the custodial and noncustodial parents including any step-parents. The income categories increase from year to year with the Consumer Price Index and the Department of Education adjusts the formula from time to time to reflect new information about taxes and other factors used in the formula. For details, see US Department of Education, Information for Financial Aid Professionals (IFAP) Library, "EFC Formula Worksheets and Tables" (ifap.ed.gov).

40. Sandy Baum, "Need Analysis: How We Decide Who Gets What," *Financing a College Education: How It Works, How It's Changing,* ed. Jacqueline E. King (Phoenix: Oryx Press, 1999), 57.

41. See Princeton, Yale, and Stanford websites for detailed financial aid information.

42. See Tulane University and University of Rochester websites for detailed financial aid information.

43. See Middlebury College website for detailed financial aid information.

44. Caroline M. Hoxby, "Benevolent Colluders? The Effects of Antitrust Action on College Financial Aid and Tuition," National Bureau of Economic Research working paper, 2002.

45. "568 Presidents' Report" (www.news.cornell.edu), Cornell University, 2001. Greg Winter, "Top Colleges, with Middle-Class Aid Seekers in Mind, Alter How They Count Assets," *New York Times,* July 27, 2003, 12.

46. Andrew W. Dick and Aaron S. Edlin, "The Implicit Taxes from College Financial Aid," *Journal of Public Economics* 65, no. 3 (1997): 295–322. Martin Feldstein, "College Scholarship Rules and Private Savings," *American Economic Review* 85, no. 3 (1995): 552–566.

47. Brown University Office of Undergraduate Admissions, "Brown Corporation Endorses Initiatives for Academic Enrichment," Brown University, 2002. Mount Holyoke College, "Task Force Recommends Considering Financial Need for Small Part of Applicant Pool: Treasurer's Report Gives Financial Framework for Proposals," *The College Street Journal,* November 8, 1996.

48. McPherson, *The Student Aid Game.* Office of Admission, "Facts and Figures, 2004–05." See Agnes Scott College website for detailed financial aid information.

49. Gordon C. Winston, "The Economic Structure of Higher Education: Subsidies, Customer-inputs, and Hierarchy," Williams Project on the Economics of Higher Education, Williams College, 1996.

50. Steve Stecklow, "Colleges Manipulate Financial-Aid Offers, Shortchanging Many," *Wall Street Journal,* April 1, 1996. See Carnegie Mellon website for detailed financial aid information.

8. The Admission Game: Strategies for Success

1. P. Arcidiacono, "Ability Sorting and Returns to the College Major," *Journal of Econometrics* 121 (2004): 343–375.

2. Terry Giffen, Director of College Counseling, Montgomery Bell Academy, interview by Malcolm Getz, 2003.

3. College Admissions Services, "Find Out Your Chances of Admission at Top Colleges and Let Us Help You Improve Them" (go4ivy.com), College Admissions Services, Inc., 2004. The website purports to predict the probability of admission at Ivy League campuses for a fee.

4. Alan Finder, "Admissions Officials Lament Practice of Signing in with More Than One College," *New York Times,* May 20, 2006. One student mentioned that more applications increase the likelihood of winning simultaneous admission to an undergraduate college and a medical school.

5. Jeffrey R. Young, "Admissions Officials at Harvard, Stanford, and Yale Call New Early-Admissions Plan a Success," *Chronicle of Higher Education* 50, no. 13 (2003): A32. Jeffrey R. Young, "Yale and Stanford End Early-Decision Options and Defy National Group," *Chronicle of Higher Education* 49, no. 13, 2002, A58.

6. "Early Decision/Early Action College Directory" (www.nacac.com/earlyadmission), National Association for College Admission Counseling.

7. Michele A. Hernandez, *A Is for Admission: The Insider's Guide to Getting into the Ivy League and Other Top Colleges* (New York, NY: Warner Books, 1997).

8. Jacques Steinberg, *The Gatekeepers: Inside the Admissions Process of a Premier College* (New York: Viking Press, 2002).

9. A problem for this statistical procedure is that the students who enroll are a select subset of all who apply. Students who are admitted but go elsewhere, those not admitted, and those who enroll but do not complete the first year will not have first year grades and so cannot be used in the statistical analysis. For this reason, the regression just using those students with first year grades is subject to selectivity bias. Jesse M. Rothstein, "College Performance Predictions and the SAT," *Journal of Econometrics* 121, nos. 1–2, pp. 297–317. This paper develops a novel approach for correcting for the selection problem. With the correction, the effect of the SAT is reduced. Alexandra Beatty, M. R. C. Greenwood, and Robert L. Linn, *Myths and Tradeoffs: The Role of Tests in Undergraduate Admissions* (Washington, DC: National Academy Press, 1999).

10. Hernandez, *A Is for Admission,* 59–89. Dmitry Kotlyranenko and Ronald G. Ehrenberg, "Ivy League Athletic Performance: Do Brains Win?" *Journal of Sports Economics* 1, no. 2 (2000): 139–150. Stephen Butler, "Admissions Bar Raised for Athletes," September 3, 2003, www.yaledailynews.com/Article.aspx?ArticleID=22894.

11. Alan Finder, "High Schools Avoid Class Ranking, Vexing Colleges," *New York Times,* March 5, 2006, 1. (Lake Wobegon is a location in Minnesota invented by Garrison Keillor.)

12. Rachel Toor, *Admissions Confidential: An Insider's Account of the Elite College Selection Process* (New York: St. Martin's Press, 2001).

13. *Boston Globe,* June 22, 2006.

14. Jay Mathews, "Admissions Obsession: As Colleges Compete to Enroll the Top Applicants, Some Educators Worry the Rivalry Has Gotten out of Hand," *Washington Post,* November 7, 2000, A18. Amy Callahan, "Early Decisions Increase in College, Engineering," *Columbia University Record,* Columbia University, January 23, 1998. University of Pennsylvania Admissions, "Incoming Student Profile: Class of 2007," www.admissionsug.upenn.edu/applying/profile, 2004.

15. Christopher Avery, Andrew Fairbanks, and Richard Zeckhauser, *The Early Admissions Game* (Cambridge: Harvard University Press, 2003), p. 137.

16. Ibid.

17. Ibid.

18. Eric Hoover, "Harvard U. Plans to Drop Its Early-Admissions Program, Rekindling National Debate," *Chronicle of Higher Education Daily,* September 13, 2006.

19. Toor, *Admissions Confidential.*

20. William G. Bowen and Derek Bok, *The Shape of the River* (Princeton: Princeton University Press, 1998), 29.

21. James L. Shulman and William G. Bowen, *The Game of Life* (Princeton: Princeton University Press, 2001), 33: in 1989, Division IA publics showed athletes as 5 percent of all male students, Division IA privates, 9 percent; Ivy League, 27 percent; and coed liberal arts colleges, 32 percent. William G. Bowen and Sarah A. Levin, *Reclaiming the Game: College Sports and Educational Values* (Princeton: Princeton University Press, 2003), 86, gives percentage of students who are recruited athletes in 1995: University Athletic Association (Division III, which includes Washington University, University of Chicago, Case, Carnegie Mellon, Emory, and others), 7 percent of males, 5 percent of females; Ivies (Division I), 16 percent of males, 13 percent of females; NESCAC (Division III, which includes Williams, Amherst, Colby, Bates, Tufts, and others), 24 percent of males, 17 percent of females; other coed liberal arts colleges, 26 percent of males, 15 percent of females.

22. On the power of coaches, see Gordon Marino, "Keeping Score on Coaches," *Chronicle of Higher Education,* March 3, 2006.

23. Bowen, *The Shape of the River.*

24. Daniel Goldin, "Colleges Ease Way for Teachers to Get Advanced Degrees," *Wall Street Journal.* 2003, 1. Bowen, *The Shape of the River,* 1998, p. 28.

25. Ibid.

26. Welch Suggs, "Tipping the Athletic Scale: Williams College Struggles with Athletics and Admission," *Chronicle of Higher Education,* March 8, 2002, A37.

9. The Choice: Comparing Offers

1. Many colleges, including the three discussed here, publish on their websites a "common data set" that provides detailed information about many dimensions of the college's operations including admissions, enrollment, financial aid, and degrees.

2. Clifford Adelman, "The Toolbox Revisited: Paths to Degree Completion from High School through College," US Department of Education, 2006.

3. Digest of Education Statistics, 2005, table 175. Author's calculation from 2002–2003 enrollment data from the National Center for Education Statistics.

4. National Center for Education Statistics, "Digest of Education Statistics 2005," US Department of Education, 2004, table 249.

5. Adelman, "The Toolbox Revisited."

6. The information provided here refers to each campus rather than individual programs because the data colleges routinely provide is for the campus.

7. Northwestern received $288 million in funded research in 2002, according to a National Science Foundation Report. William and Mary received $40 million. Haverford received $832,000. NSF, "Academic Institutional Profiles" (www.nsf.gov/statistics/profiles).

8. Data are from section B2 of the "common data set" for each college.

9. Coach Kelly McCollum has two assistant coaches plus a volunteer coach. She announced the newly signed athletes on February 15, 2006.

10. Email from William and Mary Coach Peel Hawthorne. The thirteen fraternities include 25 percent of undergraduate men and the 12 sororities include 27 percent of women in their membership.

11. The "common data set" for each campus provides information about the number of class sections in each of seven size ranges. Associating a likely middle value for the section size in each category allows an estimate of the number of student seats in each category and thereby, an estimate of the proportion of student seats in sections of each size and of the average section size from the student's point of view (see Chapter 5 for discussion). Here is a summary of the method: Compute the number of seats in a given section as a percentage of seats over all sections. Multiply the percentage of seats in a section by the seats in the section and sum to find the average section size from the student's point of view. The National Center for Education Statistics conducts an annual survey of postsecondary education, IPEDS, that reports the number of faculty on each campus by rank. The count of faculty is total for the institution and includes faculty in graduate and professional schools who do not teach undergraduates.

12. Author's estimates using data from ugadm.northwestern.edu/commondata/2004–05.

13. Author's estimate using data from www.haverford.edu/info/cds06.pdf.

14. A student with more than one major will count more than once in the denominator in calculating the percentages here. For Northwestern and Haverford, see their websites. For William and Mary, the count is from a private communication.

15. For a description of the writing programs, see the schools' websites

16. For a description of the math programs, see the schools' websites.

17. For information on honor codes, see the schools' websites.

18. Morton Owen Shapiro, "Williams Alumni Weekend Talk," Williams College, 2002.

Further Reading

ACT. www.act.org.

Allen, Andrew. *Admissions Trade Secrets*. New York: Writer's Club Press, 2001.

Avery, Christopher, Andrew Fairbanks, and Richard Zeckhauser. *The Early Admissions Game*. Cambridge: Harvard University Press, 2003.

Bain, Ken. *What the Best College Teachers Do*. Cambridge: Harvard University, 2004.

Barron's Profiles of American Colleges, 2007. Hauppauge: Barron's Educational Series, Inc., 2006.

Bok, Derek. *Our Underachieving Colleges: A Candid Look at How Much Students Learn and Why They Should Be Learning More*. Princeton: Princeton University Press, 2006.

Bowen, William G., and Derek Bok. *The Shape of the River*. Princeton: Princeton University Press, 1998.

Bowen, William G., and Sarah A. Levin. *Reclaiming the Game: College Sports and Educational Values*. Princeton: Princeton University Press, 2003.

Bureau of Labor Statistics. *Occupational Outlook Handbook*. Washington, DC: U.S. Government Printing Office, 2006. www.bls.gov/oco.

Clotfelter, Charles T. *Buying the Best: Cost Escalation in Elite Higher Education* (Princeton: Princeton University Press, 1996).

College Board. www.collegeboard.com.

CSS/Financial Aid Profile. http://profileonline.collegeboard.com.

Fastaid Scholarship Search. www.fastaid.com.

Frank, R. H., and P. J. Cook. *The Winner-Take-All Society*. New York: Free Press, 1995.

Hernández, Michele A. *A is for Admission: The Insider's Guide to Getting into the Ivy League and Other Top Colleges*. New York: Warner Books, 1997.

Hoxby, Caroline M., ed. *College Choices: The Economics of Where to Go, When to Go, and How to Pay for It*. Chicago: University of Chicago Press, 2004.

Kaplan Test Prep. www.kaplan.com.

Karab, Jerome. *The Chosen: The Hidden History of Admission and Exclusion at Harvard, Yale, and Princeton*. Boston: Houghton Mifflin, 2005.

Kirp, David L. *Shakespeare, Einstein, and the Bottom Line: The Marketing of Higher Education.* Cambridge: Harvard University Press, 2003.

Light, Richard J. *Making the Most of College: Students Speak Their Minds.* Cambridge: Harvard University Press, 2001.

McDonnell, Lorraine M. *Encyclopedia of Education Research.* New York: Macmillan, 1992.

McPherson, Michael S., and Morton Owen Schapiro. *The Student Aid Game.* Princeton: Princeton University Press, 1999.

Peterson's College Search. www.petersons.com.

Princeton Review. www.princetonreview.com.

SAT. www.collegeboard.com/student/testing/sat/about.html.

Savings for College. www.savingforcollege.com.

Shulman, James L., and William G. Bowen. *The Game of Life.* Princeton: Princeton University Press, 2001.

Steinberg, Jacques. *The Gatekeepers: Inside the Admissions Process of a Premier College.* New York: Viking Press, 2002.

Thacker, Lloyd, ed. *College Unranked: Ending the College Admissions Frenzy.* Cambridge: Harvard University Press, 2005.

Toor, Rachel. *Admissions Confidential: An Insider's Account of the Elite College Selection Process.* New York: St. Martin's Press, 2001.

US Department of Education. COOL (College Opportunities Online Locator). http://nces.ed.gov/ipeds/cool.

——— Federal Student Aid. http://studentaid.ed.gov.

——— FAFSA (Free Application for Federal Student Assistance). www.fafsa.ed.gov.

US News & World Report. "America's Best Colleges 2007." www.usnews.com.

Zwick, Rebecca. *Fair Game? The Use of Standardized Admissions Tests in Higher Education.* New York: Routledge Falmer, 2002.

Index